DELAWARE PORTRAIT

PAT CROWE

DELAWARE PORTRAIT

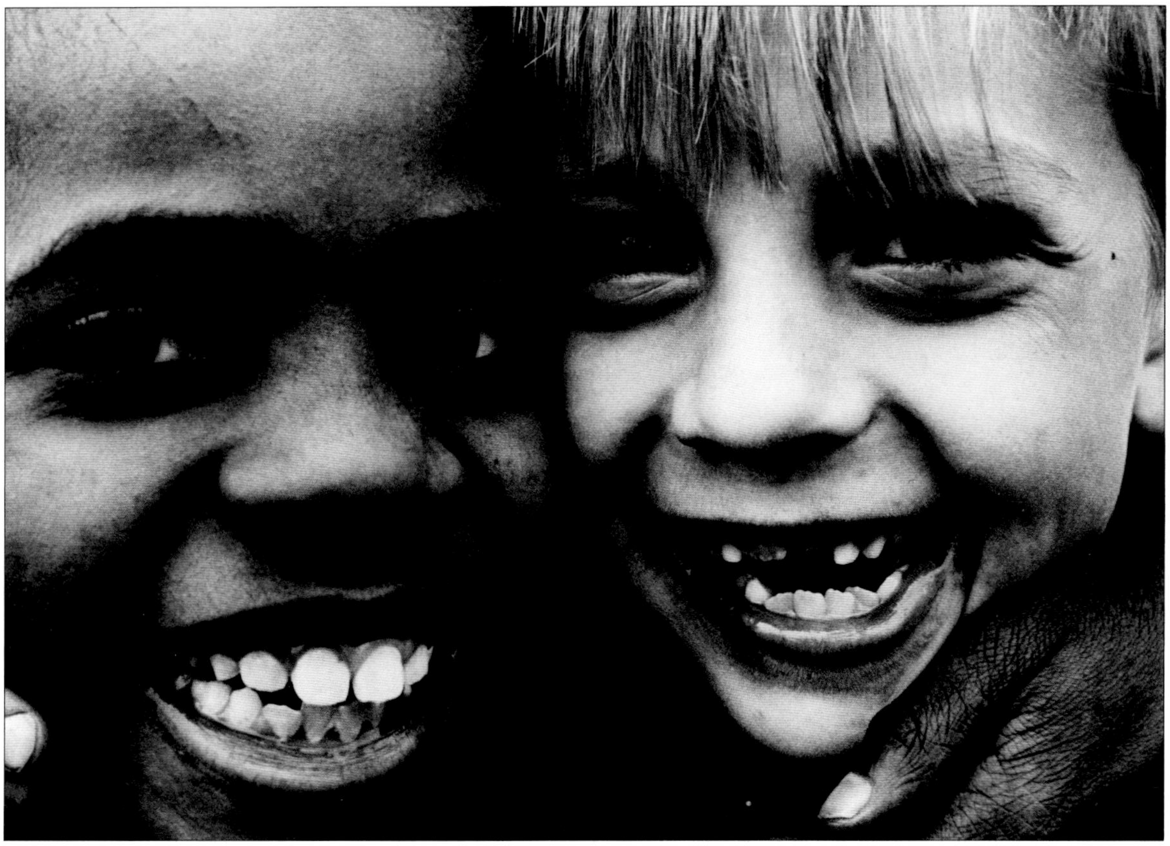

PHOTOGRAPHS FROM TWENTY YEARS AT THE NEWS-JOURNAL

PORTFOLIO PRESS, LTD.
ANNAPOLIS, MARYLAND

DEDICATION

To my mother and father, Corinne and Sonny, of Corning, New York, who have never waivered in their support of my life's endeavors.

SPECIAL APPRECIATION

To my wife, Jane, whose never ending love, energy and support has helped make this possible.

To my sons, Pat, Chris and Dan who kept saying "Go for it, Dad."

Thanks . . . . I love you all!

First edition October, 1989, by Portfolio Press, Ltd.

ISBN: 0-929518-04-7

Library of Congress Catalog Card Number 89-063188

Any inquiries or orders should be directed to the publisher:

PORTFOLIO PRESS, LTD.
P.O. Box 626, Annapolis, Maryland 21404

Photographs are used with permission of the News-Journal Company.

Frontispiece:
Greg Anderson and Scot Williams, Wilmington, 1973

Compassion, Fascination, Love, and a Sense of Humor

BY RALPH MOYED

Another photographer would have dismissed my inquiry as a classic dumb question asked by a stupid reporter. Not Pat Crowe.

"Do I count myself a photographer first or a journalist?" Pat thought a few seconds. It was clear that this was the first time he had considered the question. That surprised me, but shouldn't have. Pat Crowe is not naturally self-conscious about his work.

He thought about the dumb question and finally answered with quiet certainty: "A photographer."

Perhaps. Pat surely is an artist with a rare and indefinable talent for capturing the essential beauty and mood of even static subjects, as the photographs in this book attest. And even if he hadn't gotten that first break at the *Leader* in Corning, New York, he has no doubt that he would have made a career in photography – in or out of journalism.

Writing reporters who have shared assignments with Pat Crowe at the Wilmington *News-Journal* are proud to call him colleague. They have come to love, respect, and depend upon him as a vital part of the journalistic team. We all can recall the times when Crowe's photographs have done more to tell a story than any of our words.

It is more than just a good eye and an instant sense of composition.

"Pat Crowe has an unusual affinity for people," said Bill Hayden, the *News-Journal* theater critic. "He has sensitivity."

"An ability to put people at ease," said another colleague, business writer Maureen Milford. "Pat Crowe is disarming."

A valuable trait in a journalist. When a reporter fears a subject will be hostile, or skittish, or simply shy, it is not unusual to let Pat lead the way as a door opener. Reporters are a cynical lot, but none doubt that Crowe is entirely sincere in his approach to people.

As this book was being assembled, Pat was assigned to cover a summer project in which Girls Club members were working with retarded children in Newark, Delaware.

A few minutes into the assignment, the reporter turned to find children crawling on Pat's lap, tugging at his expensive equipment, and hugging him. He was showing one retarded boy how to take pictures.

For thanks, Pat got a hug and kiss.

To some, it might have appeared that Pat had forgotten the assignment.

He may have been lost for a moment or two in the satisfaction of bringing joy to unfortunate kids, but the assignment was not forgotten. Pat brought back more excellent photographs than could ever be published.

And that is the source of one of his great frustrations.

When he came to Wilmington twenty years ago, there was time and space for photographic essays that occupied a full page or more in the paper and that required days or even weeks of attention to a single subject.

It no longer is so. Space is tight and time is sharply limited.

"Years ago, you could get involved," he recalls. "You could get a chance to work closely with a reporter. You could get a chance to really know your subject."

A dozen years ago, after many of us had written volumes about miserable conditions at Delaware State Hospital without changing a thing, Pat Crowe was assigned to go with a reporter to get what photographs he could. Photographers had never been allowed inside one particularly notorious building.

"Somehow, I got into the inner, inner sanctum

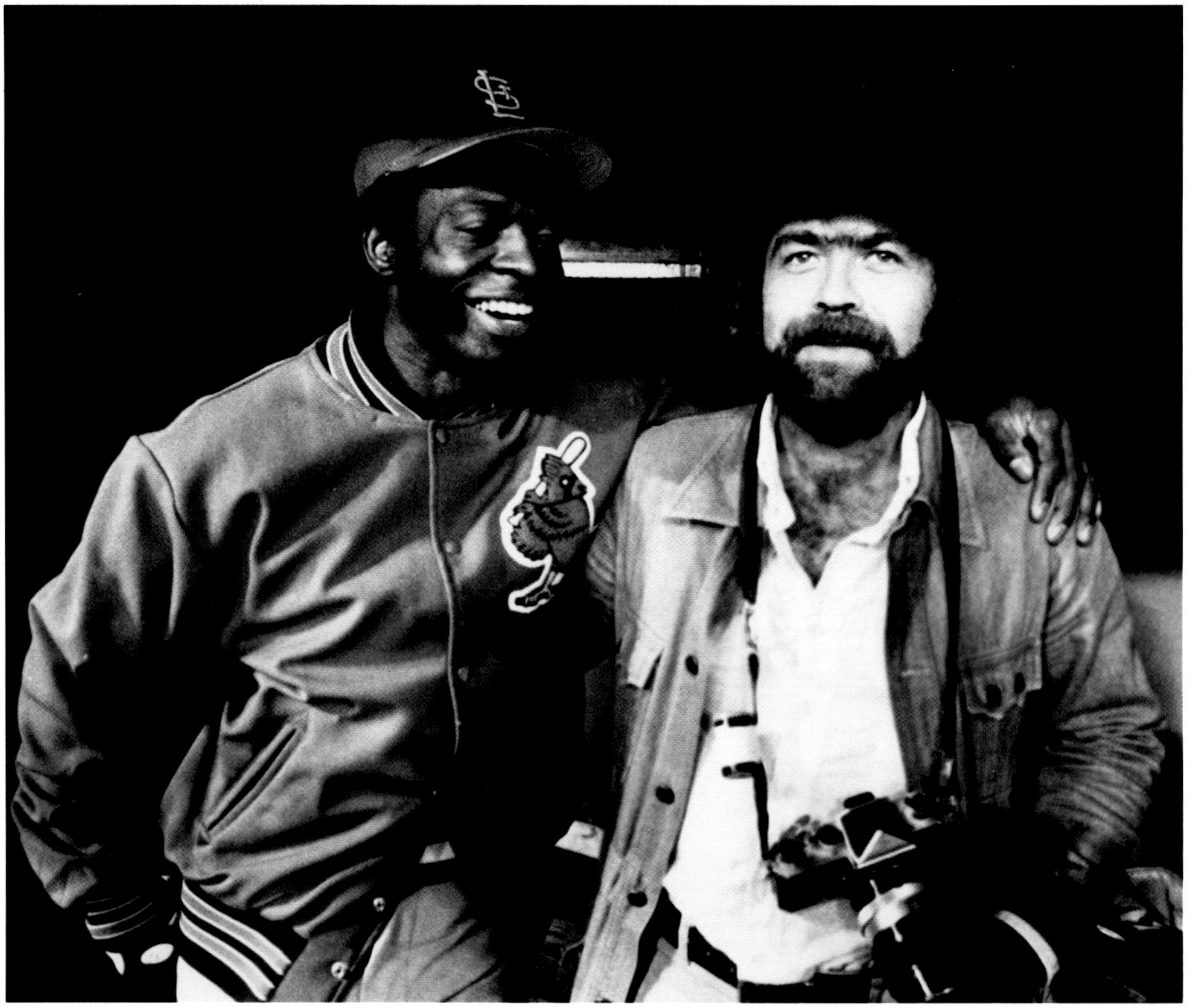

Pat Crowe with Lou Brock of the St. Louis Cardinals *by Leo S. Matkins*

for about an hour and shot five or six rolls of film." The *News-Journal* published a photo essay. "These were stark mental health pictures. They may have made a difference. The state kicked in a million bucks or so to fix up the place."

From the start, Crowe's main interest was people. Imbued with a thirst for adventure by his father (who toured Ireland by bicycle as a teenager), Pat decided to become a photographer out of the blue – literally.

The story has the makings of a legend. Starting back from leave at his home in Corning to his Army base in Frankfurt, West Germany, Pat picked up two photography magazines to read on the plane. "By the time I reached Europe I knew what I wanted to do. I decided in those six hours that I wanted to be a people photographer."

Pat Crowe never had college training, but taught himself and absorbed the rest by watching his senior colleagues as he moved from Corning to Ithaca to Rochester and finally to Wilmington.

He is a sucker for fledgling photographers. From his early days in Wilmington, he has had them tagging after him. When they show talent and enthusiasm, he takes the time to teach them what he knows.

"For me," he has said, "it was intense energy and devotion that put me where I am. I couldn't refuse a kid who had fire, who had spirit."

Some have gone on to success. One, John Kaplan of Wilmington, was barely in his teens when he began going on assignments with Pat Crowe. "He was on fire at 14," Crowe remembers. At 30, John Kaplan was a staff photographer at the *Pittsburgh Press* and winner of the 1988 Newspaper Photographer of the Year Award.

Crowe won the same prestigious honor himself in 1975.

The best evidence of Pat Crowe's affinity for people may be found on the succeeding pages of this book. Besides the exceptional beauty and exquisite composition, you will find compassion, fascination, love, and a sense of humor.

I envy you who haven't scanned the photographs before reading this foreword. Your joy is yet to be.

Photographing the Soothing Side of Life

BY PAT CROWE

A photographer, like a writer, always hopes to see his work published in a book. I've thought about this one for some time and I'm thankful to photographer and publisher Kevin Fleming for making it possible. I hope the book reveals my affection for the state that's been my home for twenty years.

I was reminded how warm and accepting the people of Delaware have been as I sorted through stacks of photographs. Having shot in the neighborhood of 600,000 frames for the Wilmington *News-Journal,* I no longer remember every name, but each face brought a rush of memories.

People have always been my favorite photographic subjects. On assignment I've covered celebrities – fighters Jake LaMotta and Michael Spinks, baseball all-star Hank Aaron, Gloria Steinem, and my boyhood idol, Roy Rogers.

But more often my subjects have been everyday Delawareans. I'm more grateful to them than they'll ever know. They proved to me there are no ordinary people, only people of extraordinary talent and character. I hope their faces show something of what I've felt as I traveled this intimate state — that the wonder of the human spirit is its ability to endure. Their faces illustrate this like nothing else, and speak to us of stoicism, humor, and goodwill.

Landscapes and wildlife have been my second love. I've spent many hours roaming the rolling countryside around Wilmington in search of nature's serenity. This may be because my father, a mailman who loved jazz drumming and poetry, painted pastoral settings around our home in Corning, New York, and taught me to see the elegance of a faded wooden barn and the grandeur of a tree on an autumn hillside.

I've been lucky that my editors have encouraged this work, in addition to asking me to cover robberies, fires, accidents, floods, and murders. Because of all the tragedy I've seen, I've felt that people would breathe easier on finding something calming and fun in the paper. Providing the more soothing side of life has been one of my missions.

In pursuing this goal I've had the opportunity to learn from a host of talented photographers who have practiced their craft in Delaware: Fred Comegys, Chuck McGowen, Leo Matkins, Ron Cortes, Bill Ballenberg, Bob Herbert, and Kevin Fleming — to name a few.

Their inspiration paid off when I was named 1975 Newspaper Photographer of the Year, an award given by the National Press Photographers Association with the University of Missouri and Nikon. The award is considered the highest honor a newspaper photographer can receive. Working with creative, competitive colleagues gave me the incentive to do good work. Their drive also explains why the *News-Journal* has excelled in photography.

I had no direction when I graduated from high school in 1960. I enlisted in the Army, mostly because I wanted to travel. I admired my mother's spirit and energy, and took my father's sense of adventure as my own. The Army was my means of seeing the world, and Uncle Sam obliged by sending me to Frankfurt, West Germany. At age twenty-two I was on my way back to the base, after a thirty-day leave at home, when my life changed. My father stopped at a newsstand before dropping me at the airport so I could buy something to read on the flight across the Atlantic. Two magazines, *Modern Photography* and *Camera 35* leaped into my hands. One had an article about W. Eugene Smith, often called the father of modern photojournalism. When I was invited to Columbia, Missouri, to receive the Newspaper Photographer of the Year Award I met Eugene Smith, who was being honored that year for his

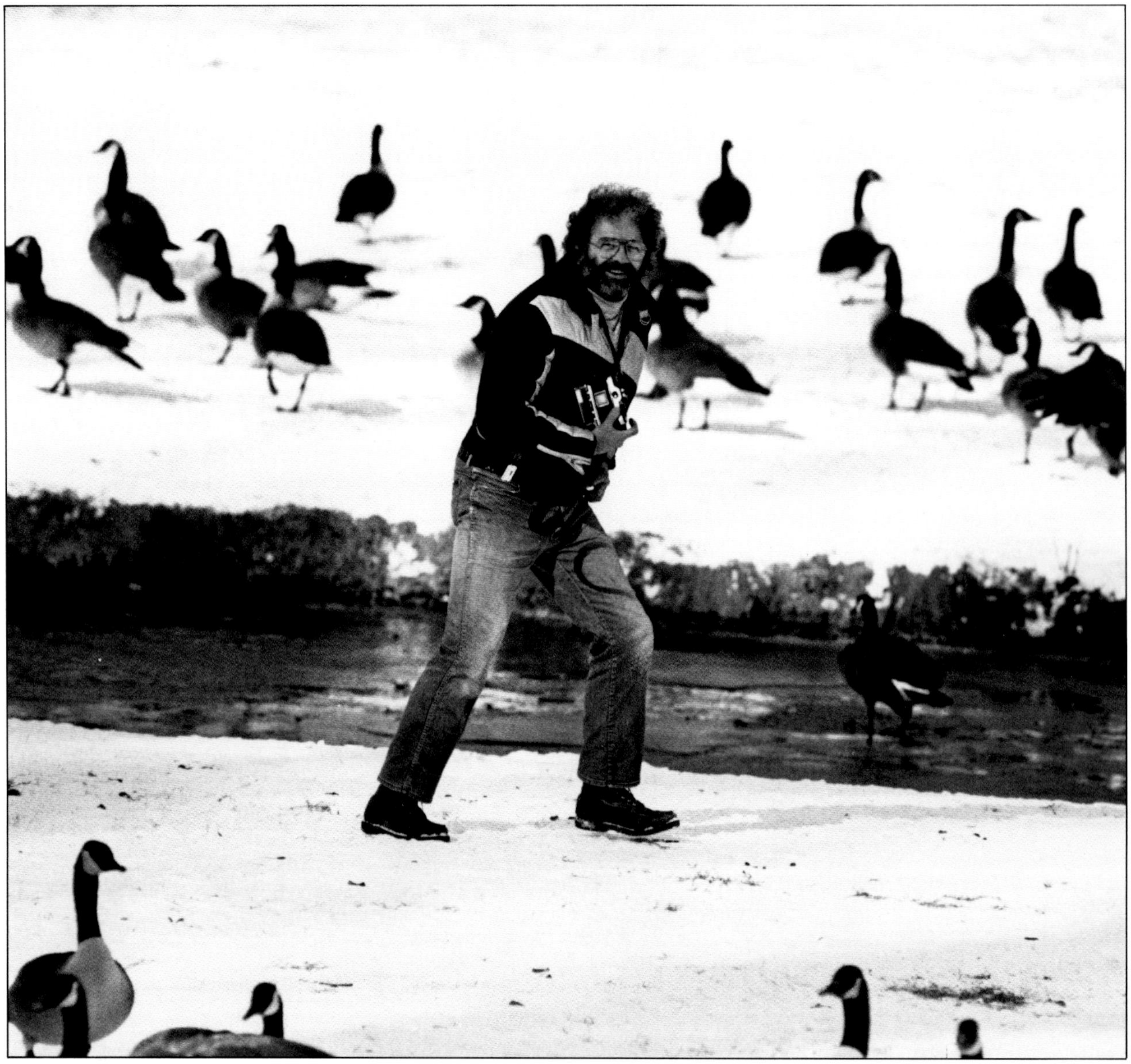

Photograph by Fred Comegys

lifetime's work. Unbeknownst to him, he had started me in photography. It was Smith who inspired me to become a storyteller.

An Army buddy sold me my first camera, a Minolta Autocord. It's a two-and-one-quarter-inch-format camera; I still have it on a shelf at home. I located a darkroom and dove into the work, learning as I went along. A lab instructor encouraged me by entering two of my early photographs in an armed services competition. I won two honorable mentions.

I returned home in 1963 with a stack of pictures. They were street scenes and shots of people I'd met all over Europe. I also came back with the desire to work for a newspaper. My hometown newspaper, the *Leader*, gave me my start. It was a small daily and I was the only photographer. I joined the National Press Photographers Association and read everything I could find. Two of the most influential books were Henri Cartier-Bresson's *The Decisive Moment* and Yousuf Karsh's *Portraits of Greatness.*

I won a few prizes given by the Associated Press. I also moved to a larger paper, the *Times-Union* in Rochester, New York. By 1969 I wanted to work for a more picture-oriented paper and applied to several around the country. The Wilmington *News-Journal* and *Newsday* offered jobs. Not being able to imagine myself happy on suburban Long Island, I chose Wilmington with its nearby mills, stone barns, and spring houses.

It was a good choice.

DELAWARE PORTRAIT

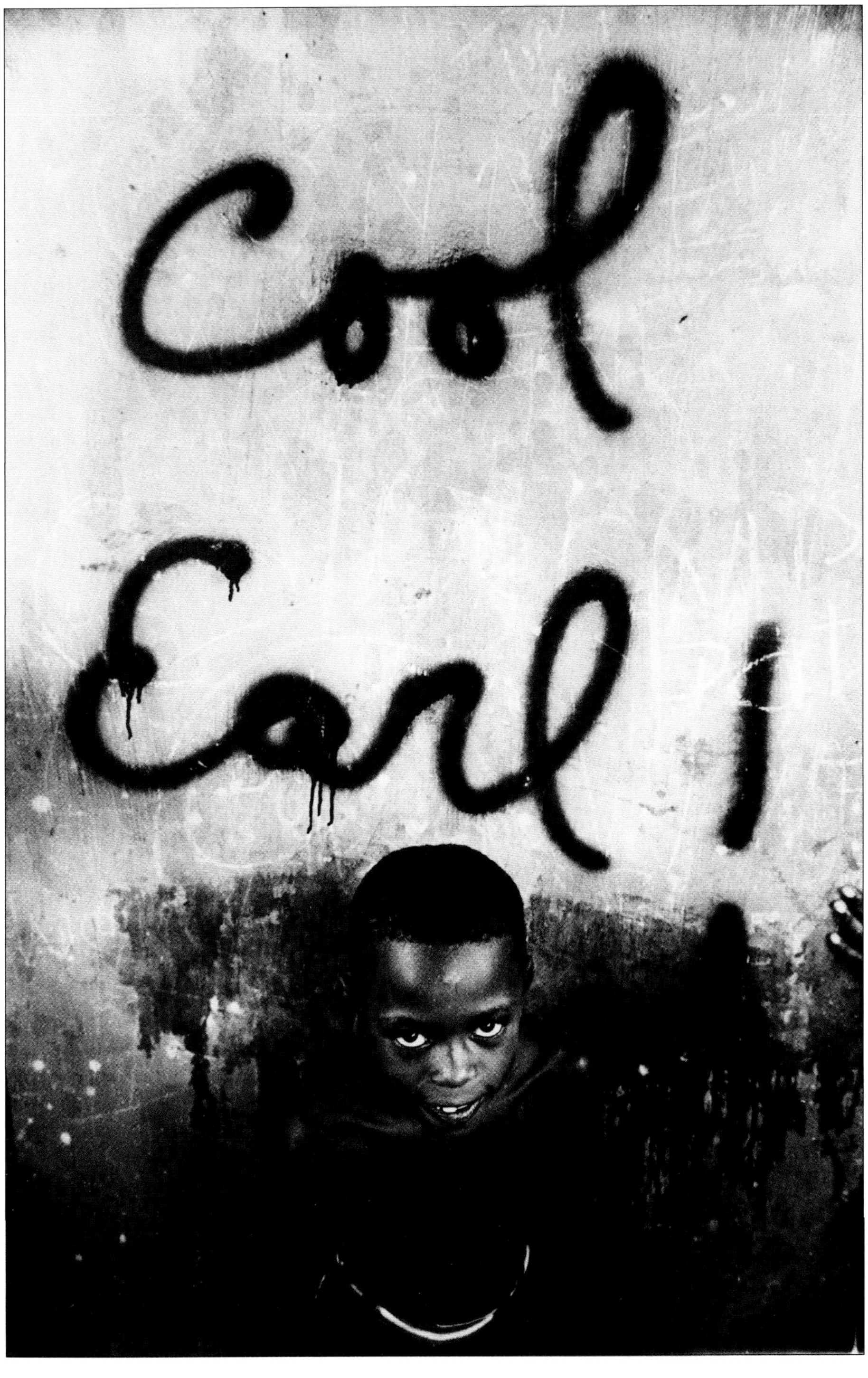

Wilmington, 1973

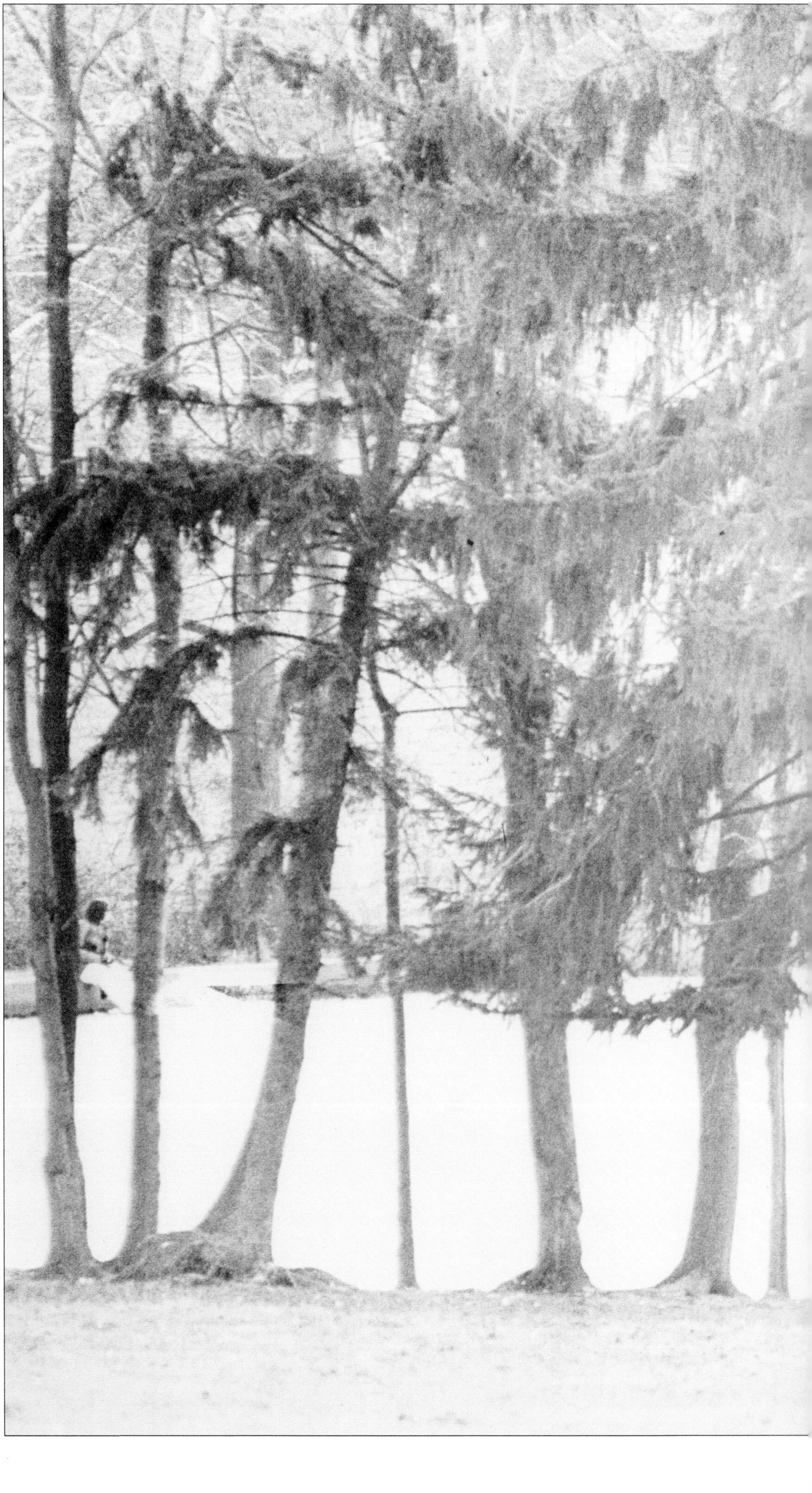

Twin Ponds, Greenville, 1986

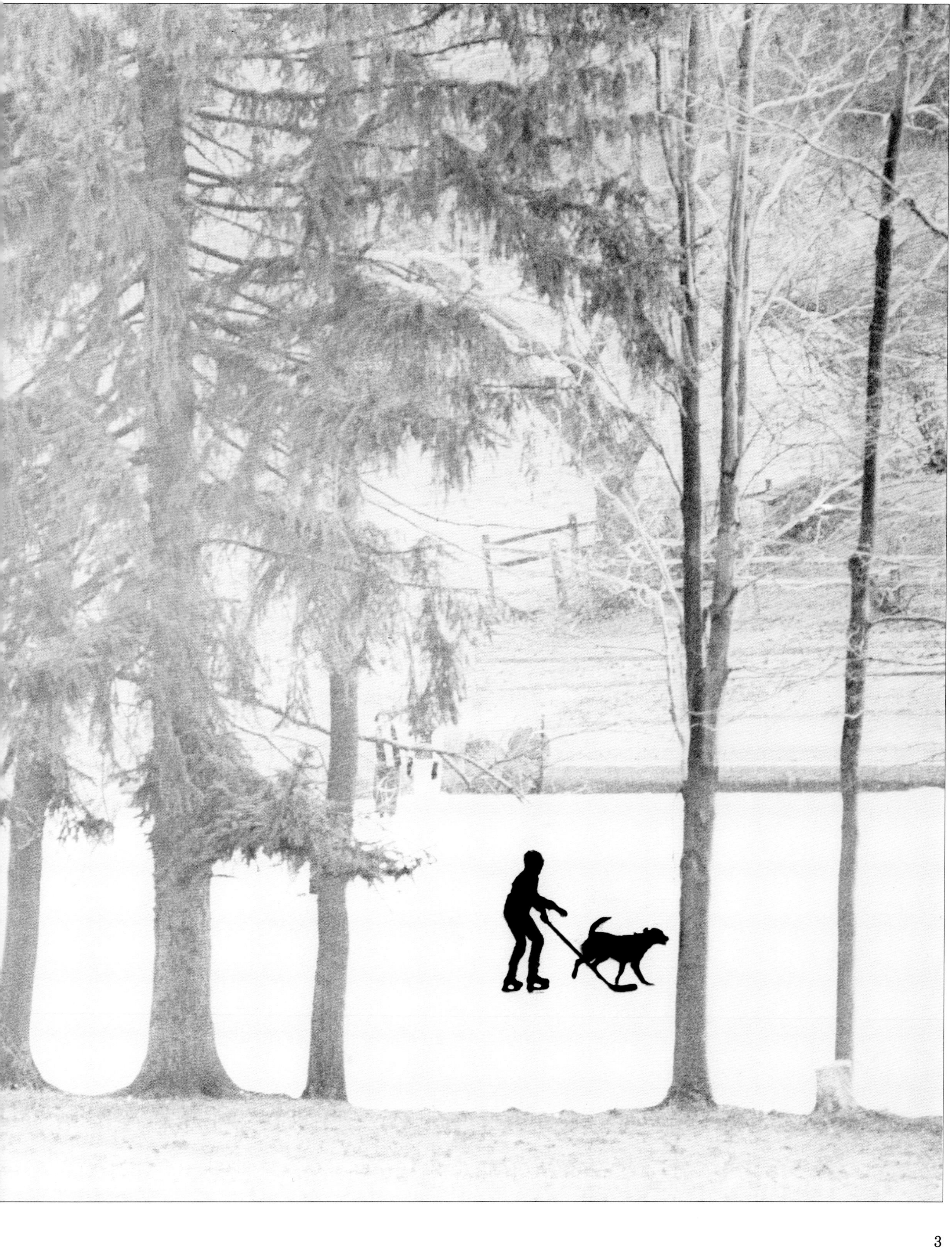

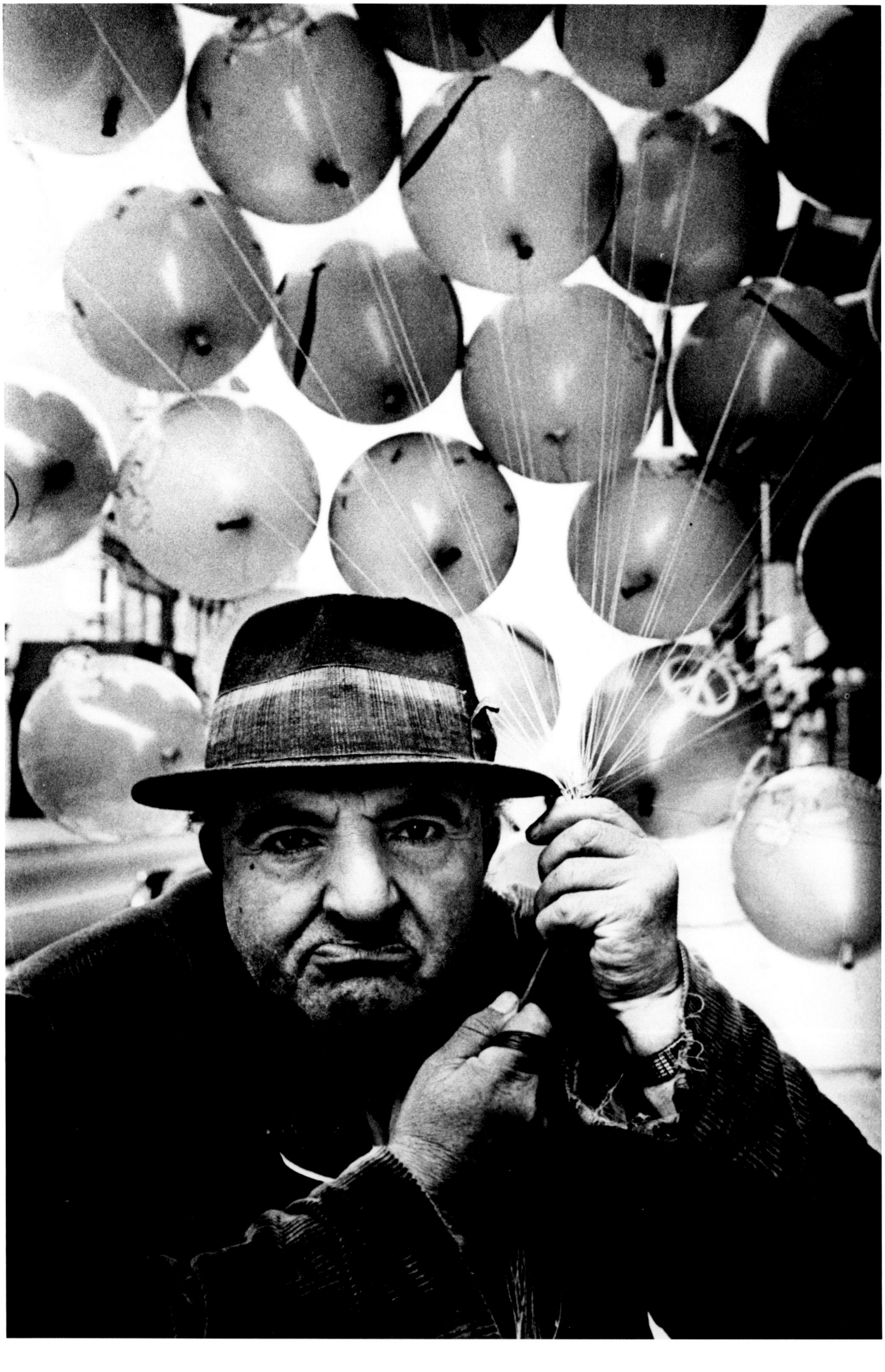

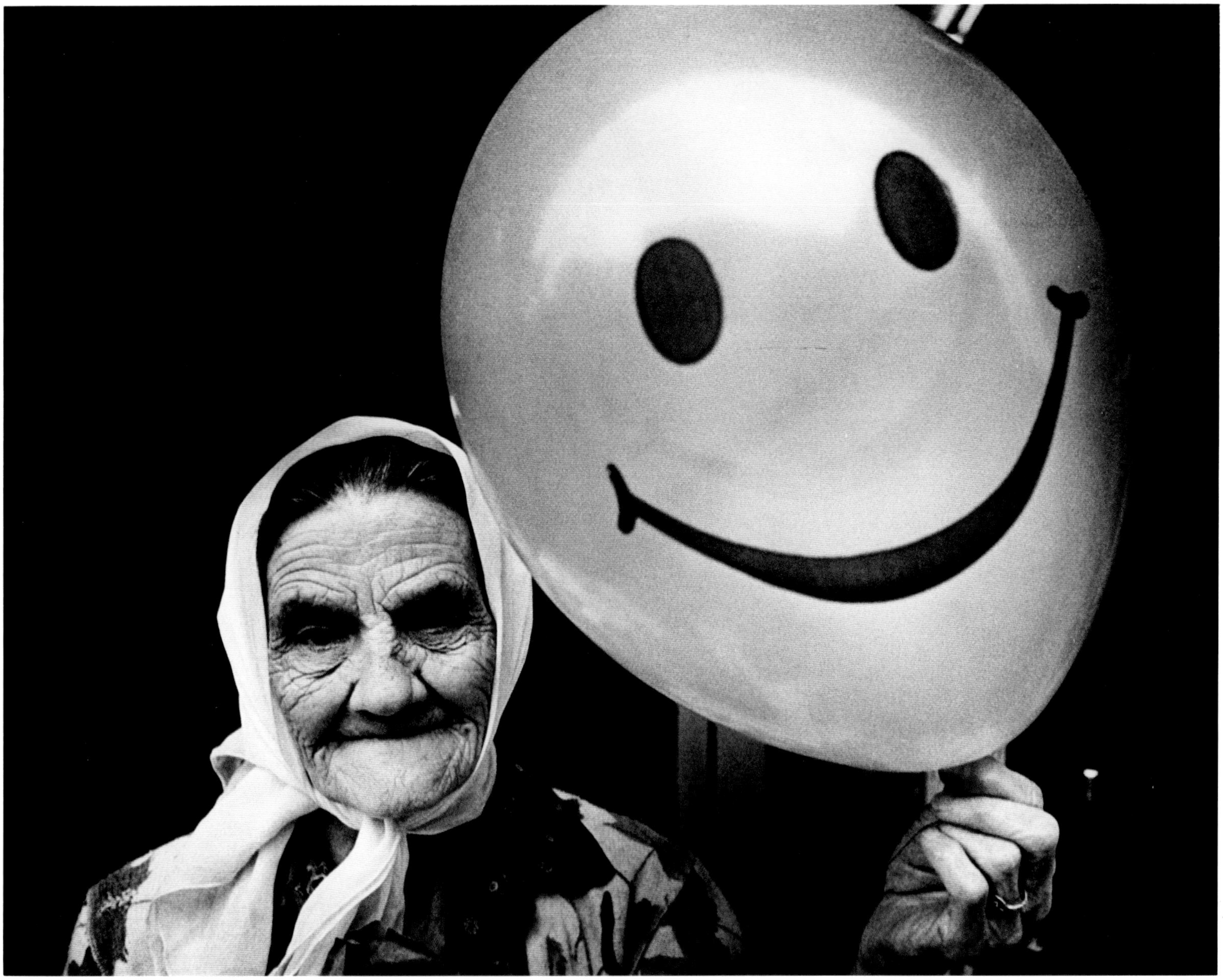

Memorial Day Parade, Market Street, Wilmington, 1974

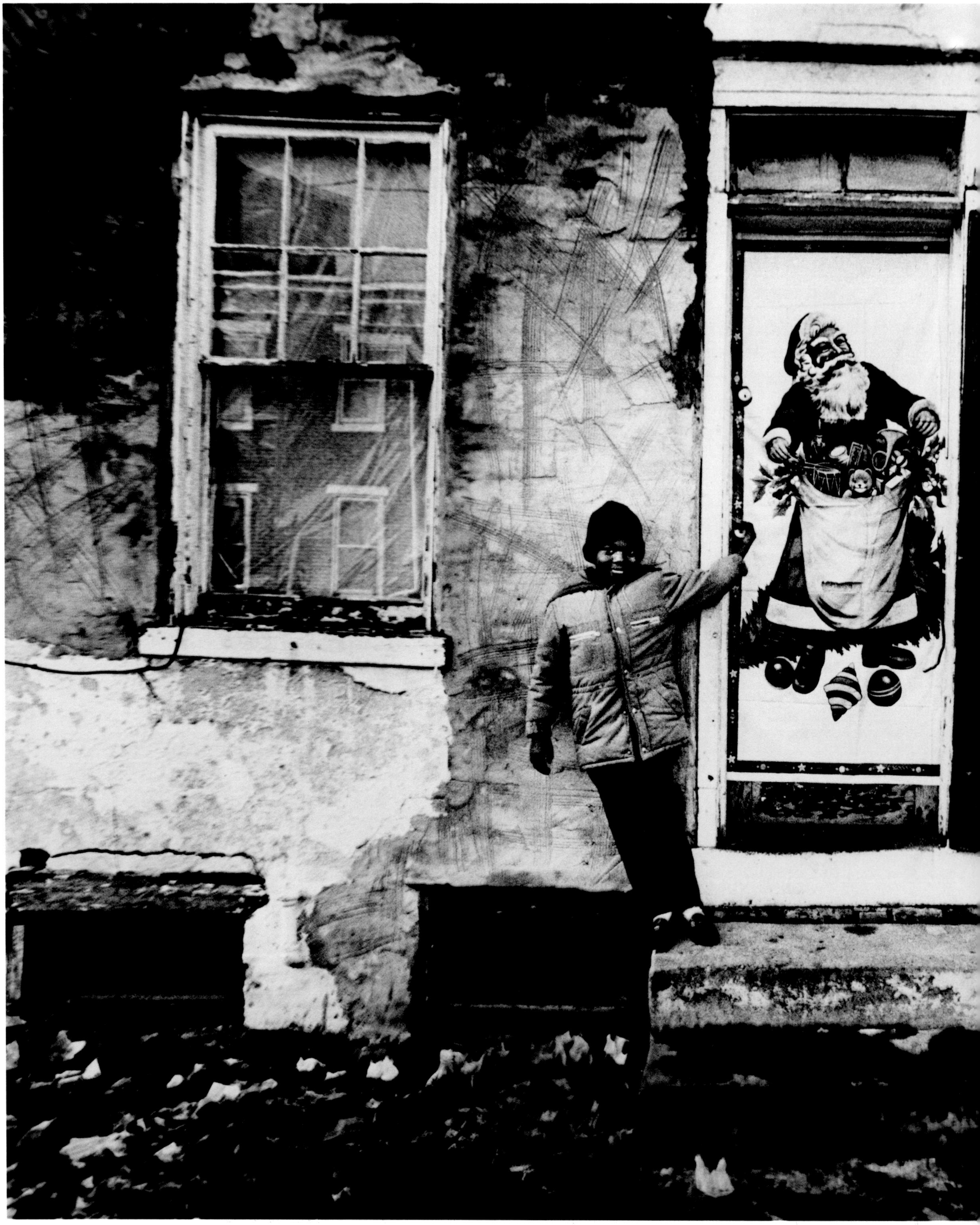

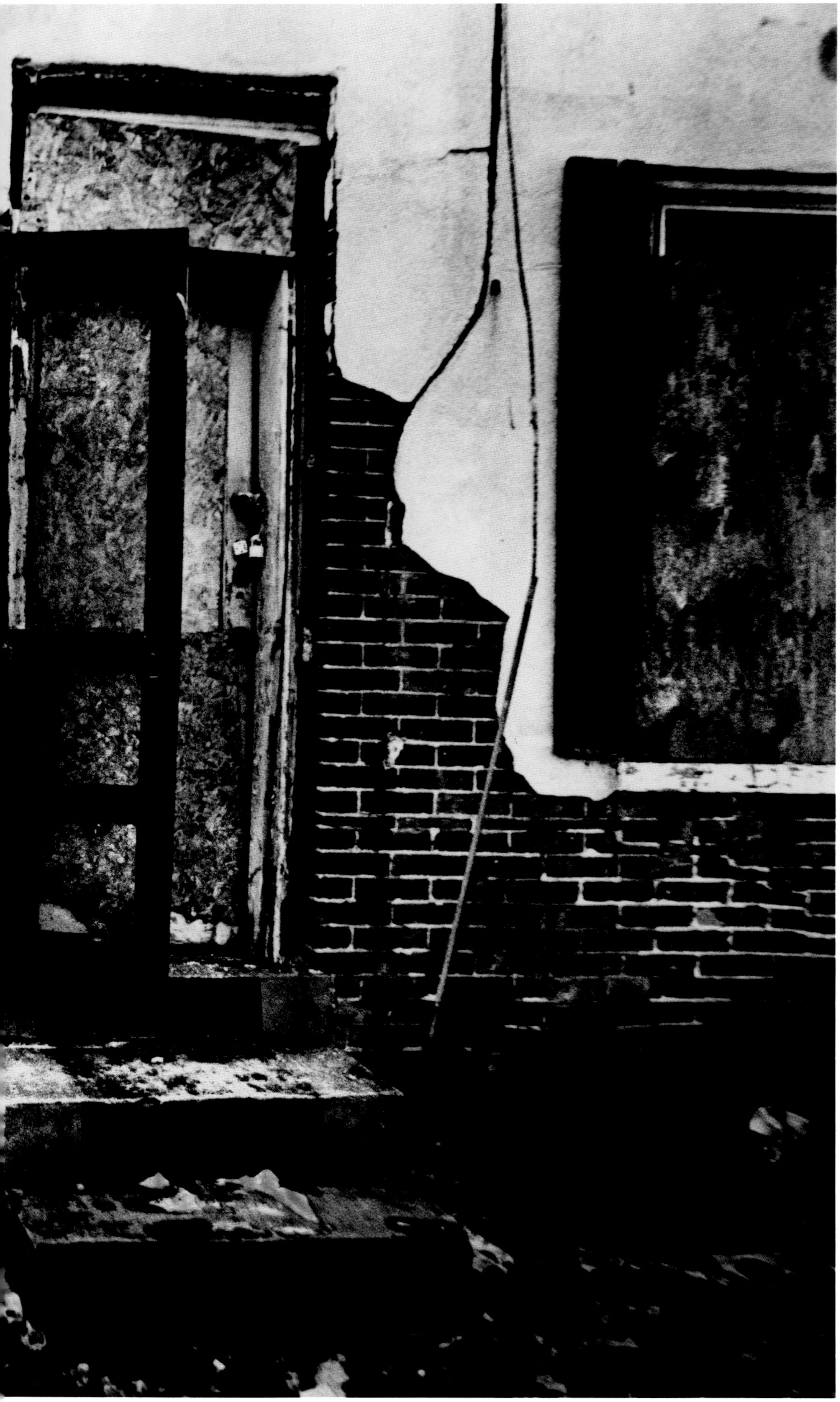

William Howard Draper, East 22nd Street, Wilmington, Christmas, 1985

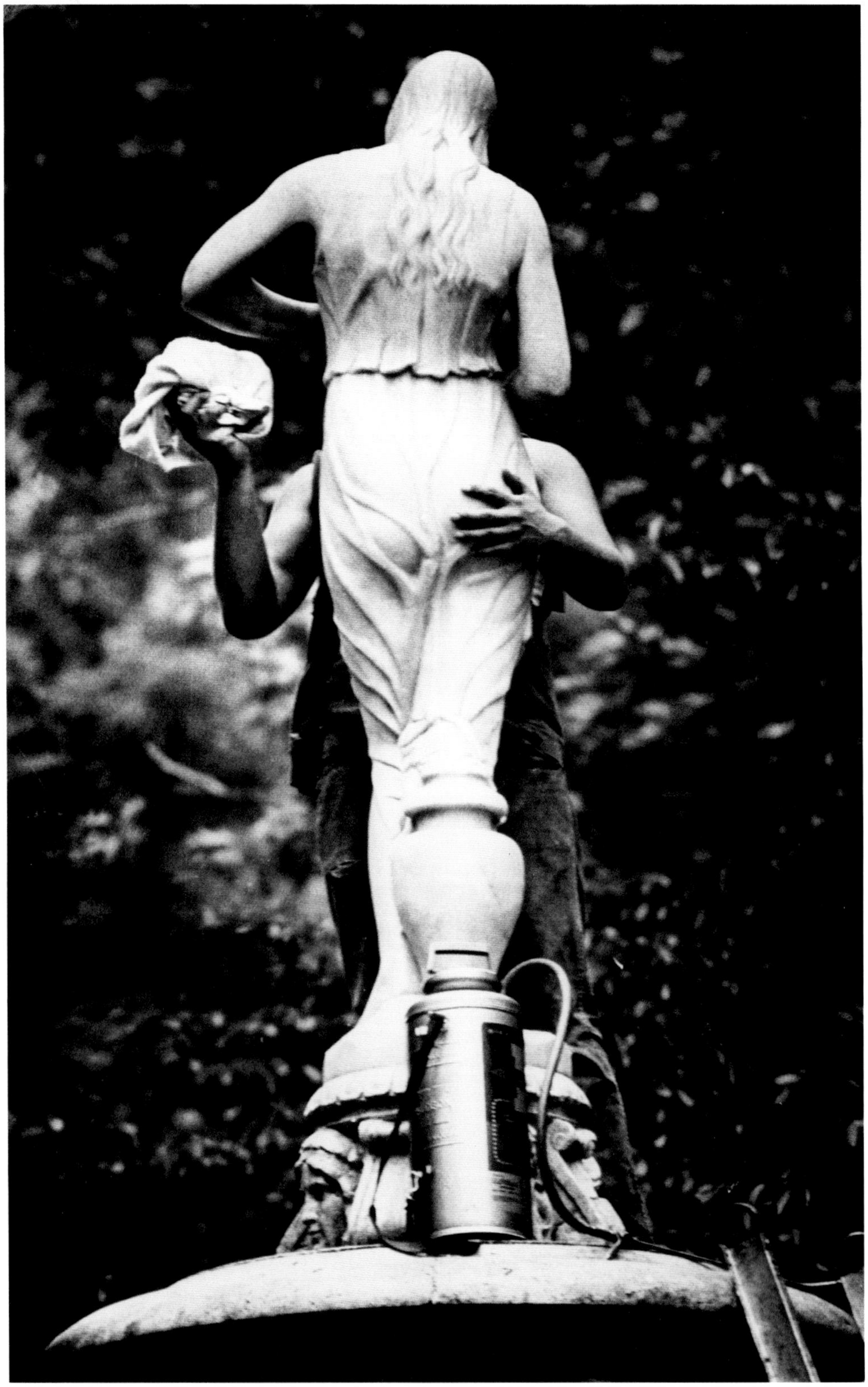

Josephine Gardens, Wilmington, 1971

Bill Ott, Wilmington art show, 1973

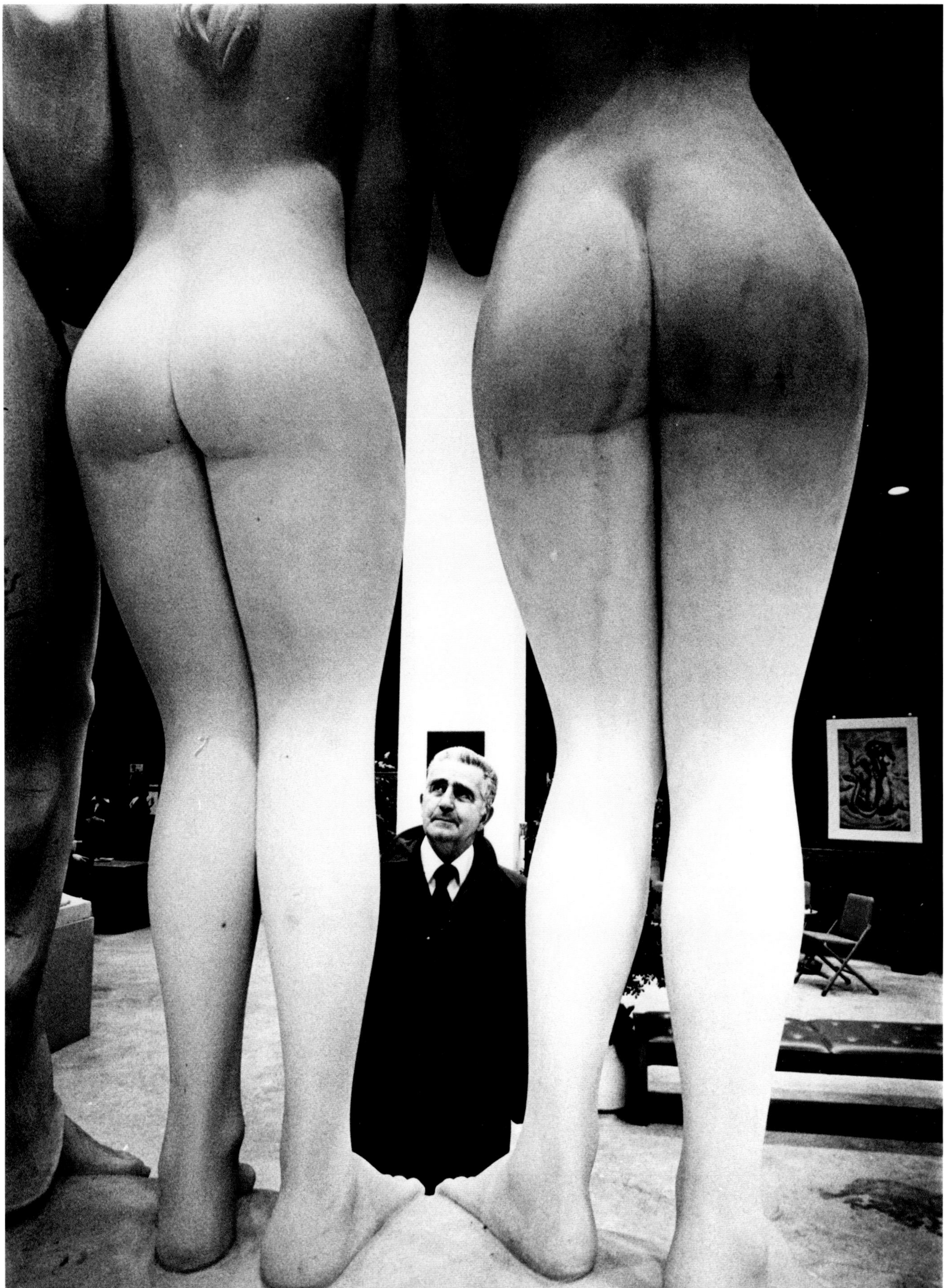

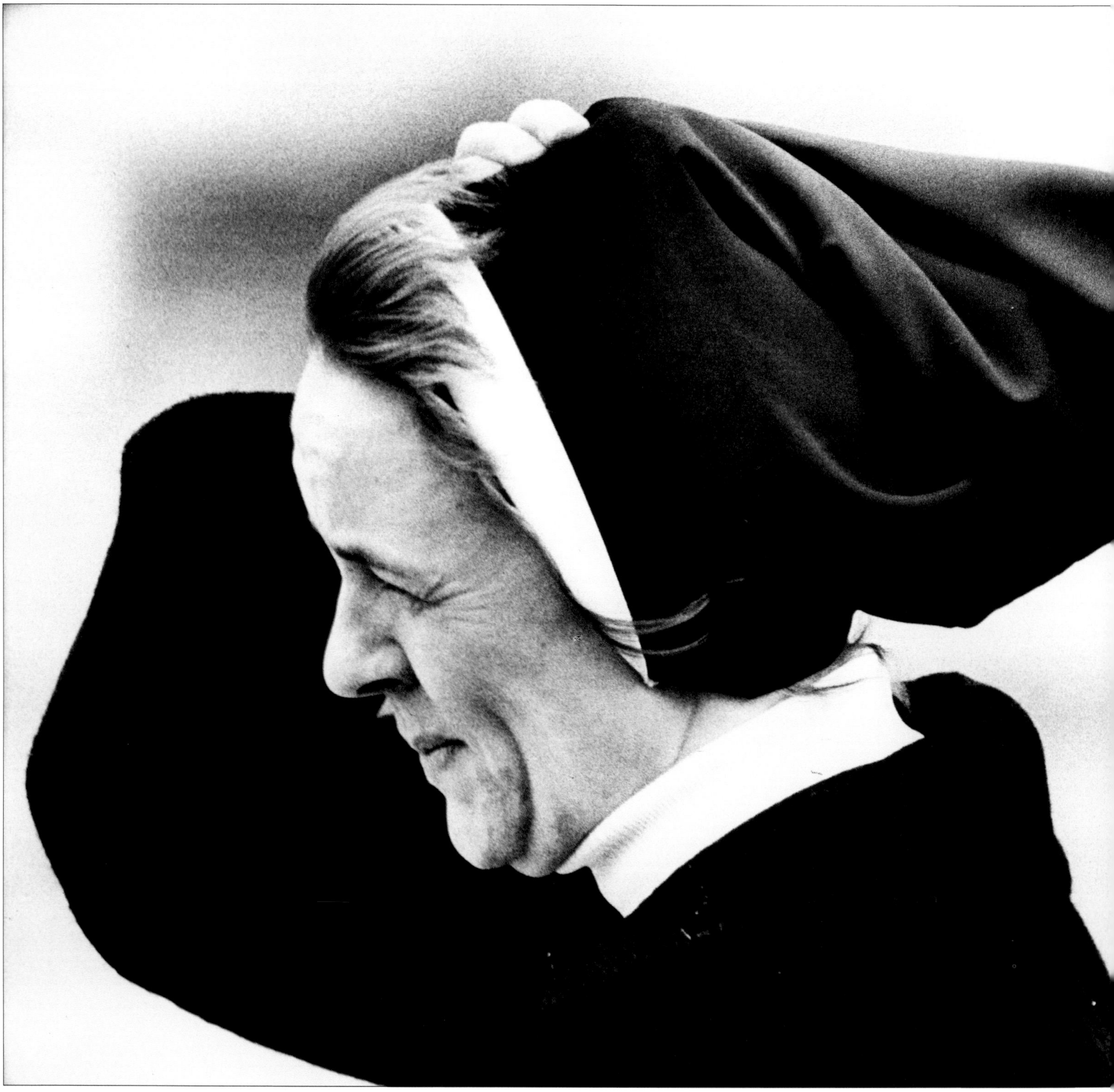

Sister Helen MacLennan, St. Anthony's School, Wilmington, 1975

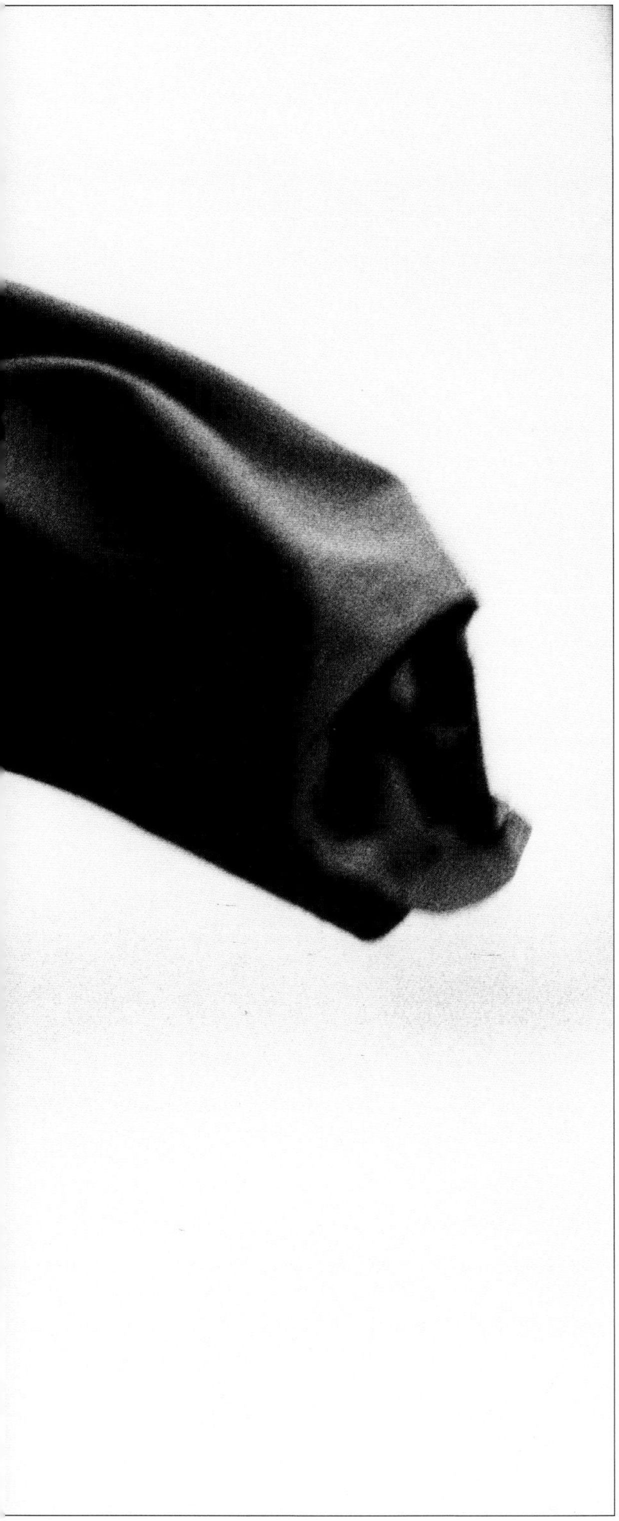

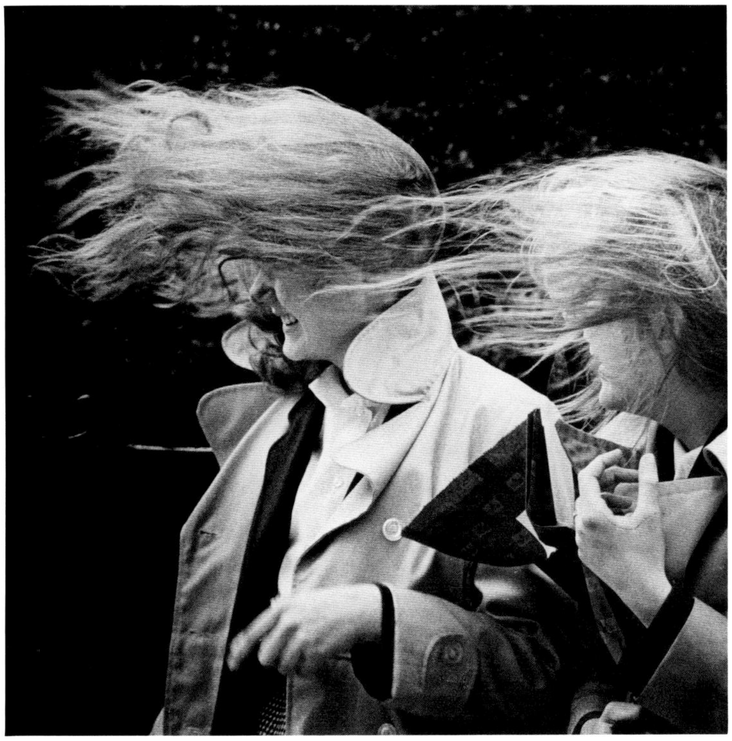

Hurricane winds, Market Street, Wilmington, 1970

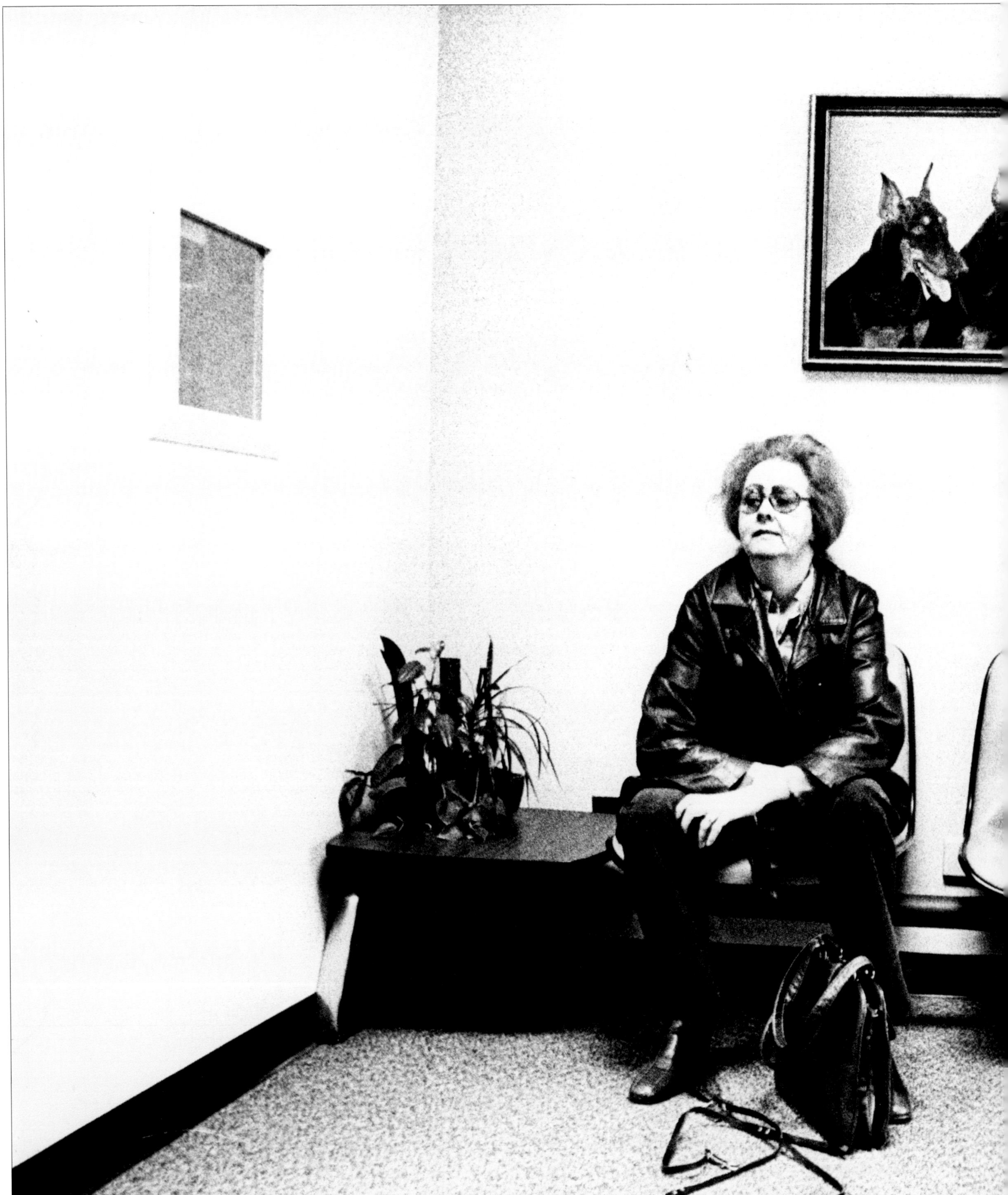

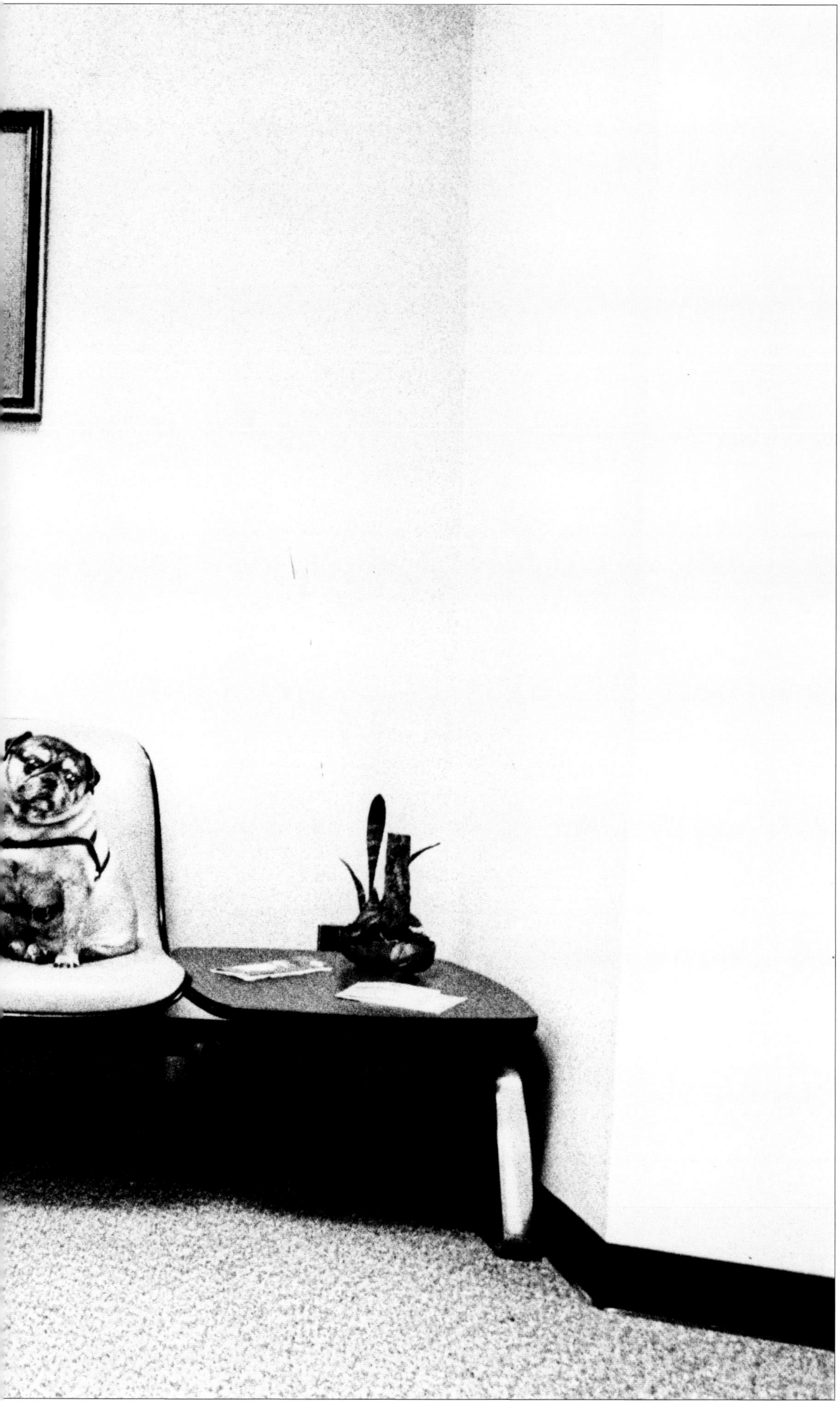

Nancy Curren and Mugg,
her Chinese pug,
Brandywine Hundred
Veterinary Hospital, 1979

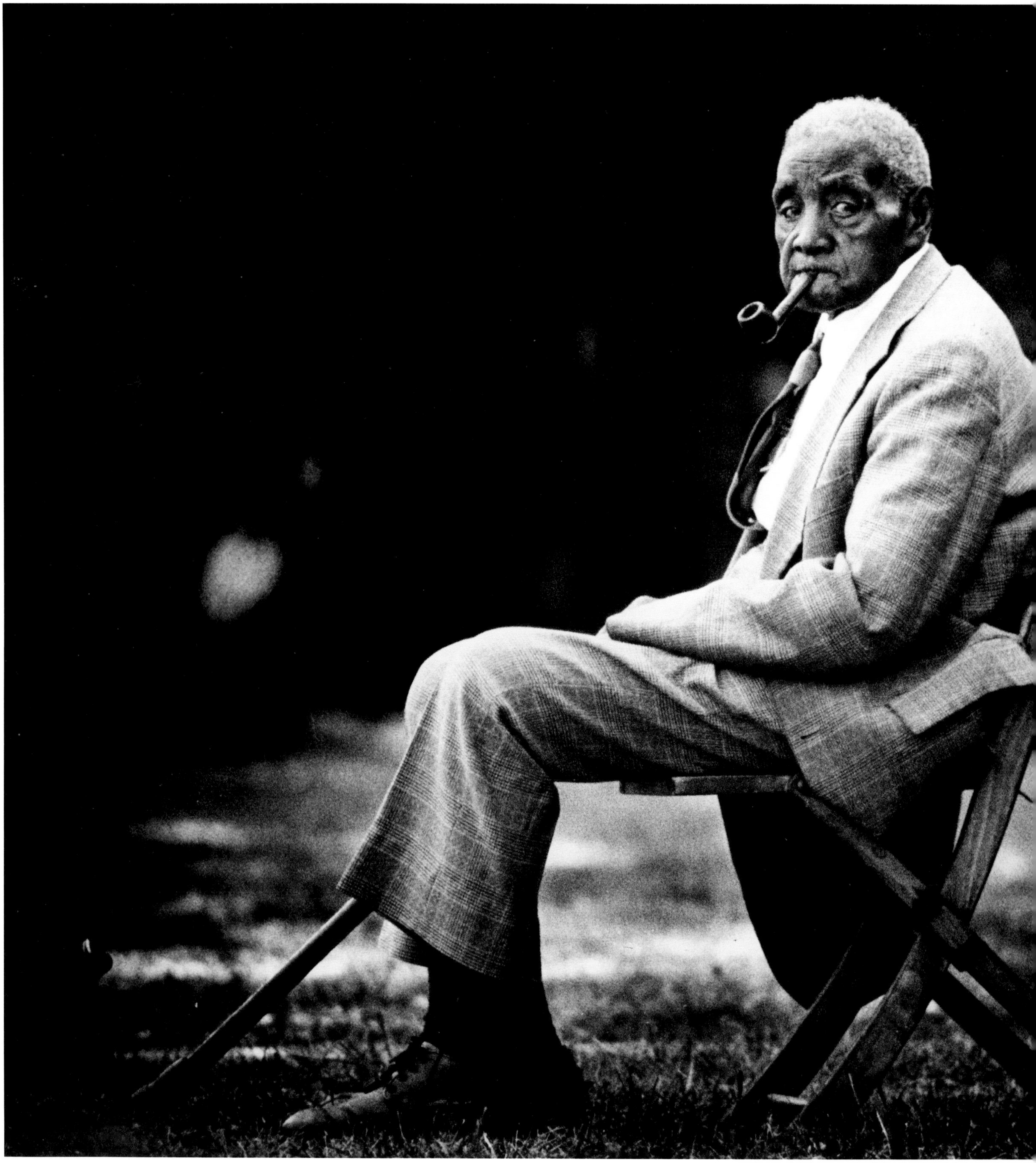

The Reverend Johnson Henry Williams at 100, Wilmington, 1980

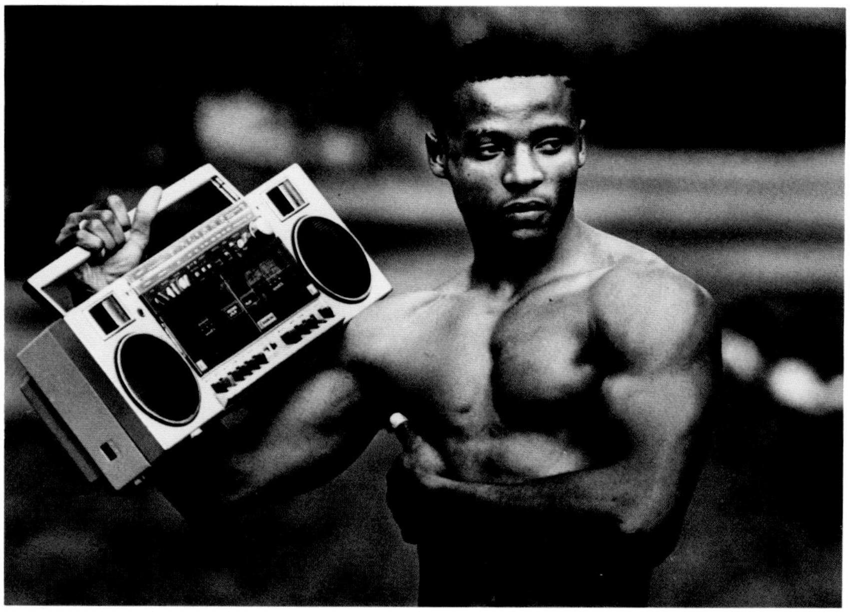

Nate White, Brandywine Park, Wilmington, 1985

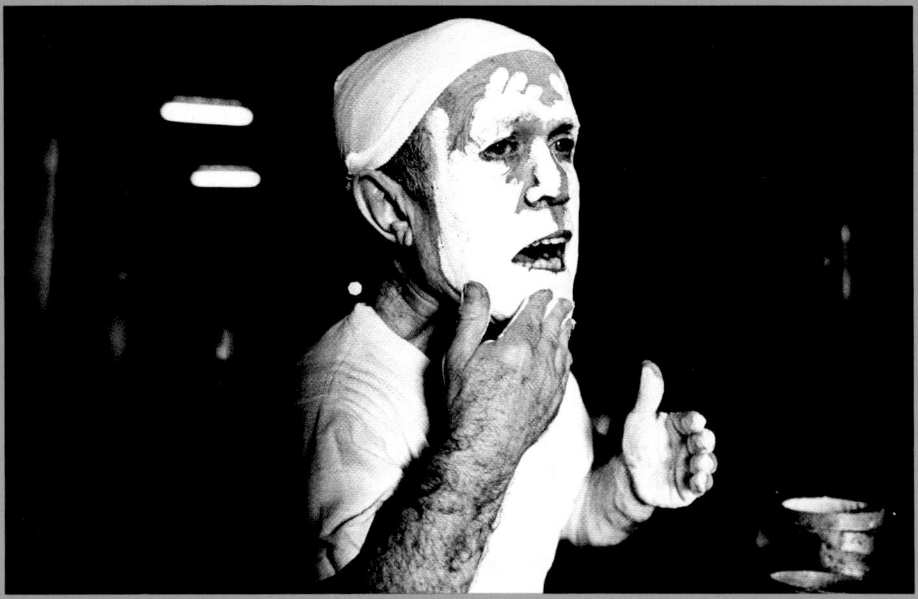

Prince Paul *1974*

I met Ringling Brothers' Prince Paul at the A.I. duPont Institute where he was entertaining the hospital's children. Impresed by his talent, his pride, and his ability to make children laugh, I asked if I could photograph him backstage at the Spectrum in Philadelphia. A world-renowned clown, he talked about his 28 years with the circus. "It would have been easy for me to stay at home and miss the fun and challenge. Being a little guy, I'd probably be a nobody. But with the circus, when I get a reaction out of people, I'm somebody."

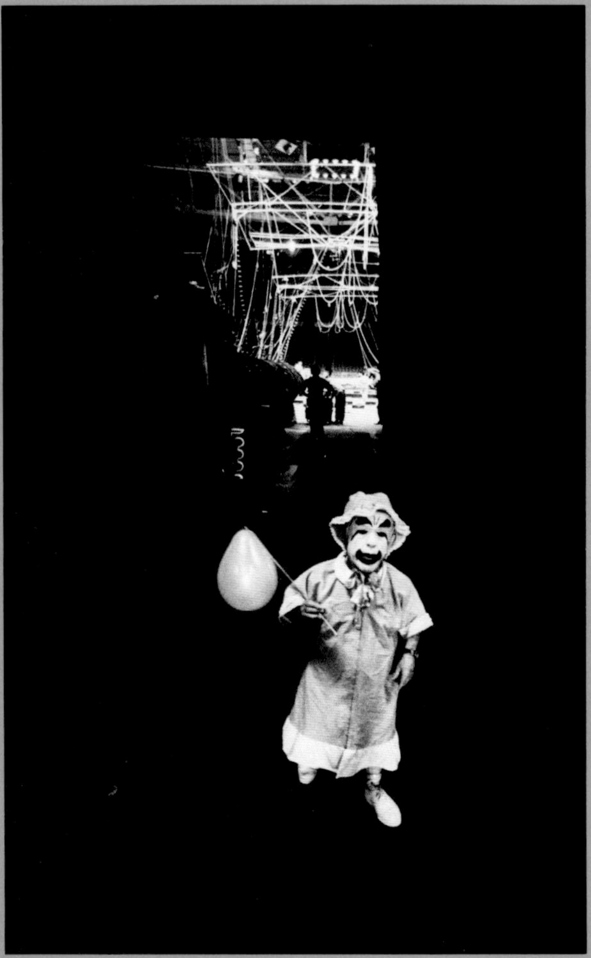

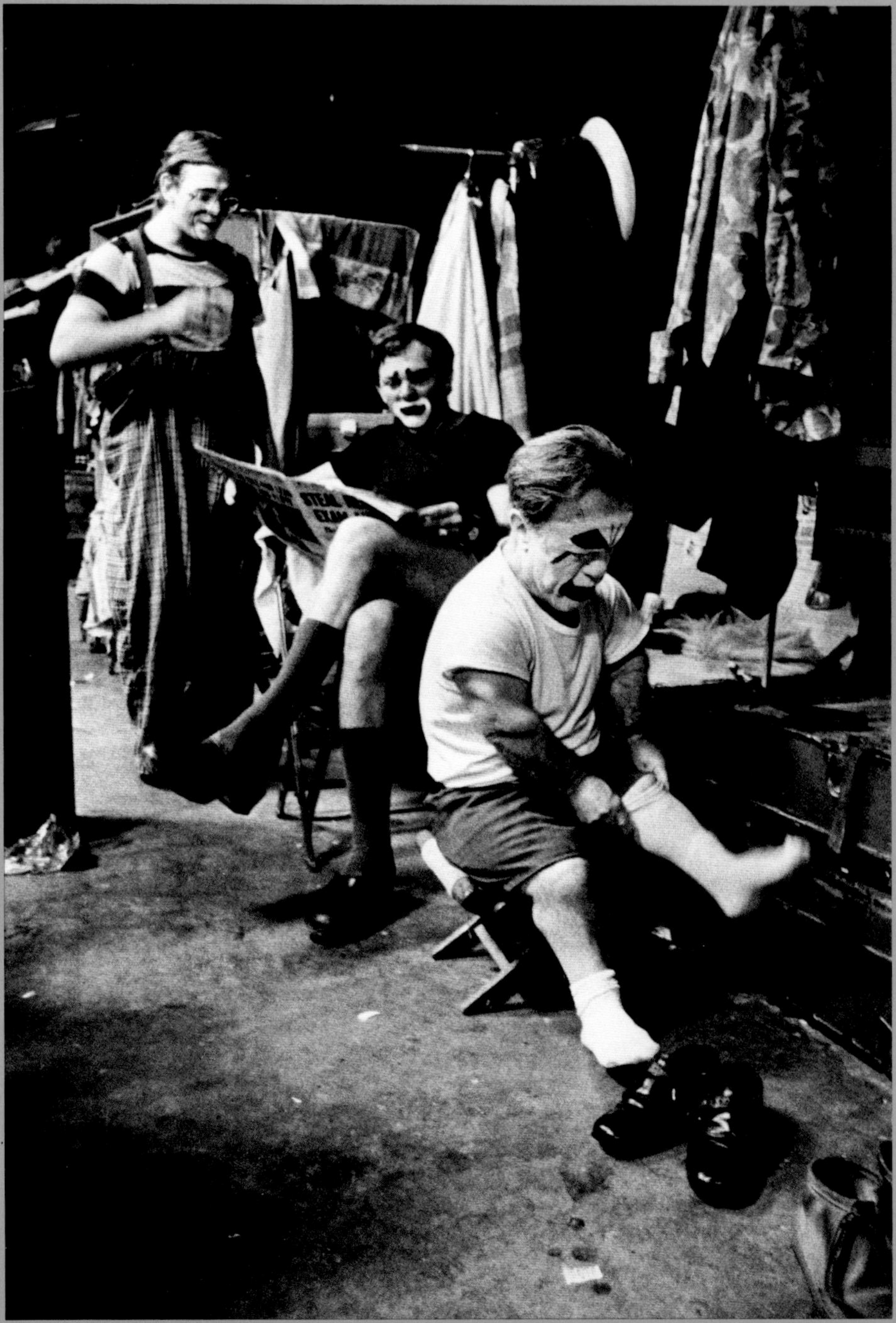

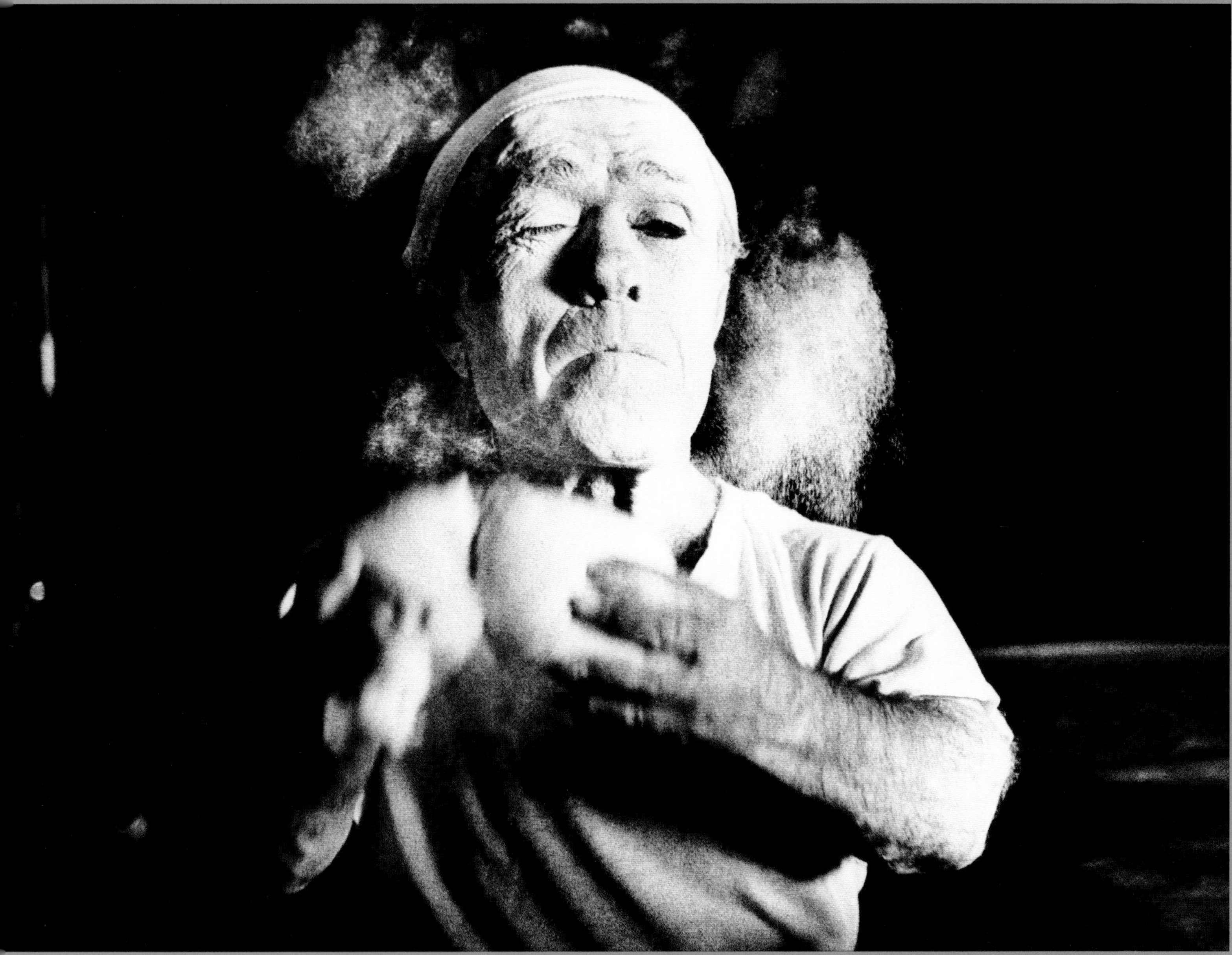

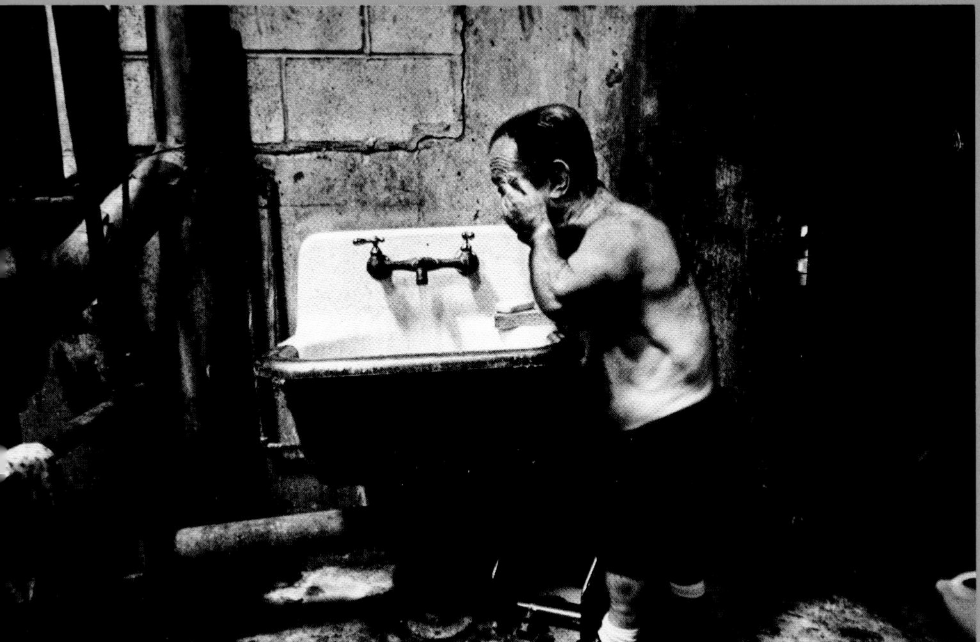

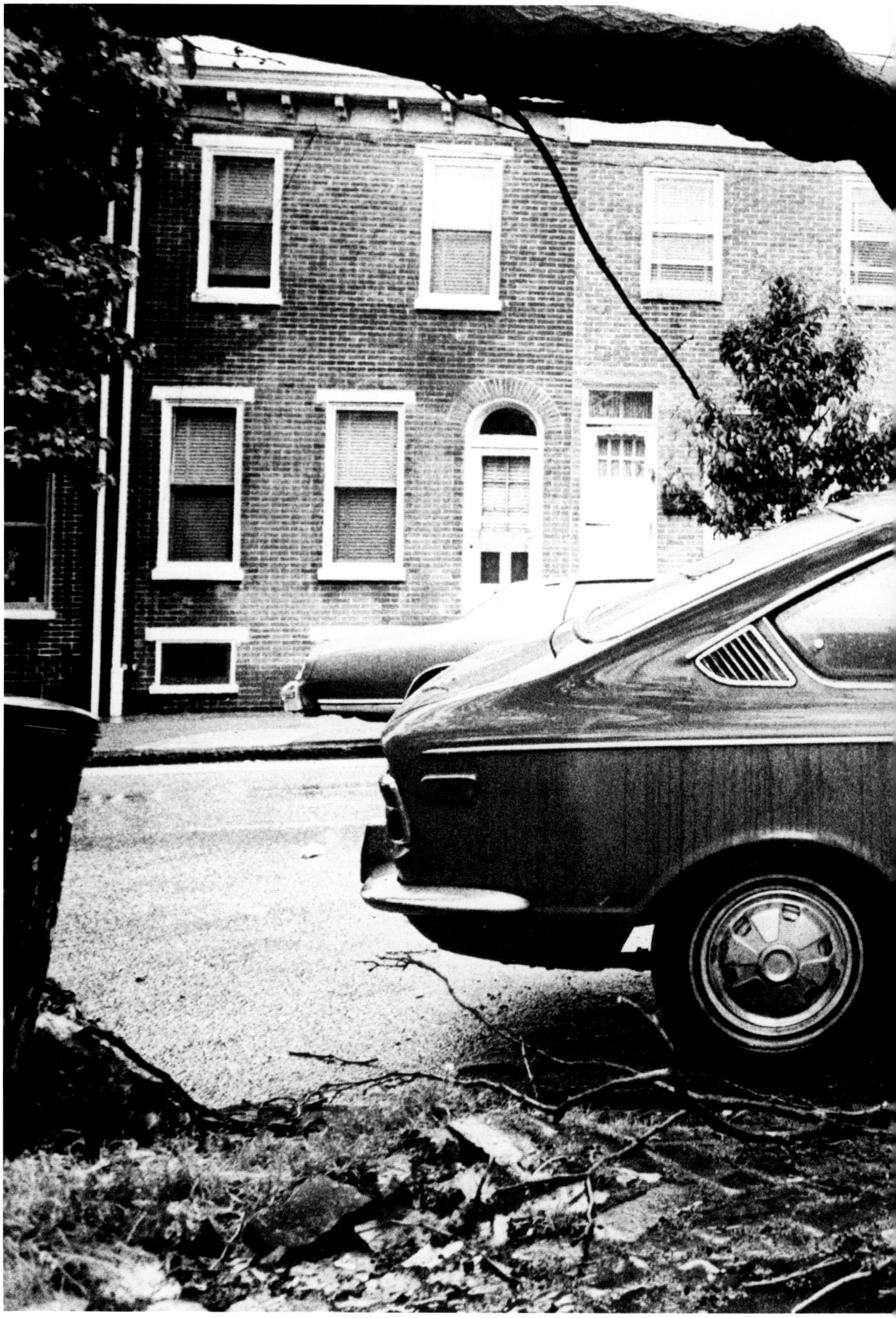

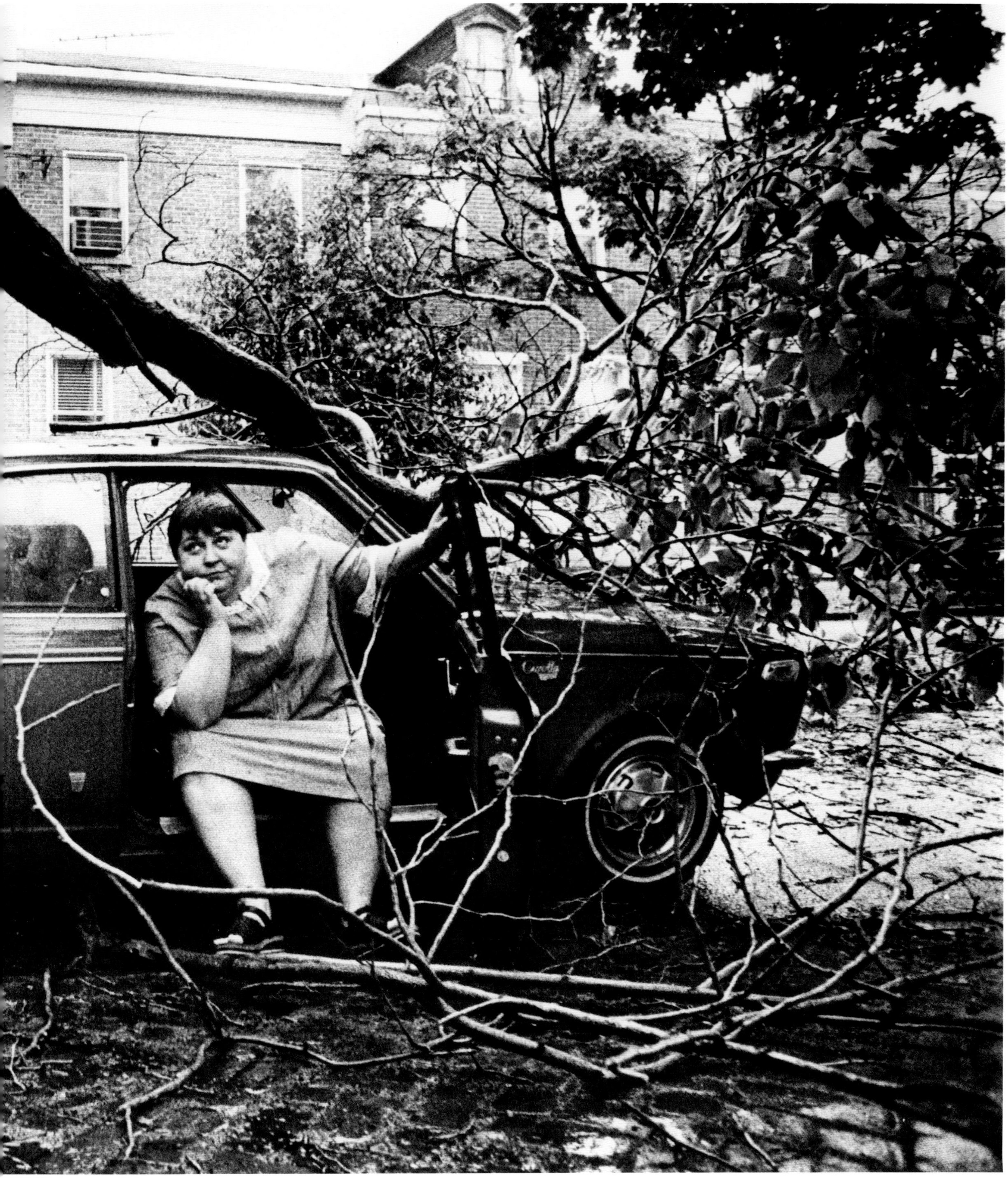

Antoinette Klonowski, Van Buren Street windstorm, Wilmington, 1981

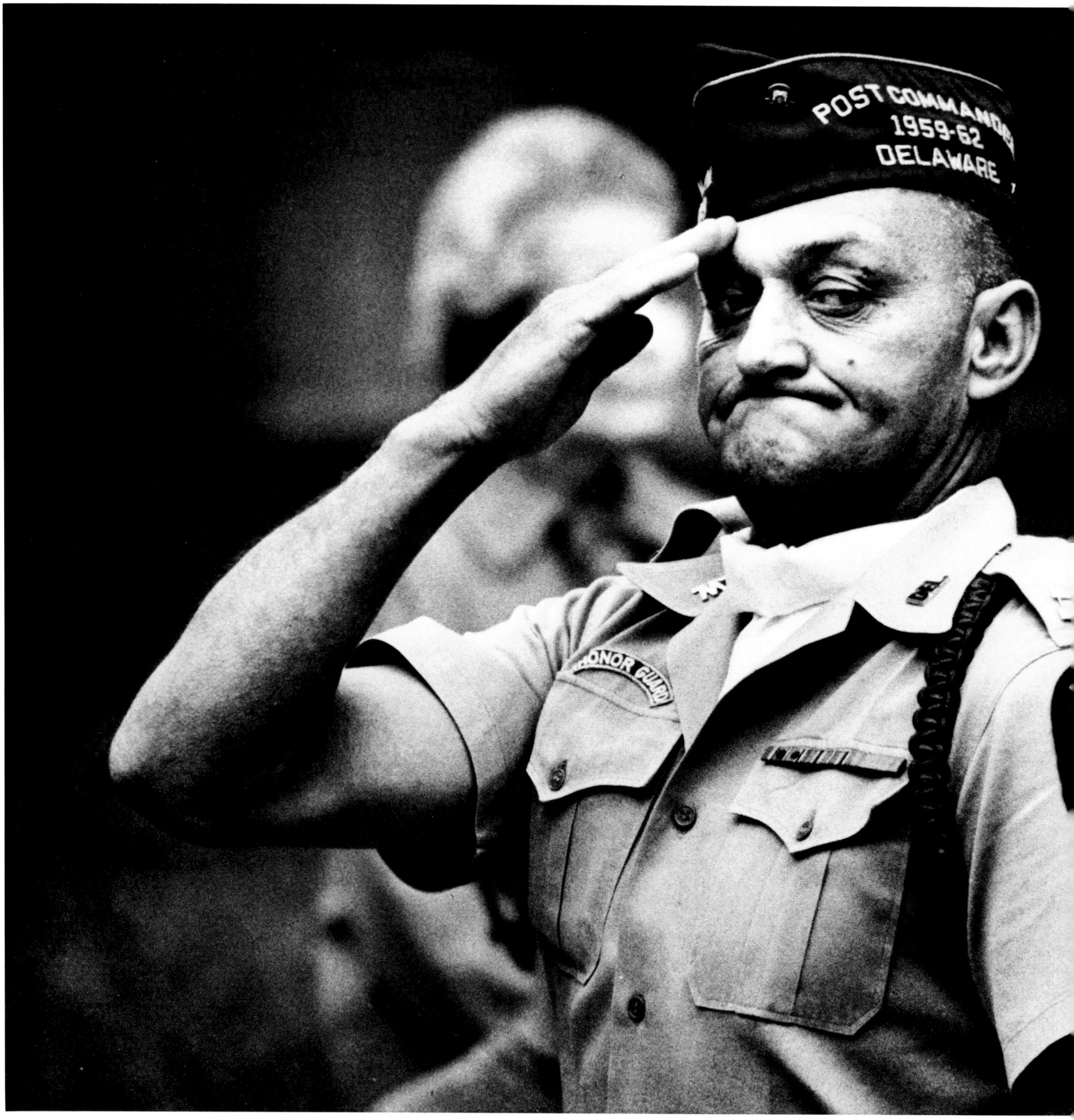

Memorial Day, Wilmington, 1974

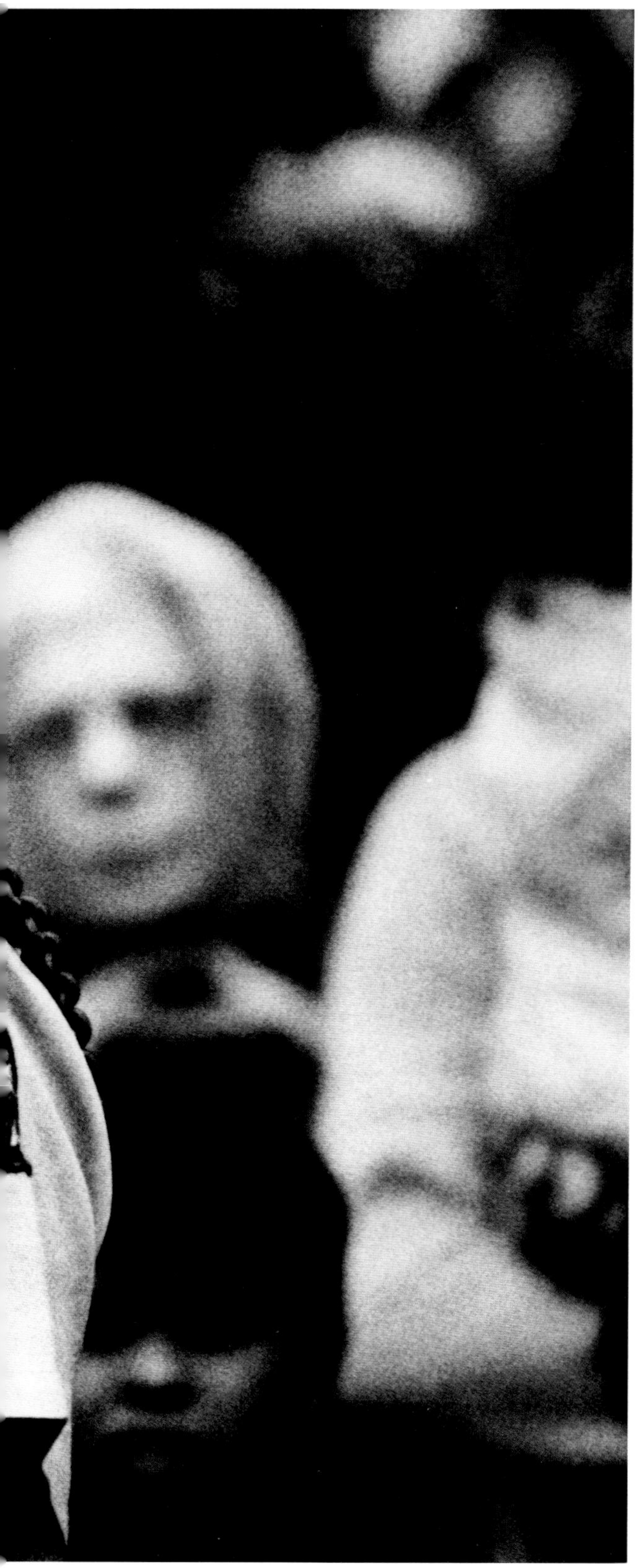

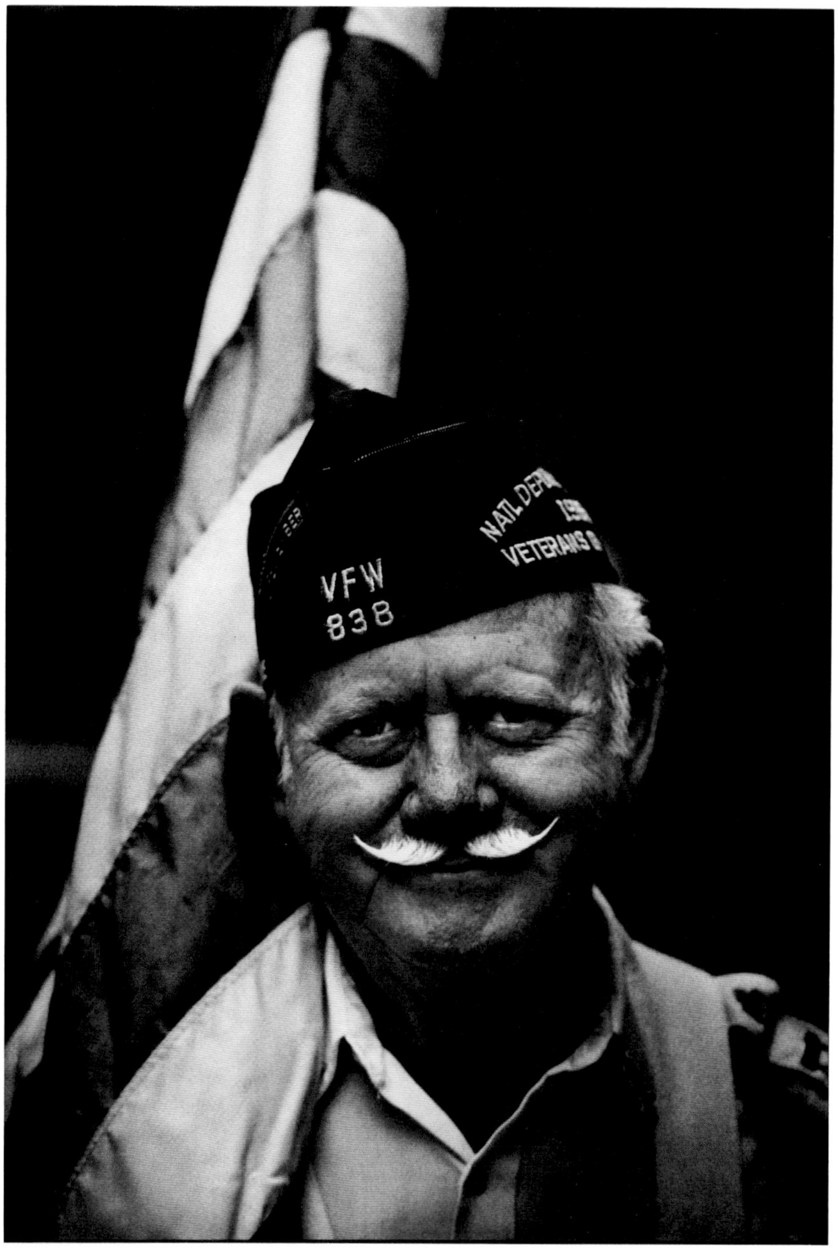

Memorial Day, Wilmington, 1986

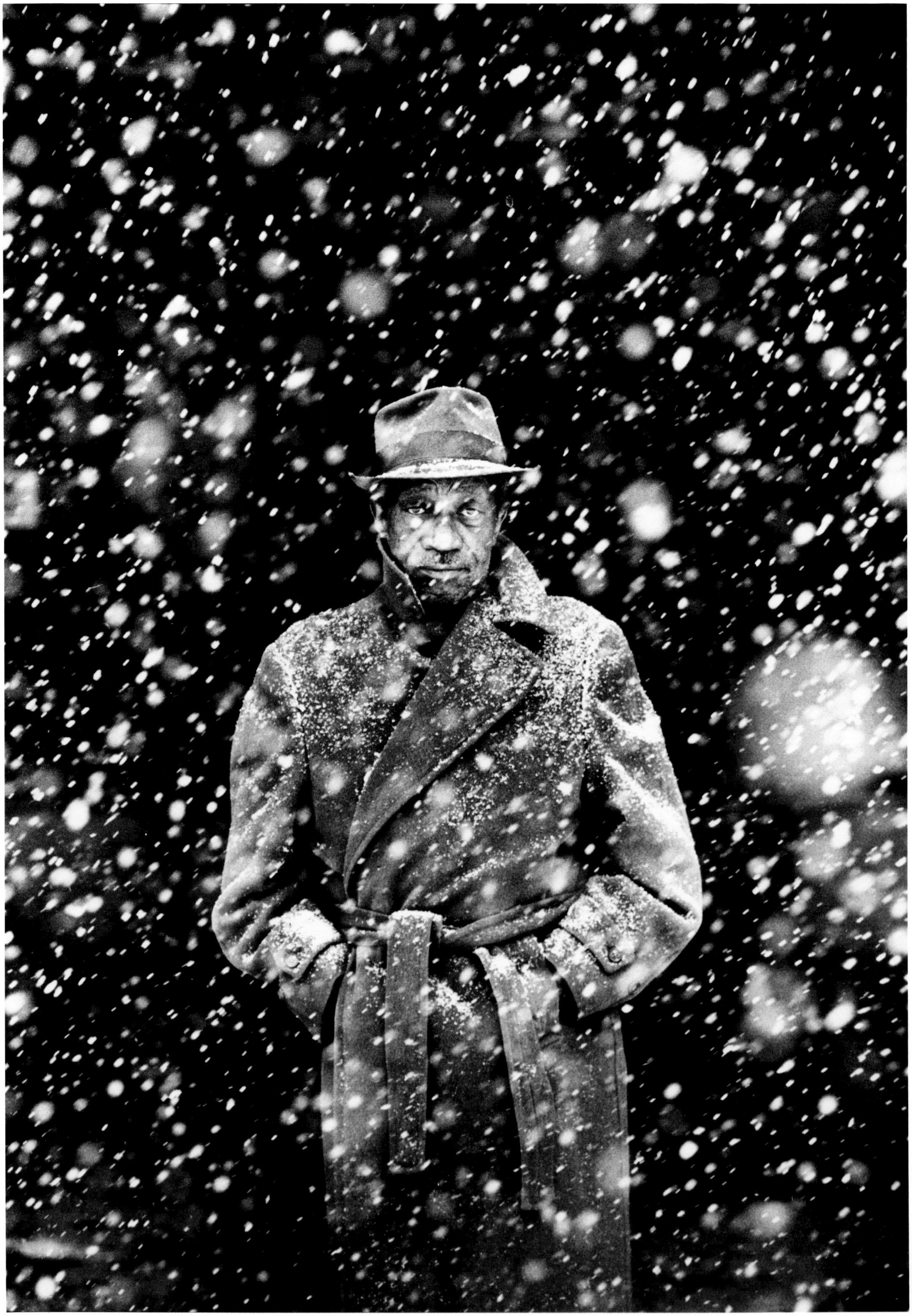

Wilmington, 1987

Wilmington, 1974

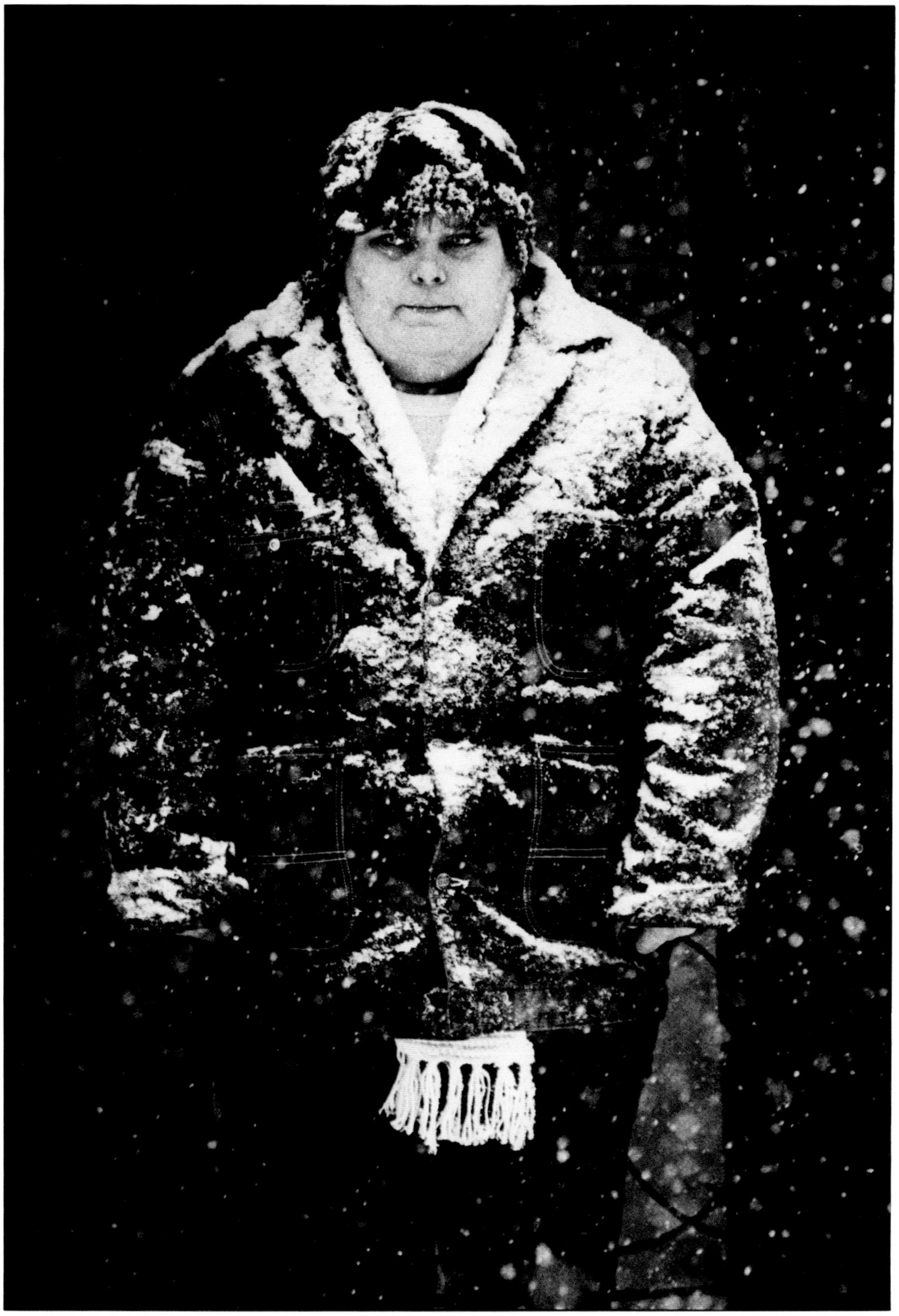

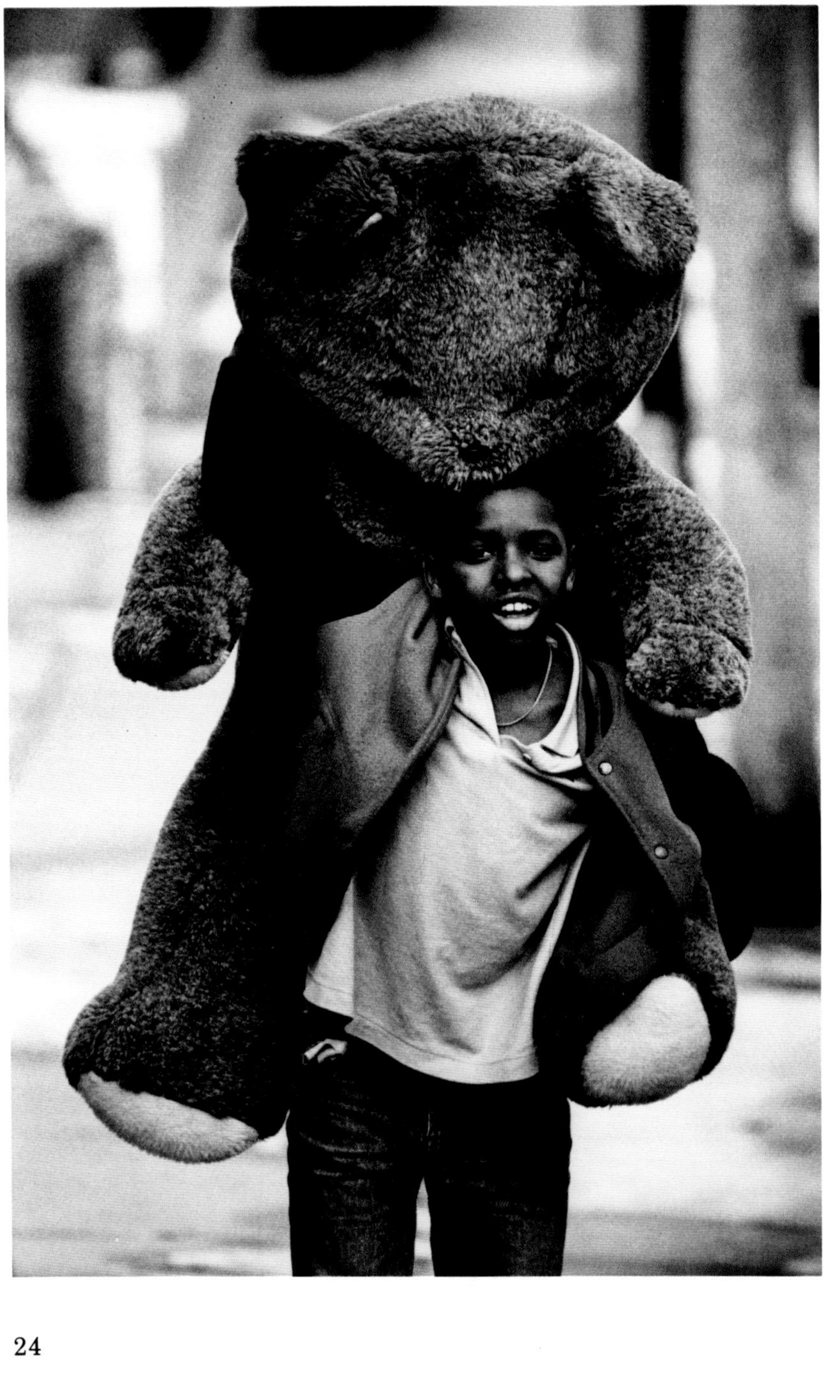

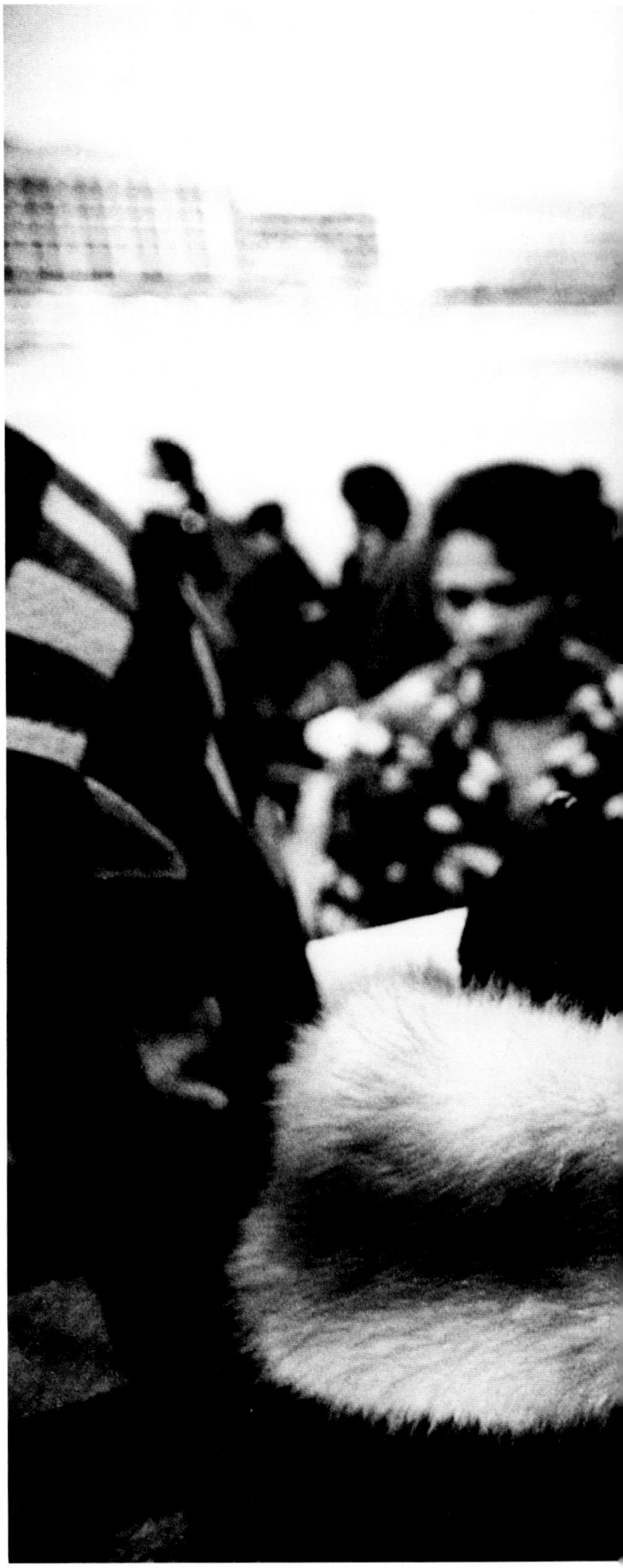

Lancaster Avenue, Wilmington, 1988

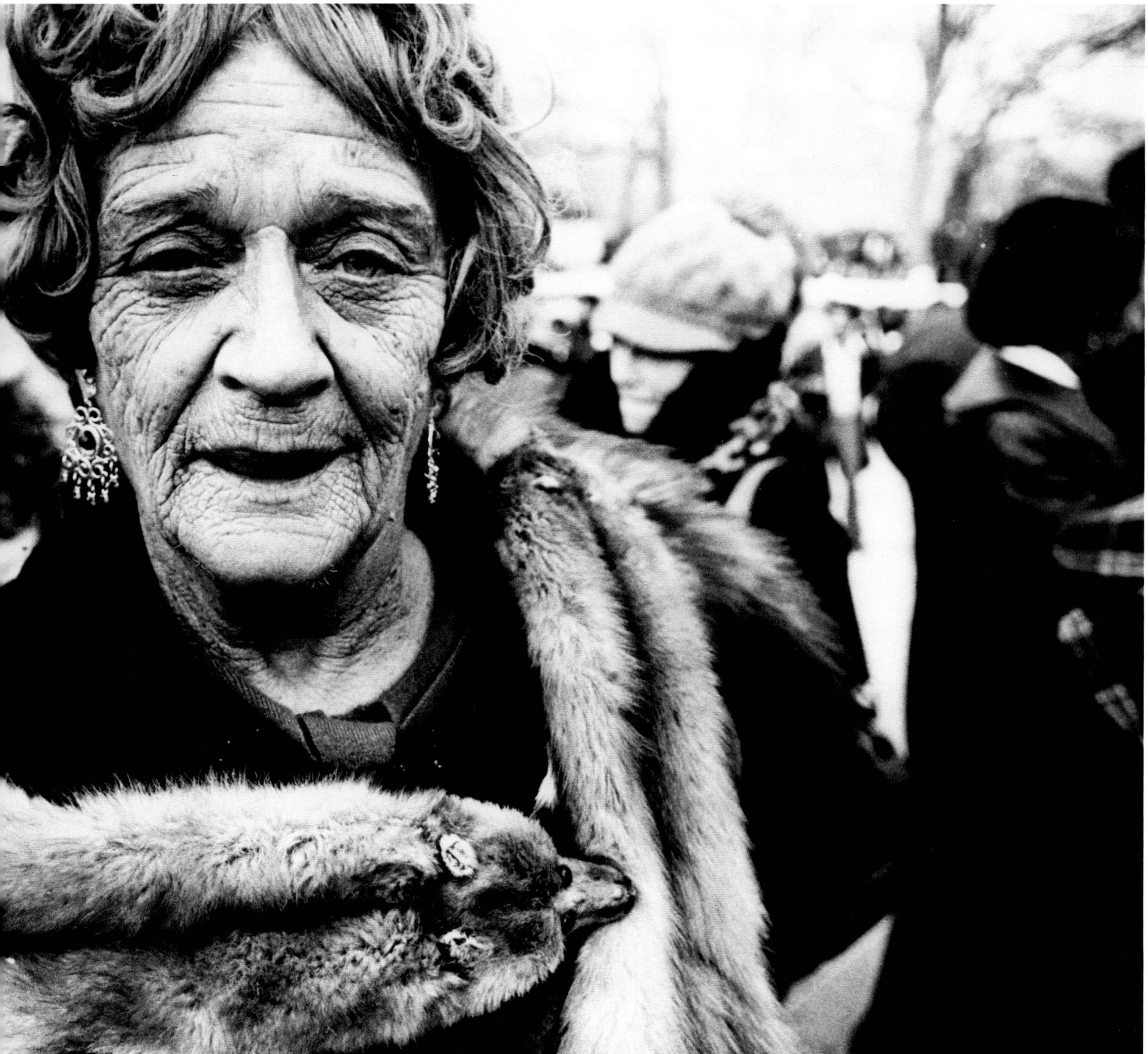

Social Security cutback protester, Washington, D.C., 1972

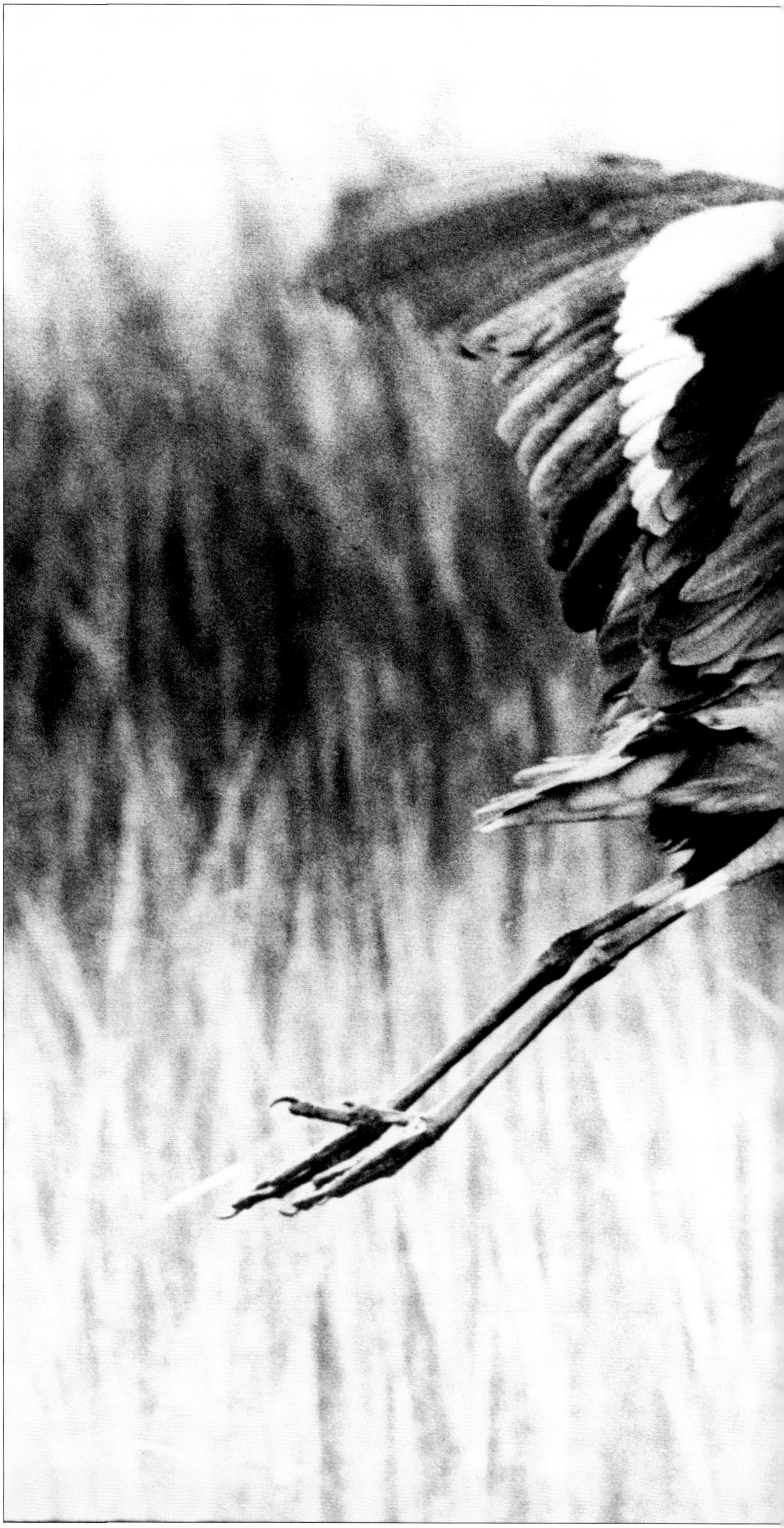

Great blue heron, Bombay Hook National Wildlife Refuge, 1987

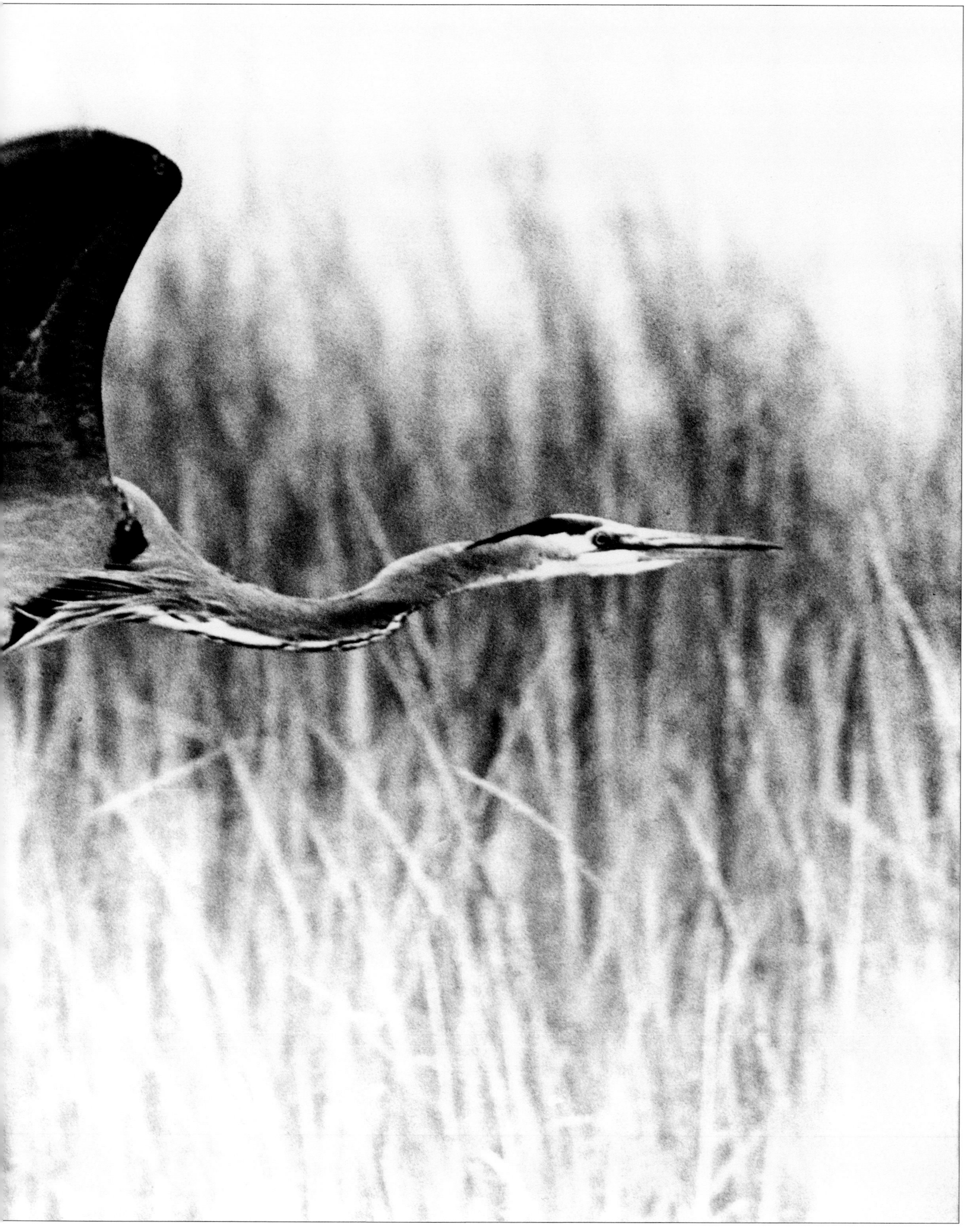

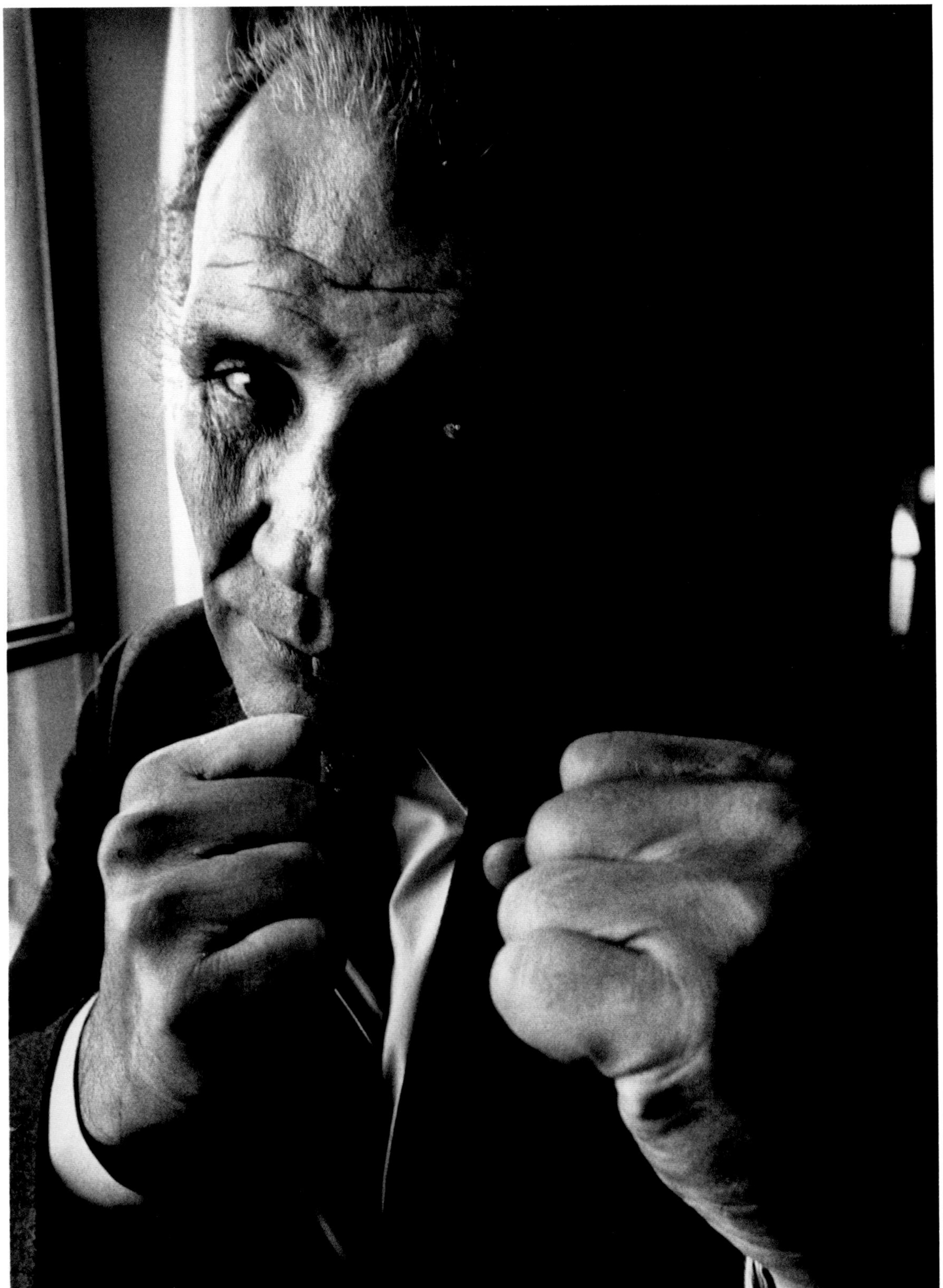

Jake LaMotta, Philadelphia, 1981

Michael Spinks, Hotel duPont, Wilmington, 1988

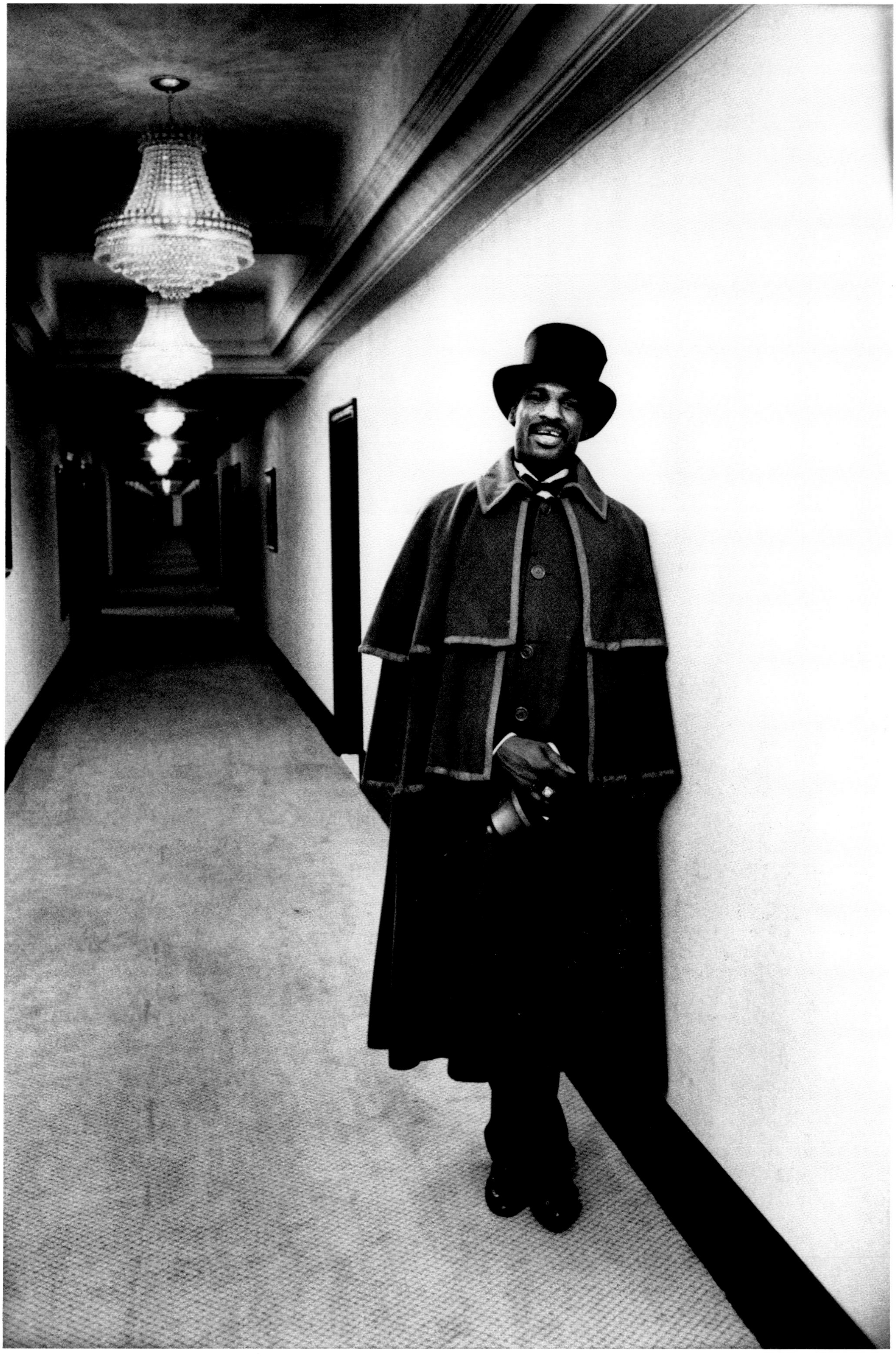

Wheelchair Tom 1974

Wheelchair Tom was a World War II Navy vet who had a special way of talking with kids. In the backyard of the Cherokee Nursing Home in New Castle, Tom Maher would sit for hours with the children who were his friends. Tom would share his stories and neighborhood children would share their ice cream, rabbits, and rubber alligators.

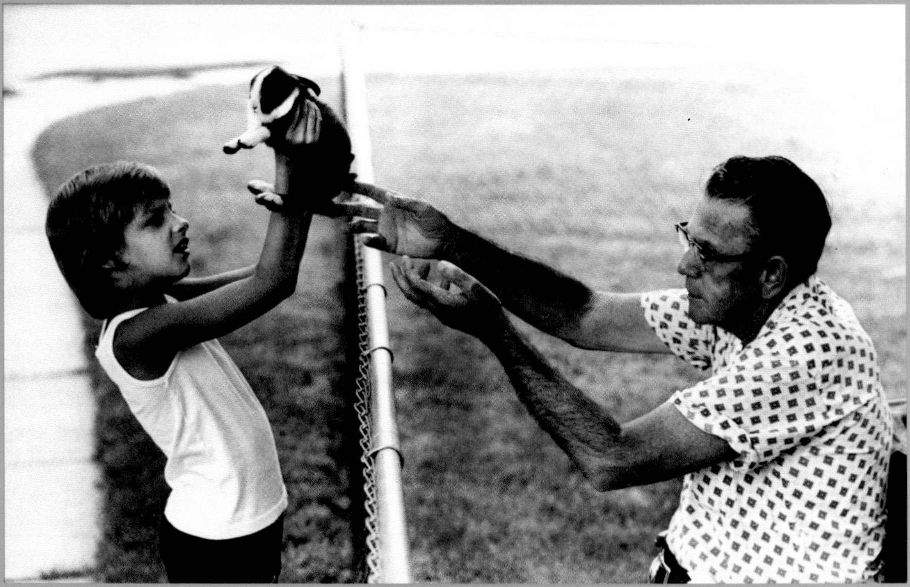

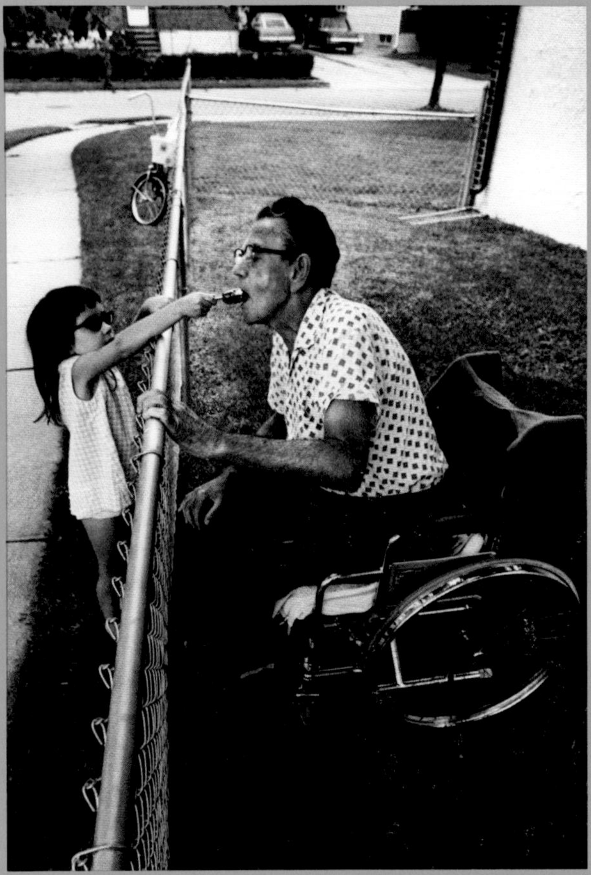

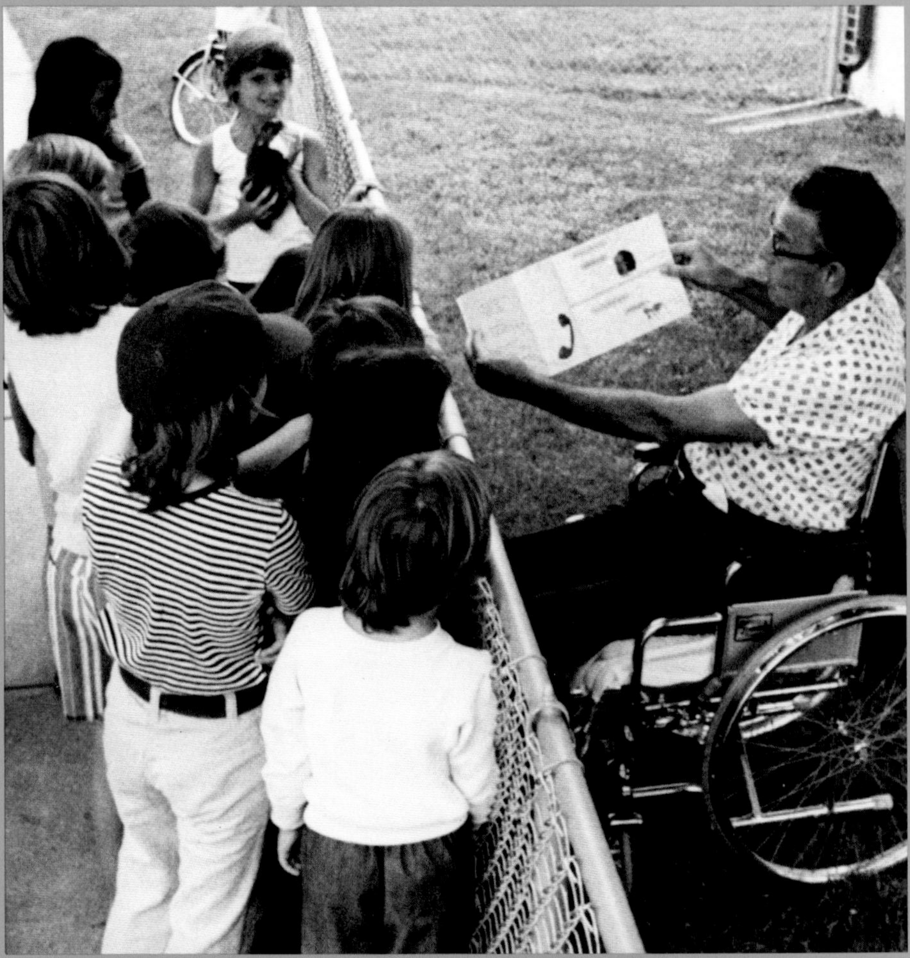

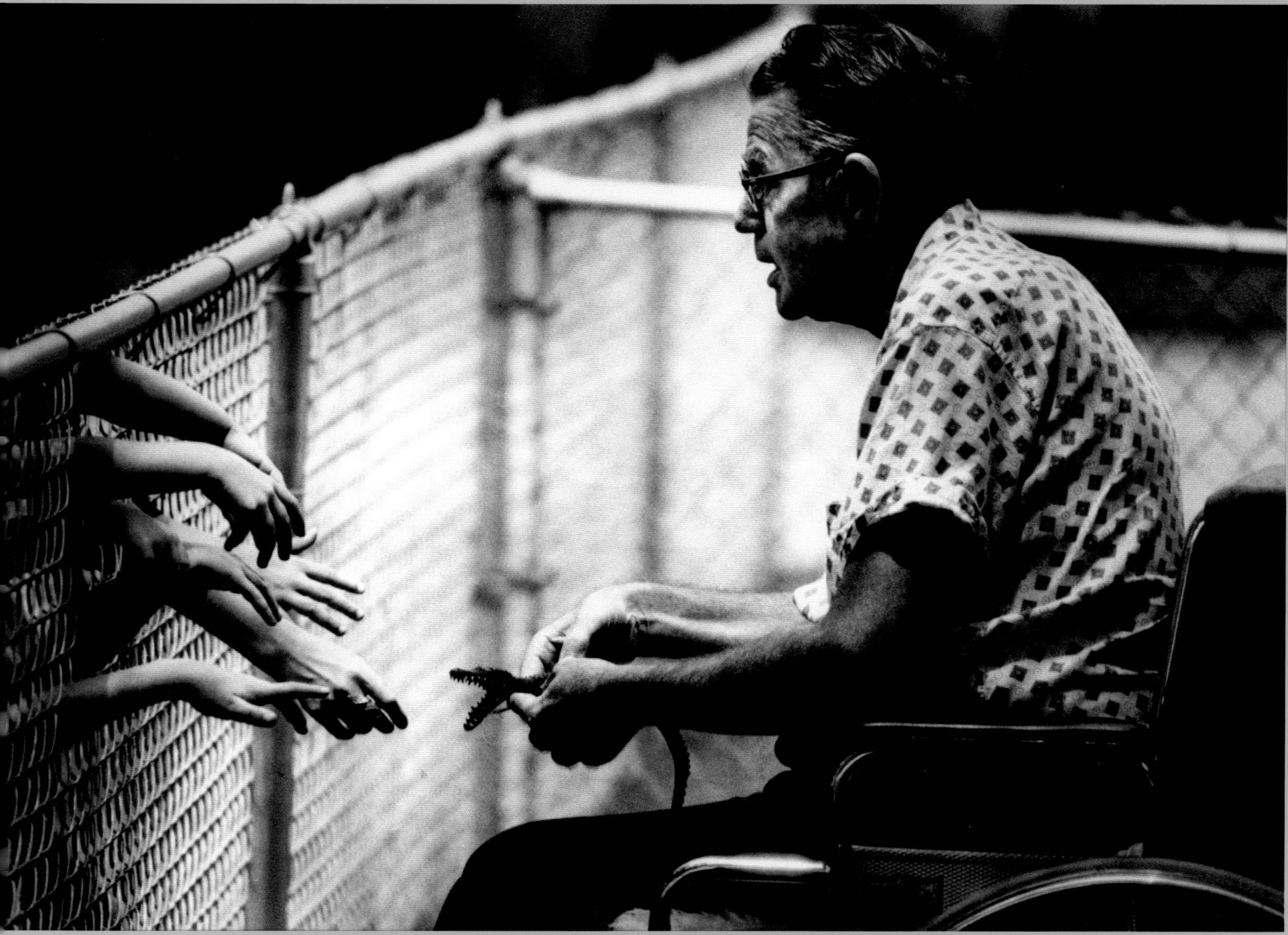

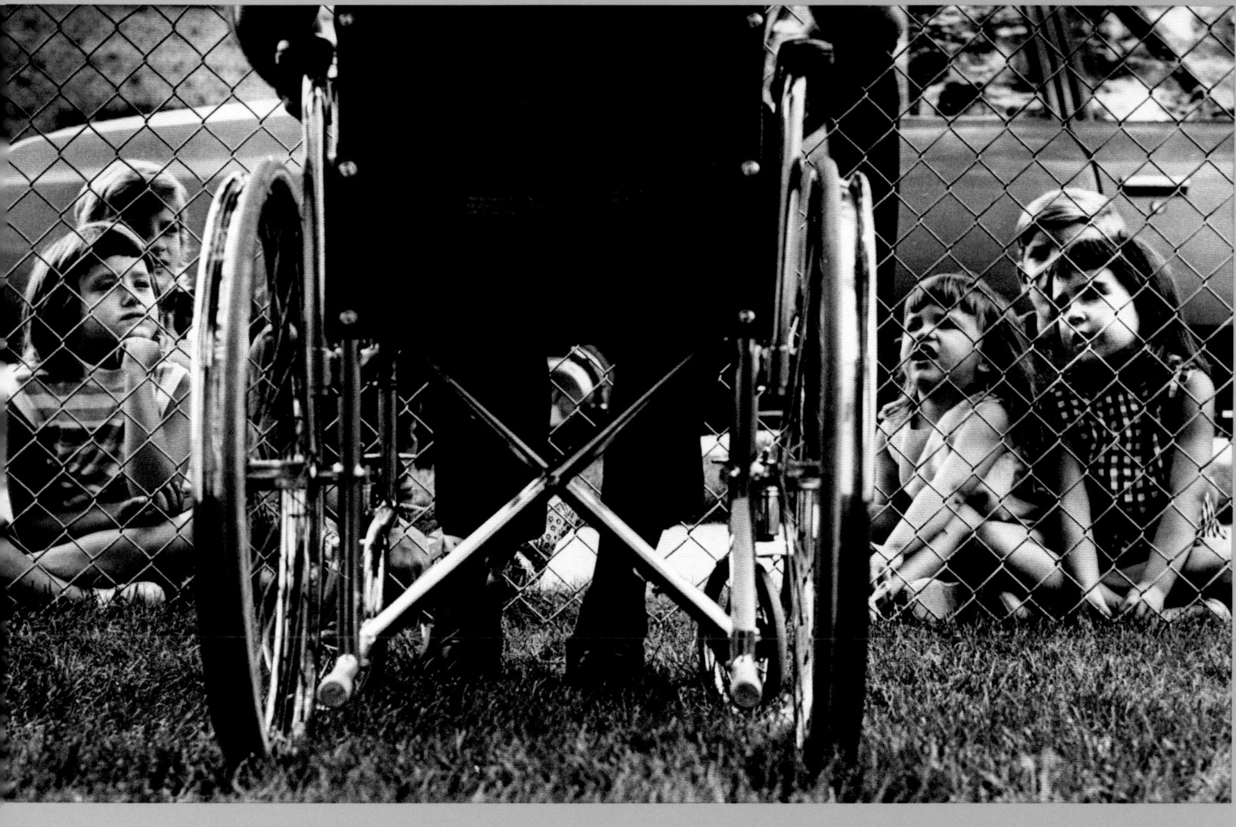

Pike Creek, Wilmington, 1987

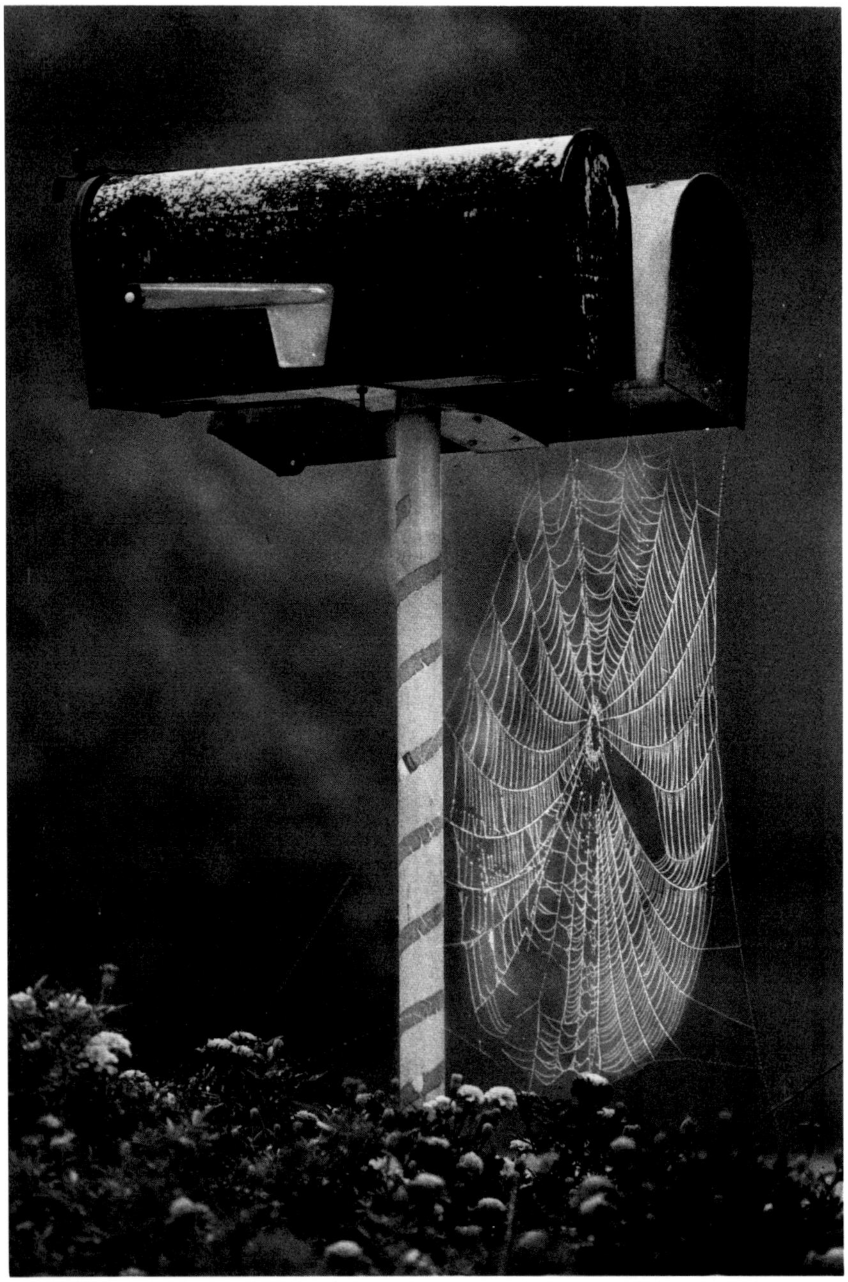

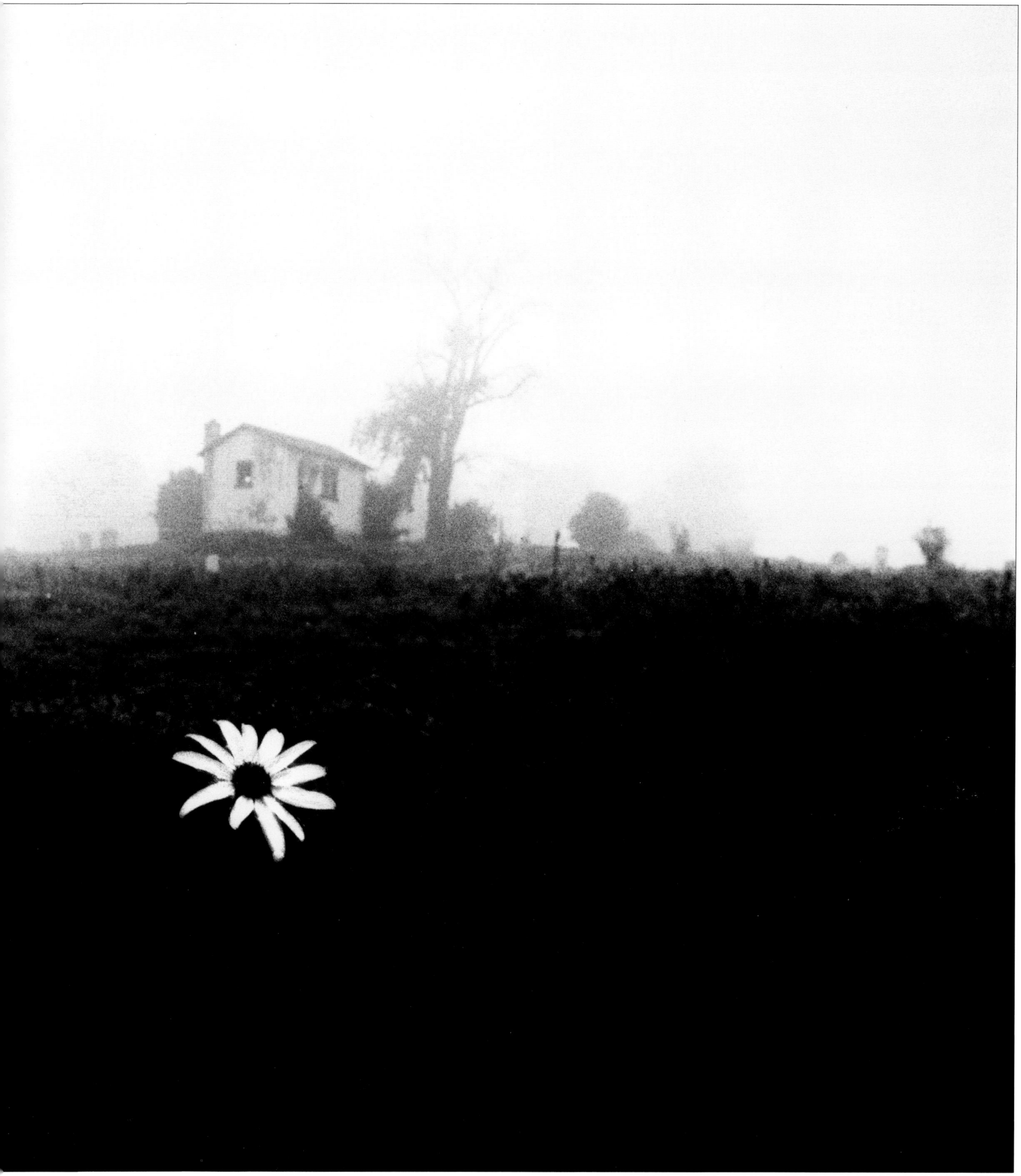

Graveyard, Lancaster Avenue, Wilmington, 1971

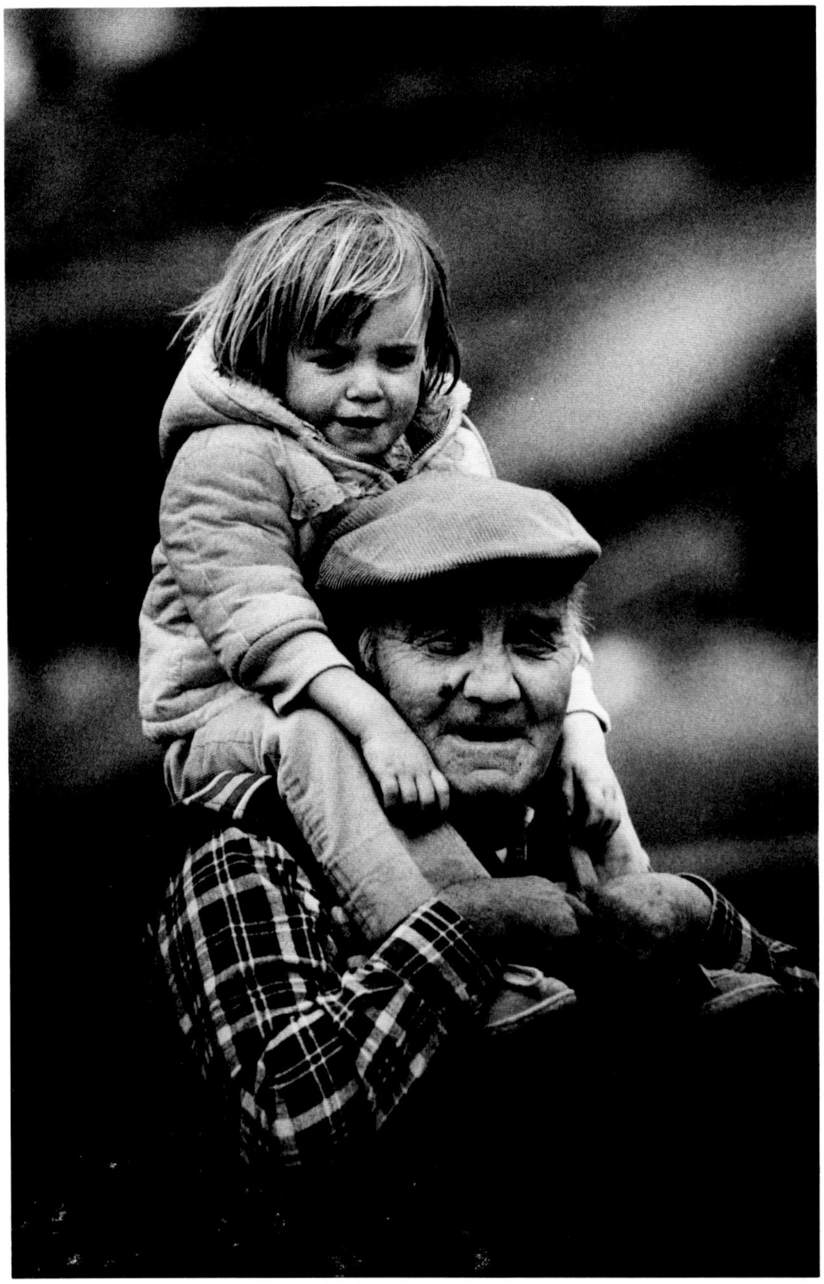

Stanley Brzozowski and granddaughter Heather, Kosciuszko Park, Wilmington, 1987

The Reverend Wilmer E. Abbott Sr. holds his great-great grandson, the fifth generation, St. Mark's United Methodist Church, Wilmington, 1984

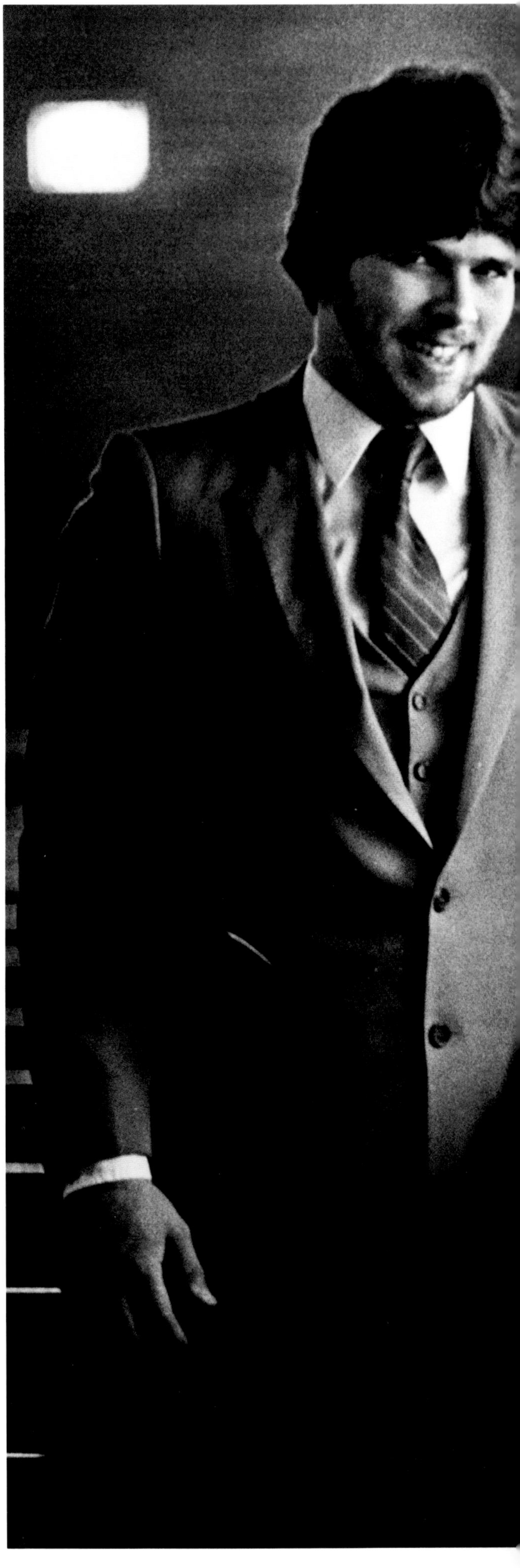

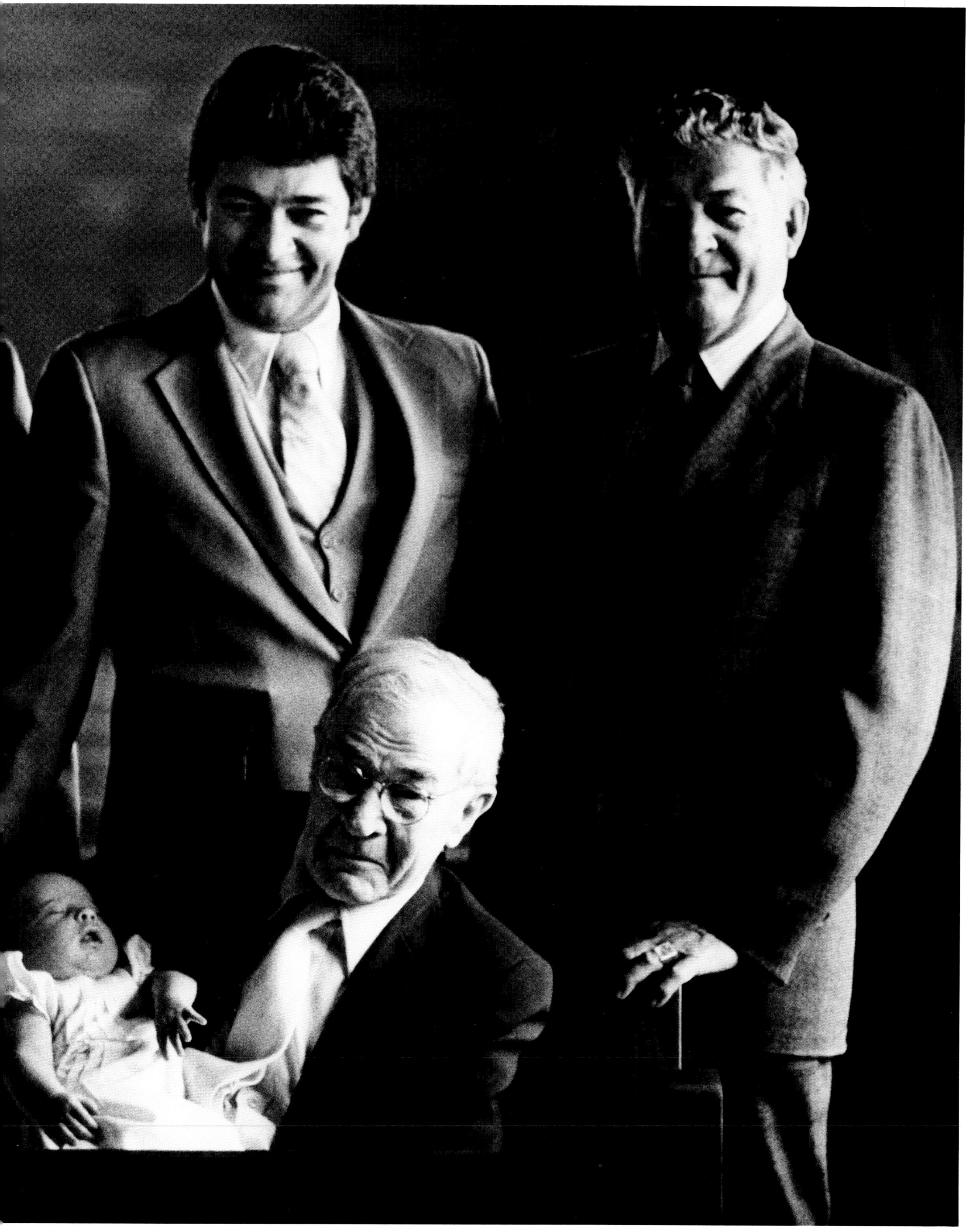

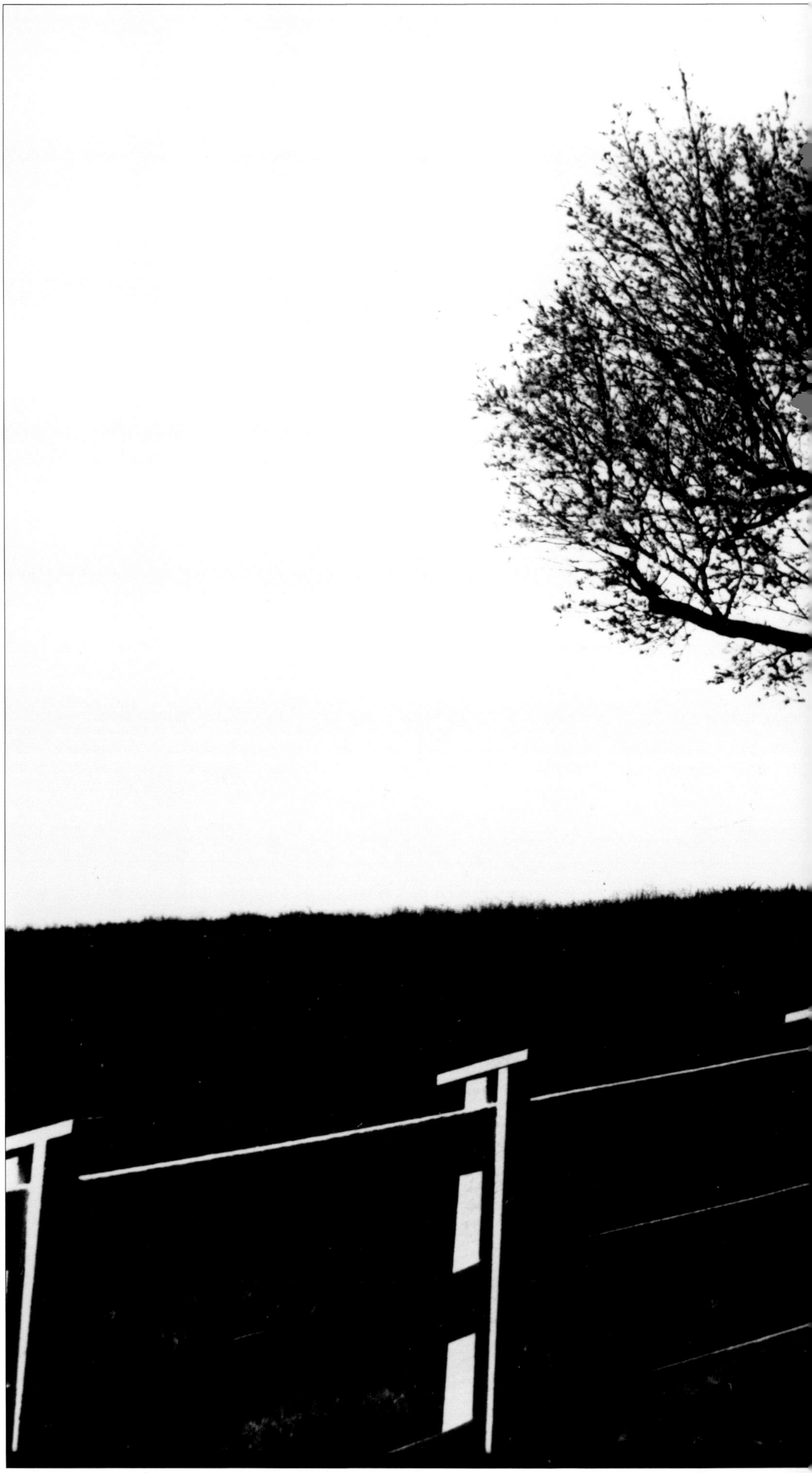

Kennett Pike and Snuff Mill Road, Centerville, 1974

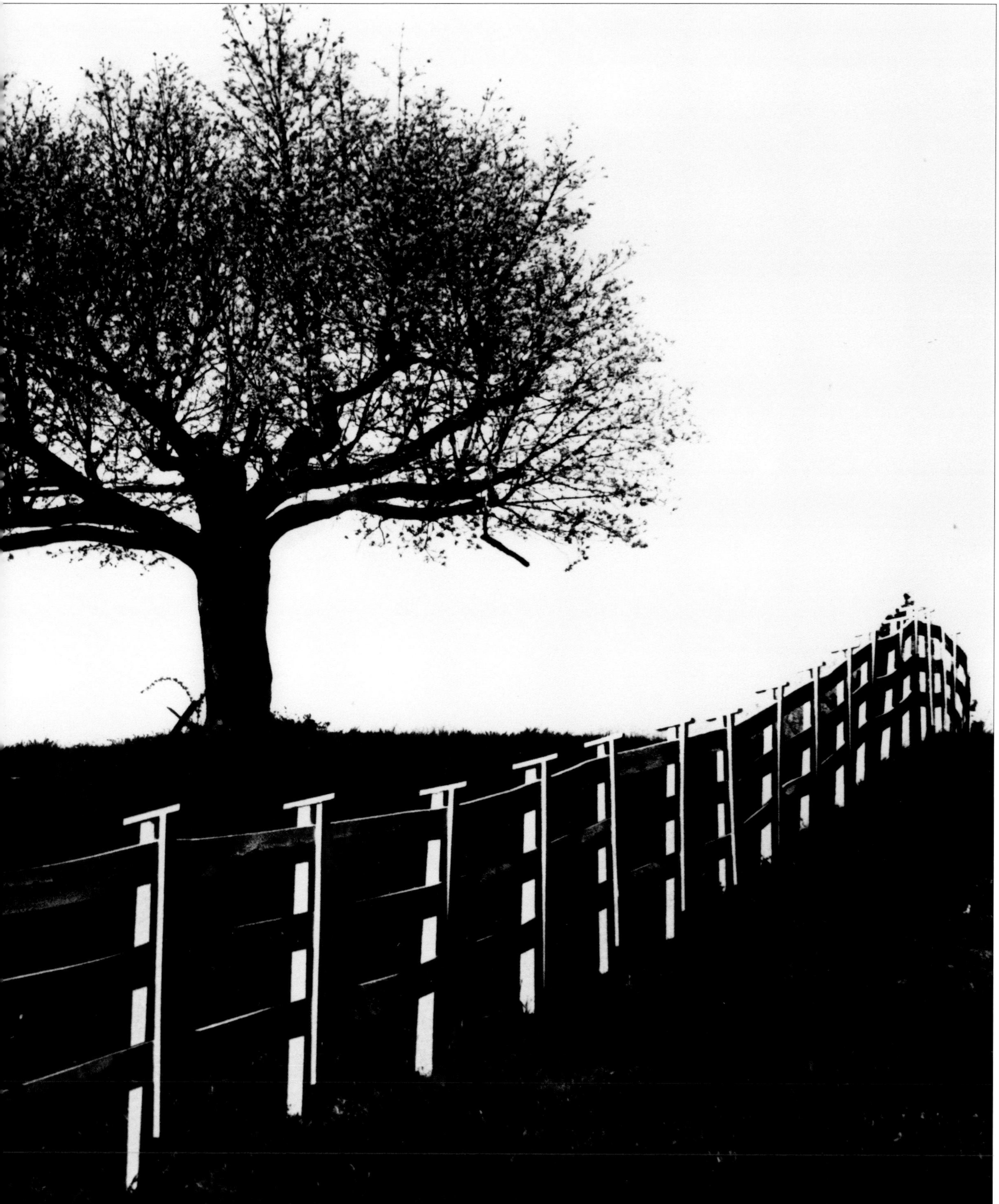

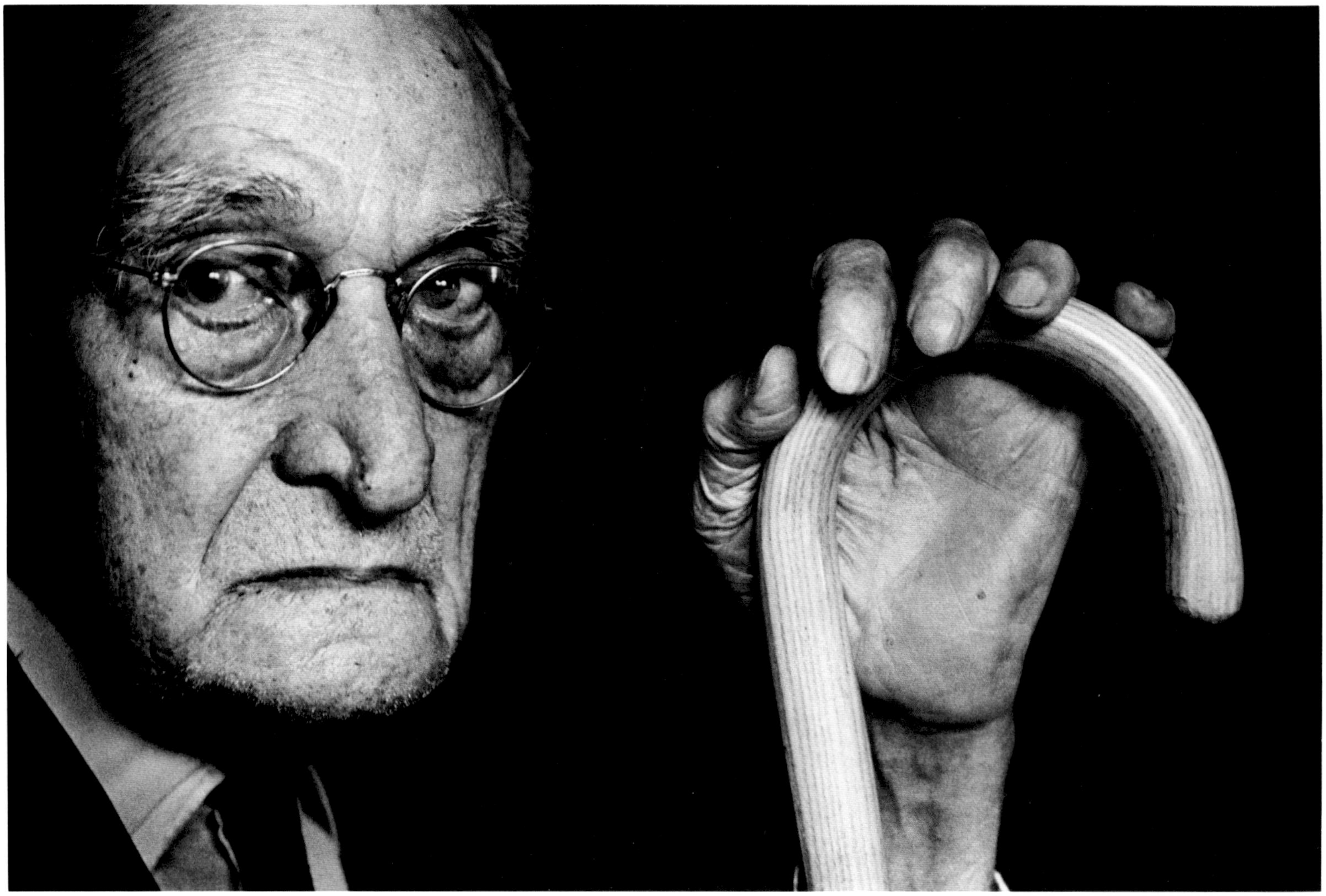

Clarence M. Wright, Spanish-American War veteran, Wilmington, 1970

Mary Starr Fowler at 100, Claymont, 1972

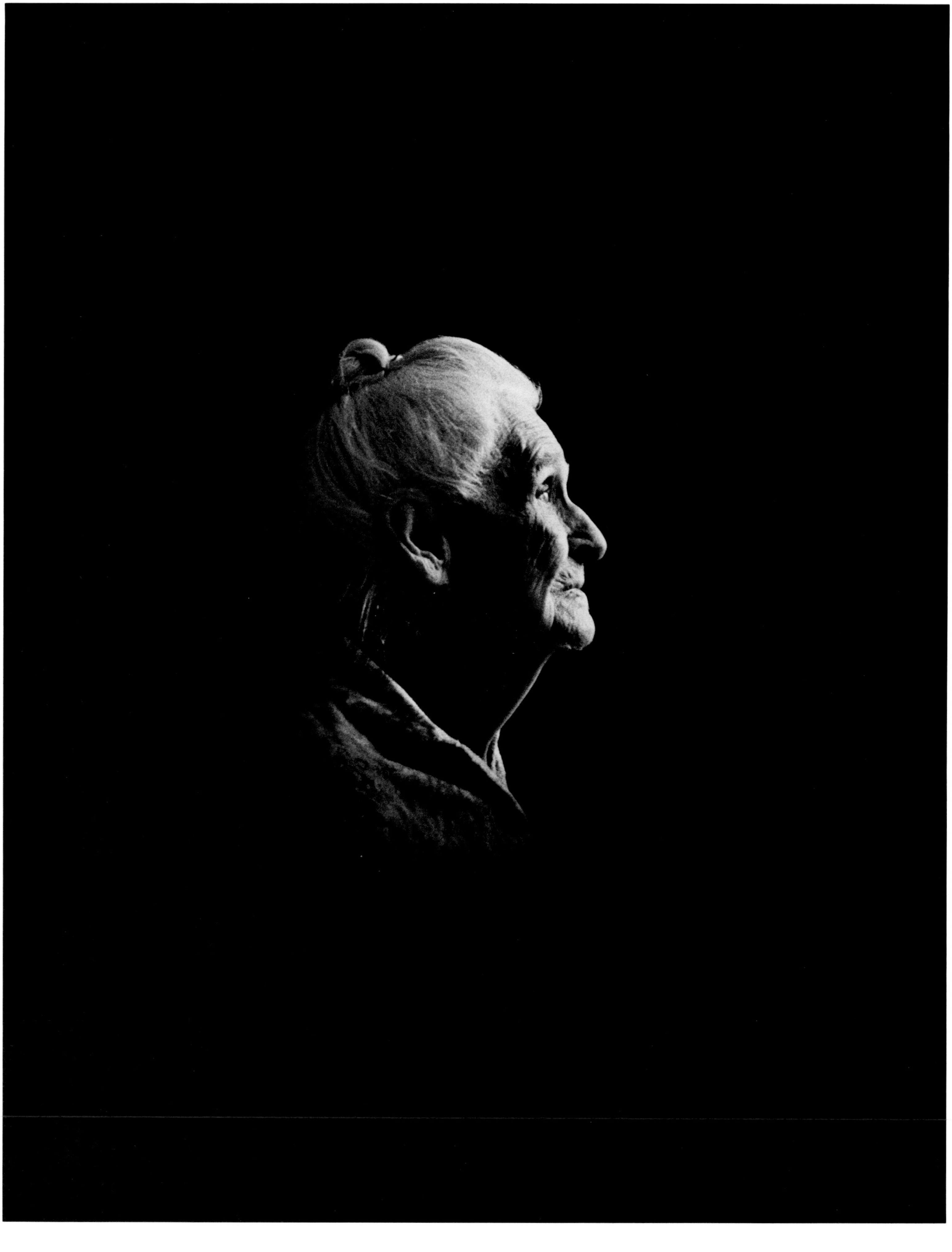

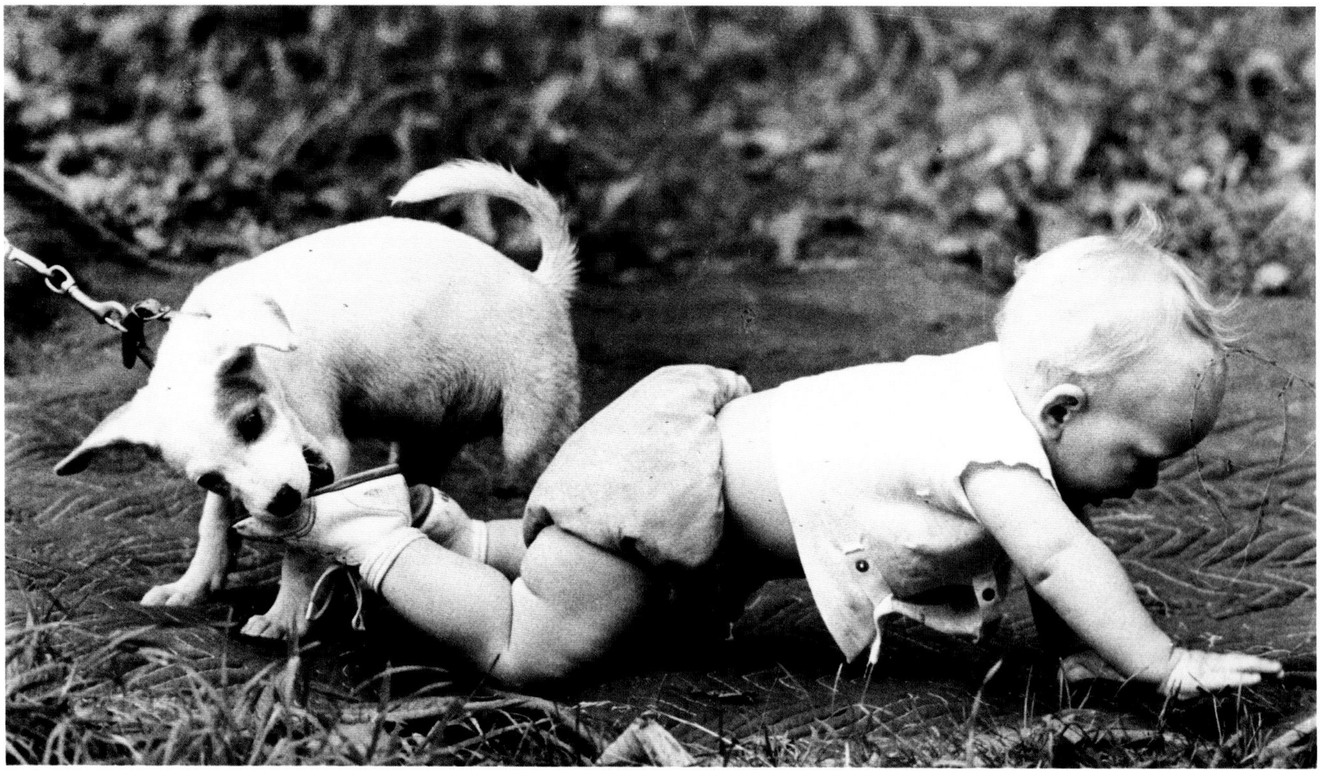

Brandywine Park, Wilimington, 1969

Rockford Park, Wilmington, 1970

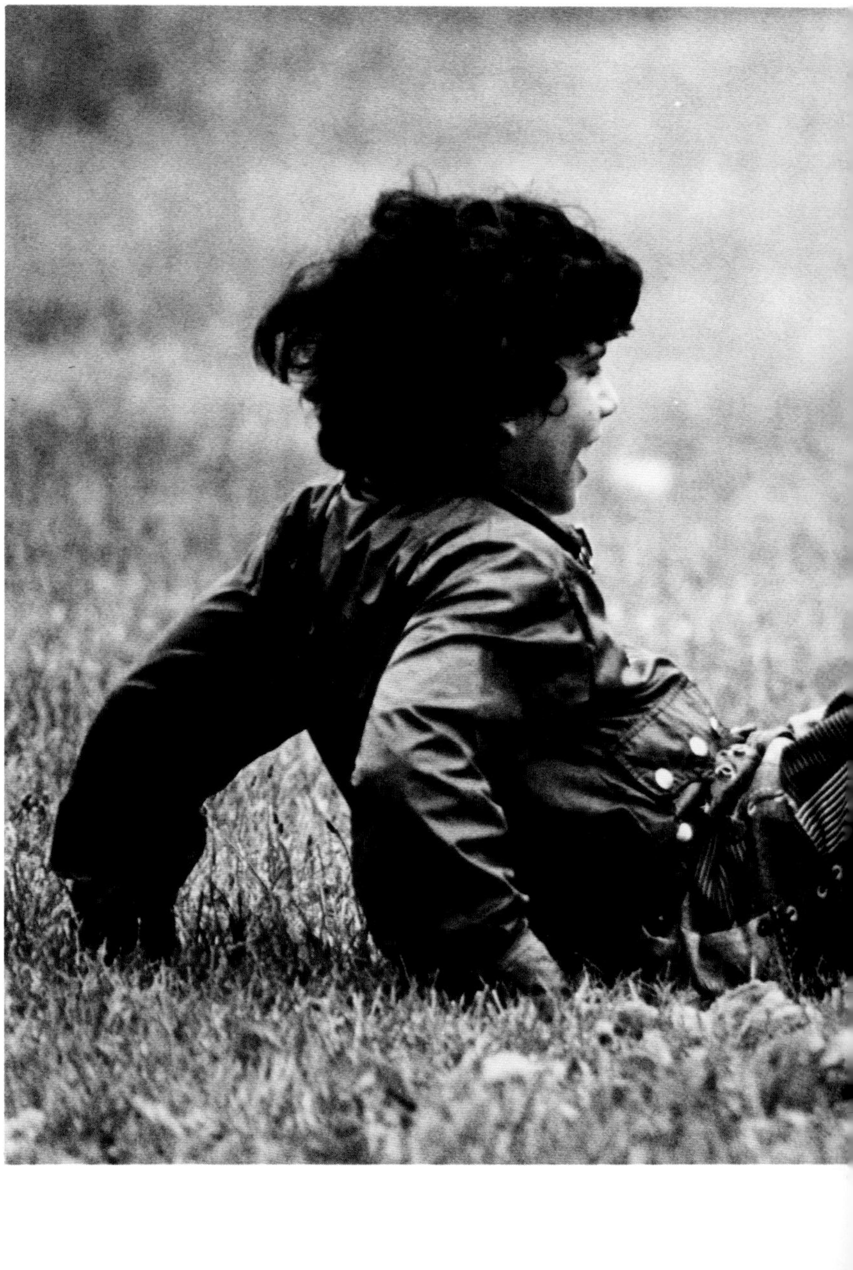

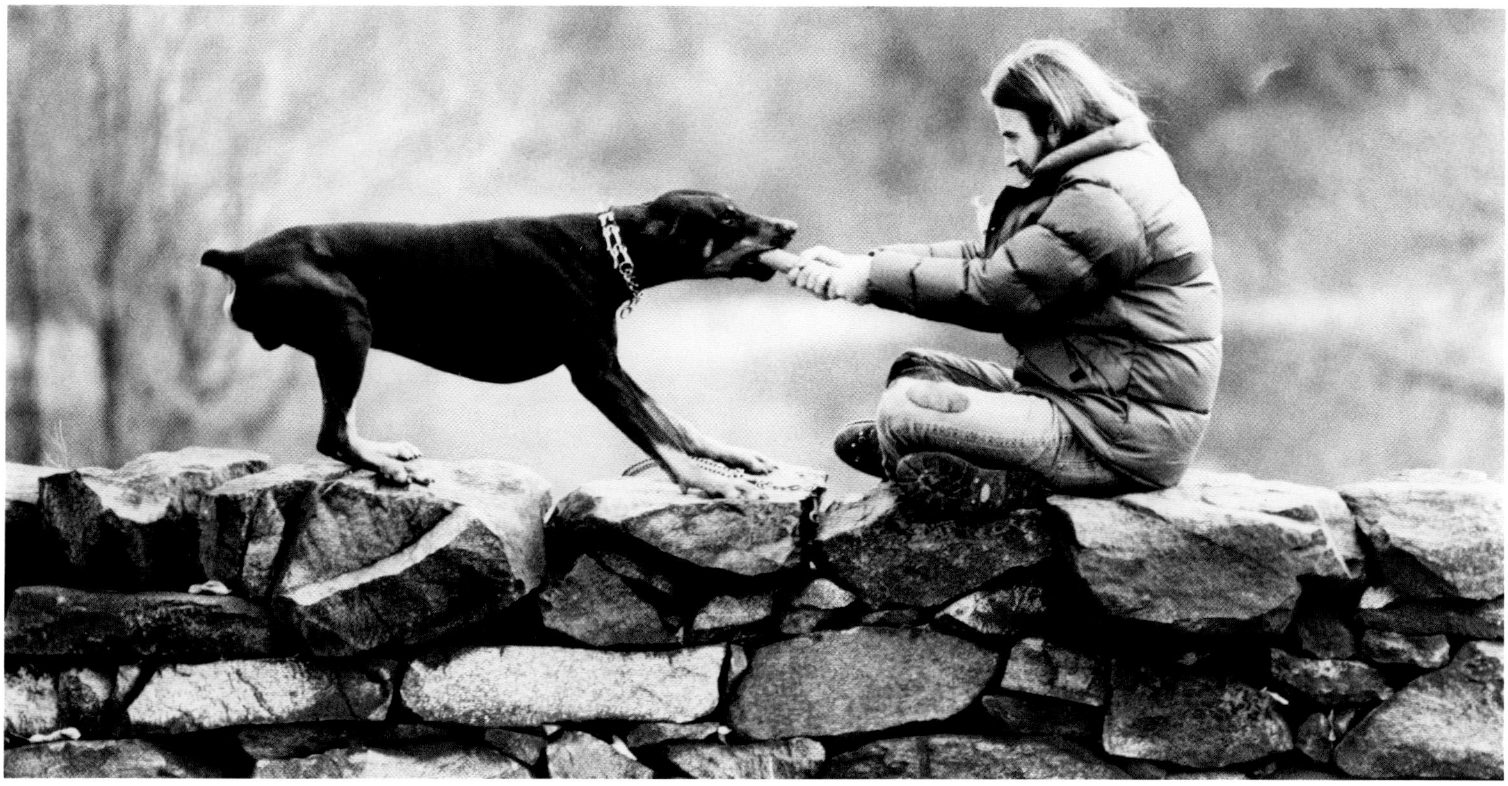

Brandywine Creek State Park, 1981

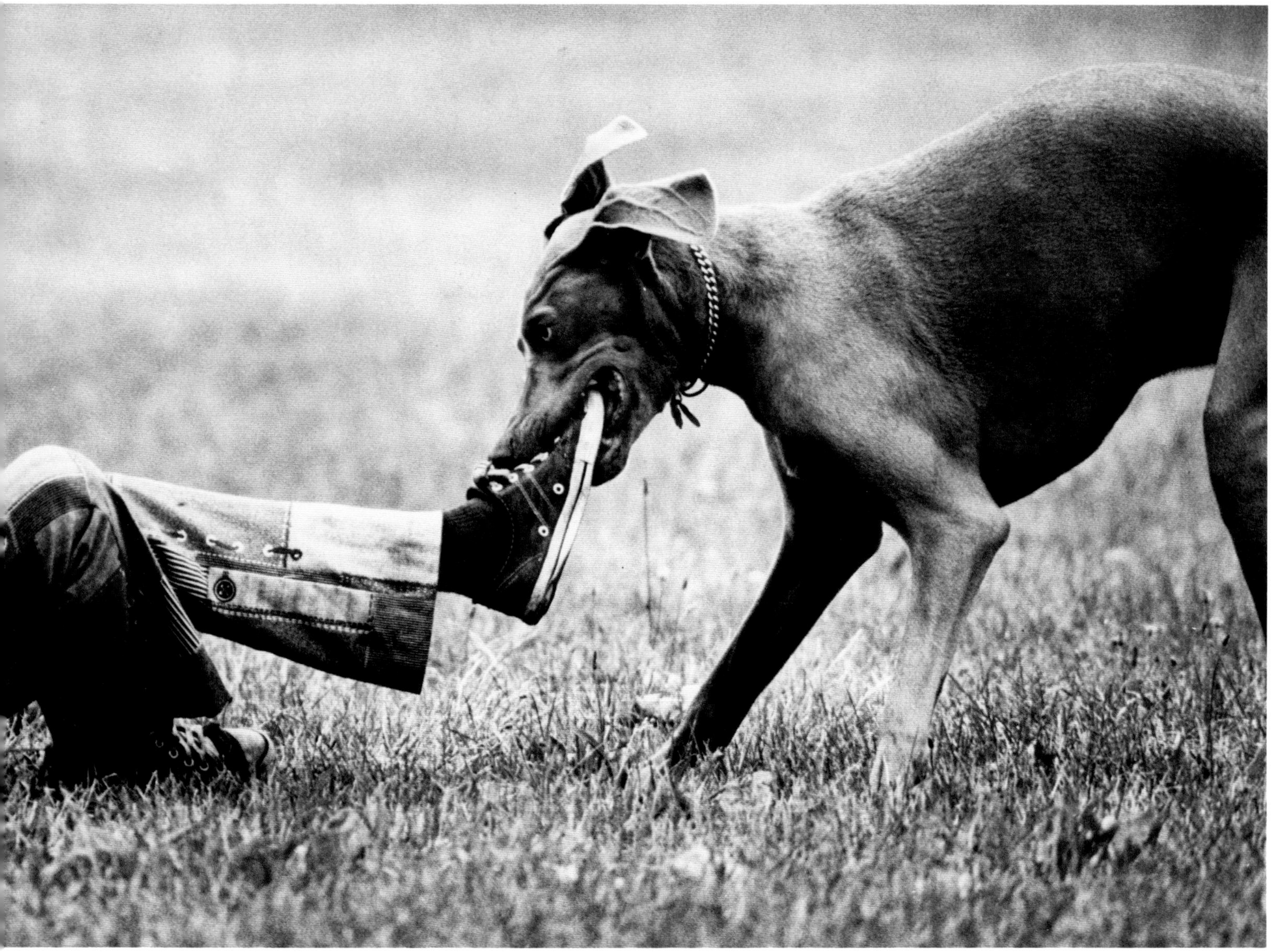

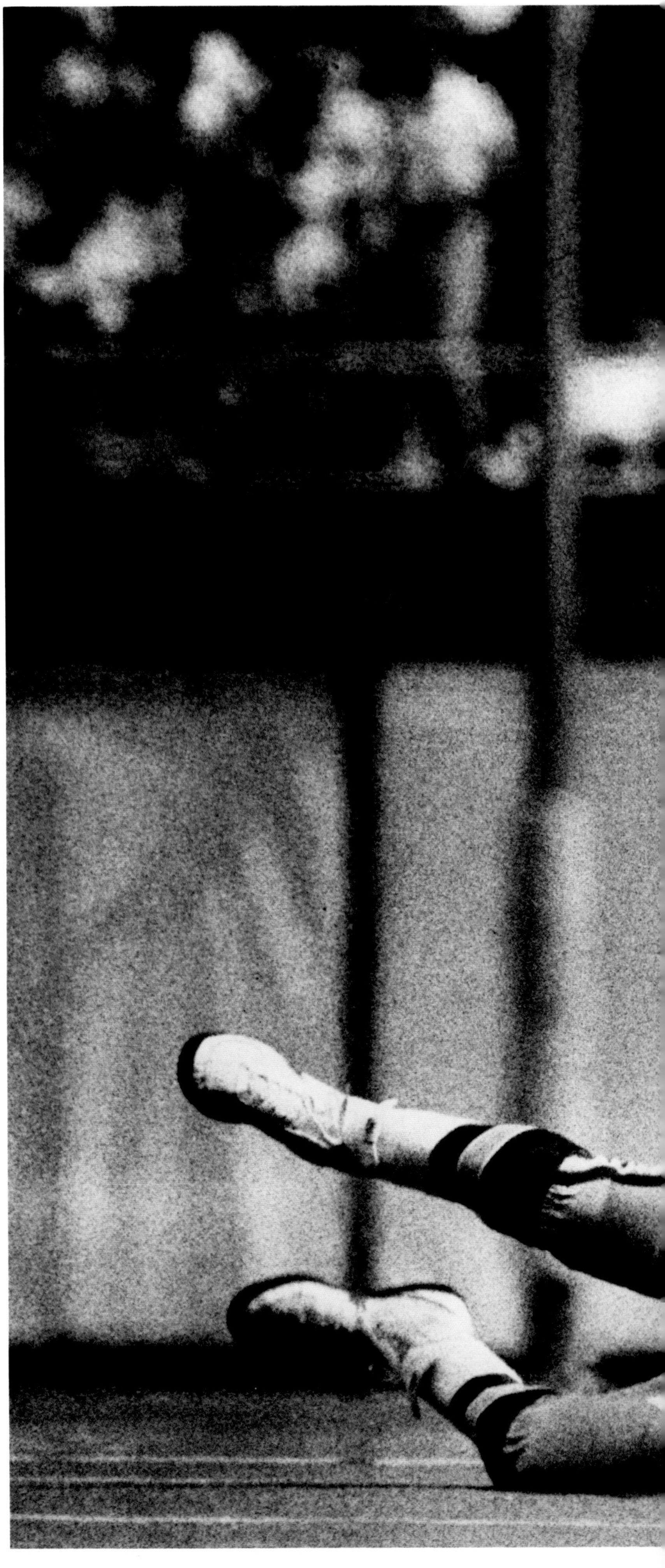

Philadelphia Eagles linebacker Jerry Robinson; Washington Redskins running back John Riggins, Philadelphia, 1984

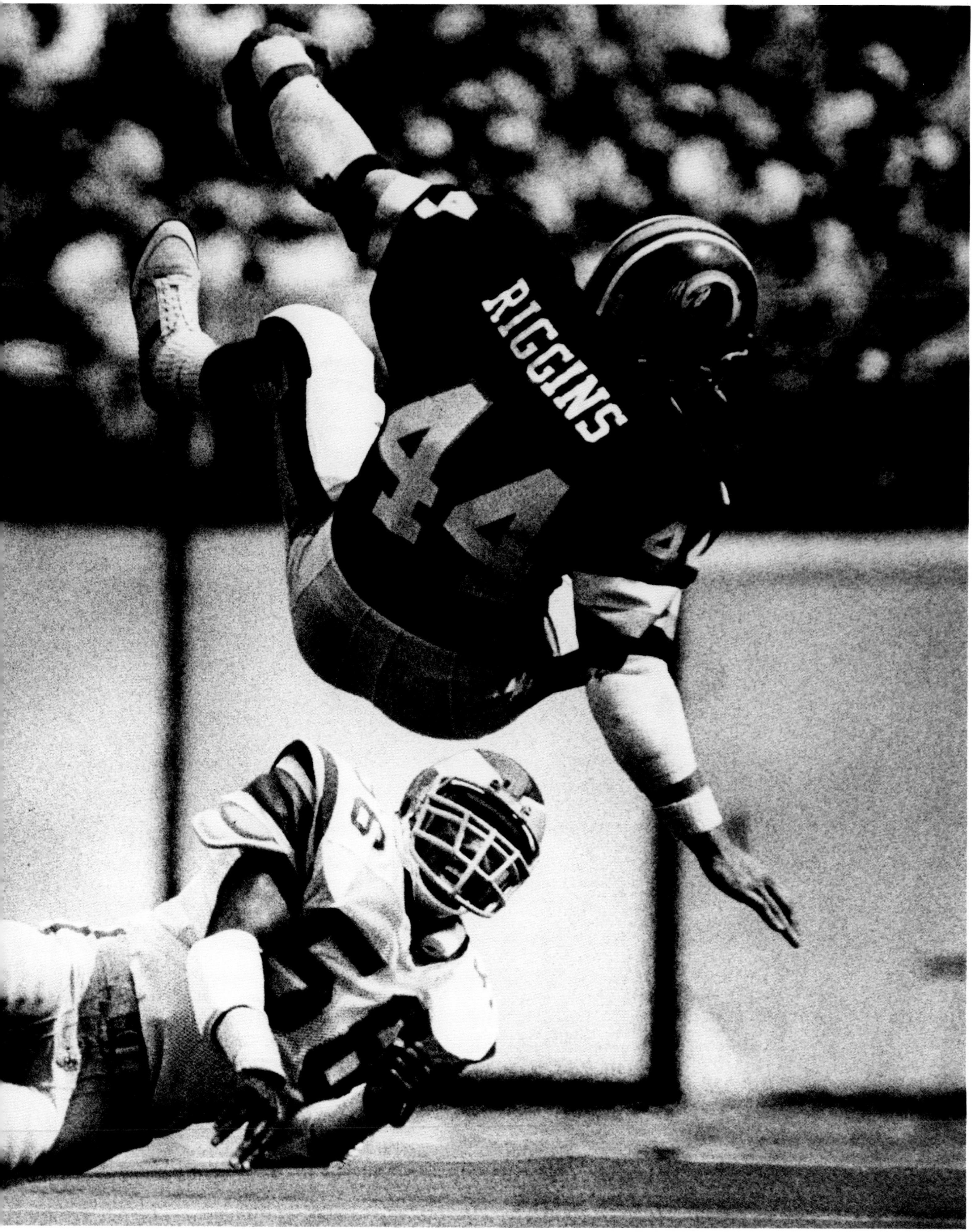
RIGGINS
44

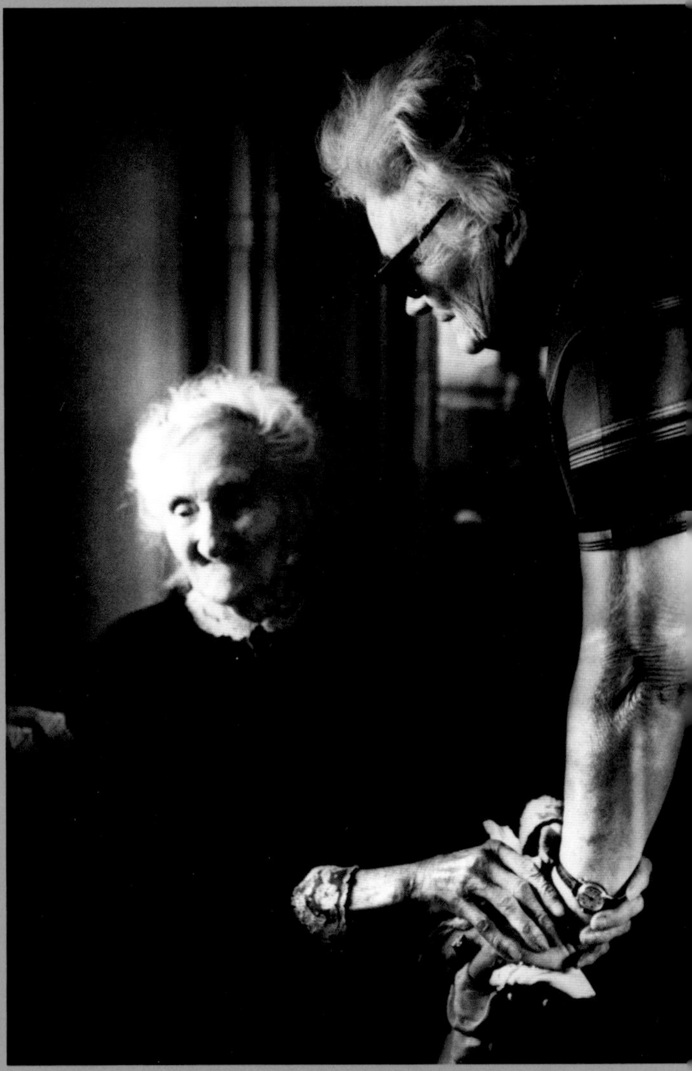

Muddie, It's Time to Leave Now

I met Florence "Muddie" Crumlish through News-Journal *reporter Betty Burroughs. Betty had written about Muddie many times and loved this vital 108-year-old lady, a fiery fighter not above telling a raucous joke. When I was introduced to Muddie in 1973 she was moving from her house into a retirement apartment building. It was a day of intense emotion. Family and relations came to say goodbye and extend good wishes. Muddie cried and laughed. I felt privileged to be included in this rite of passage. Not long after, at age 109, she died.*

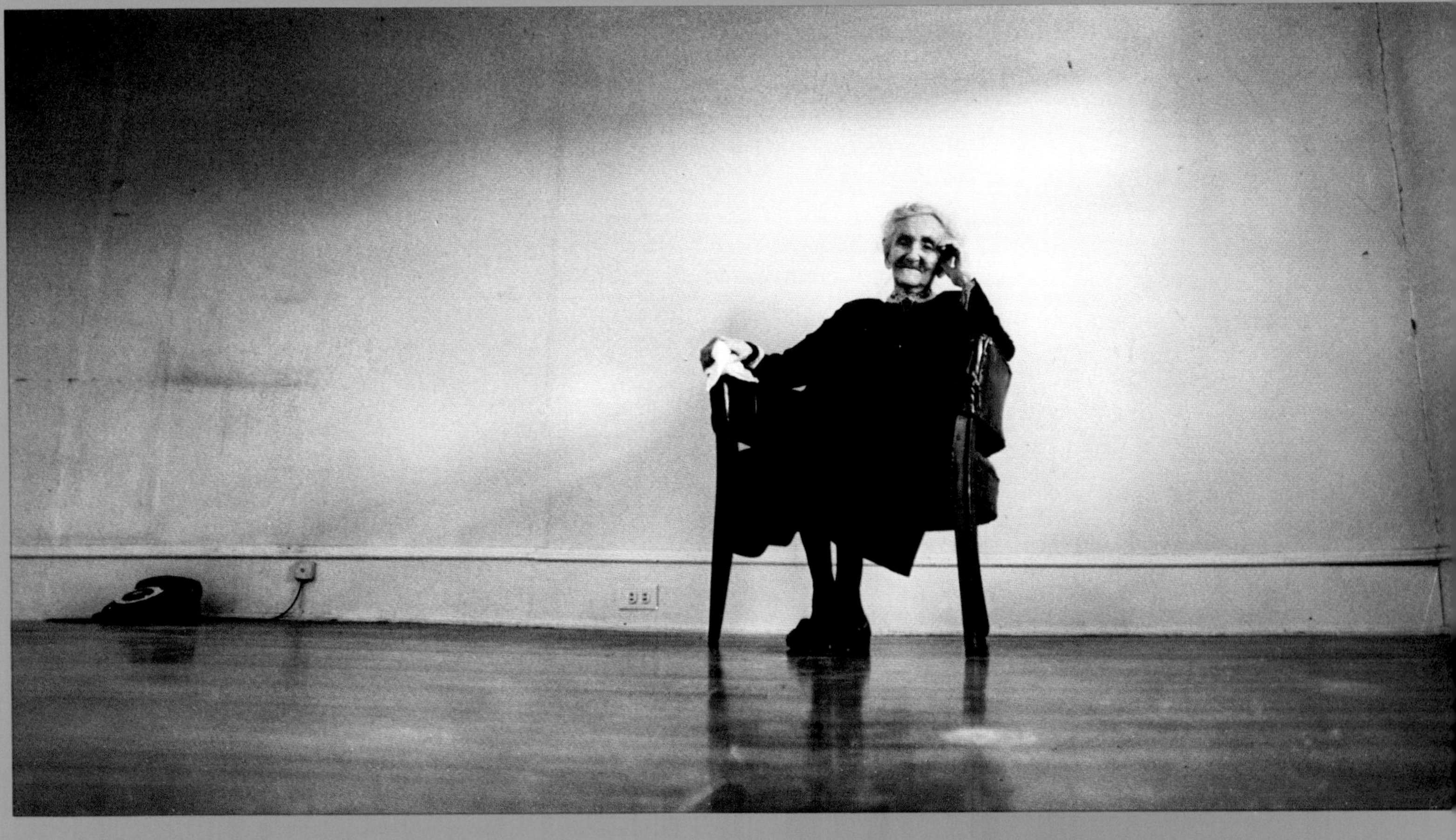

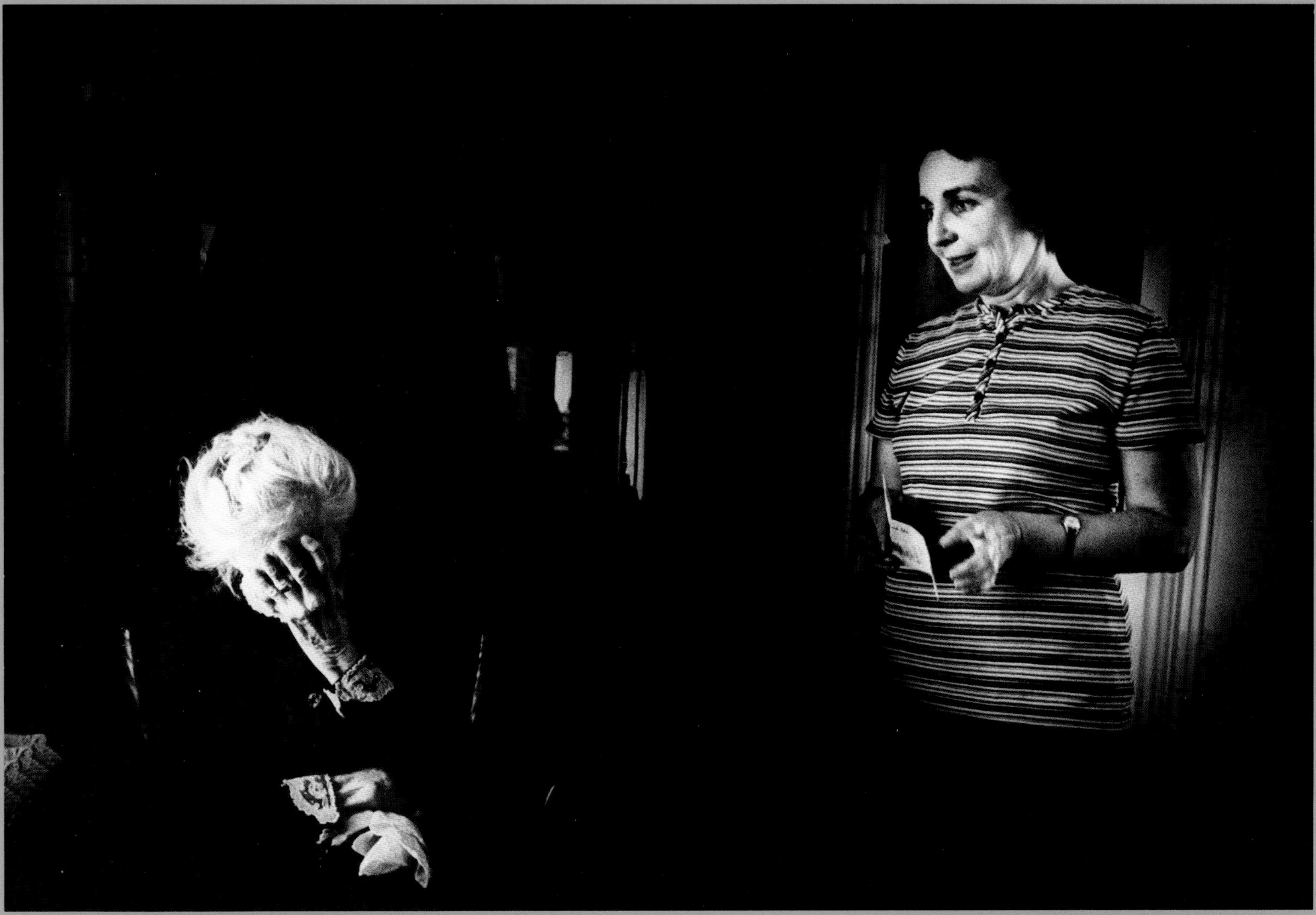

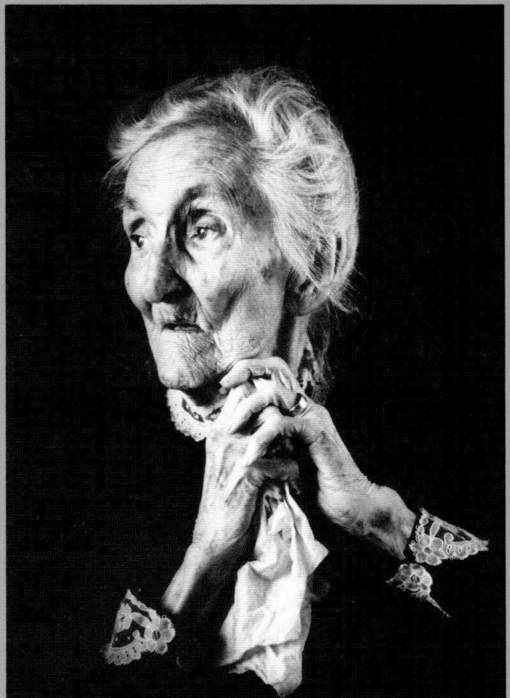

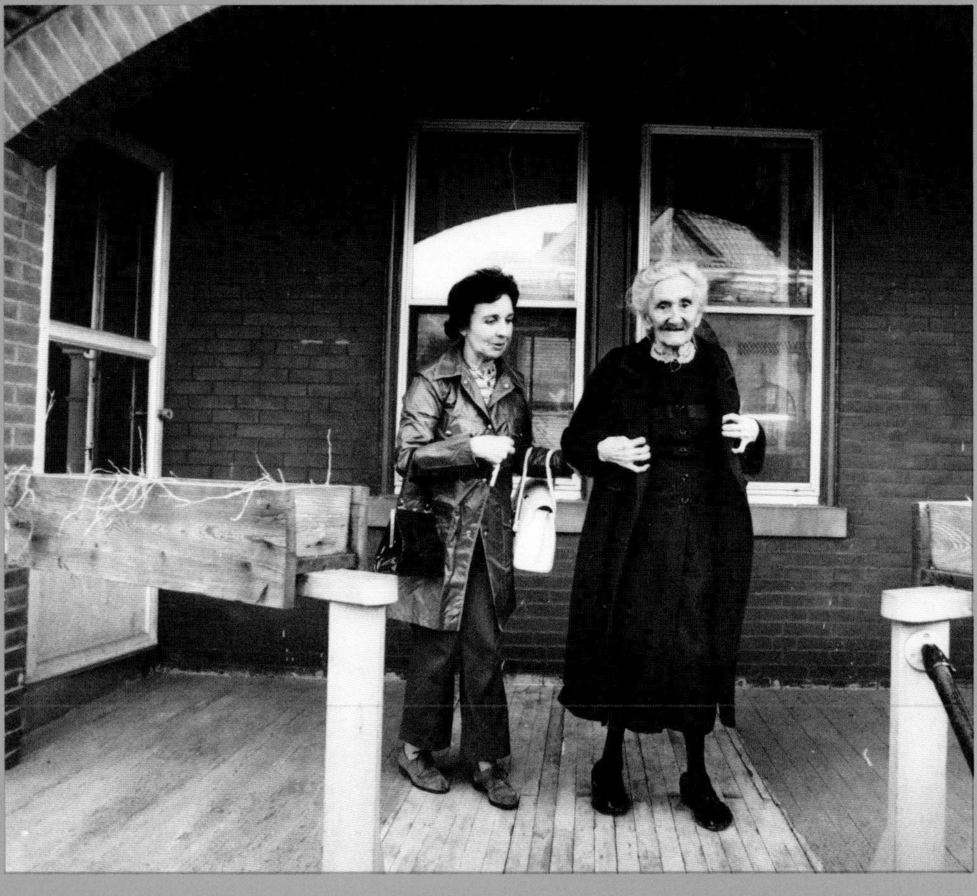

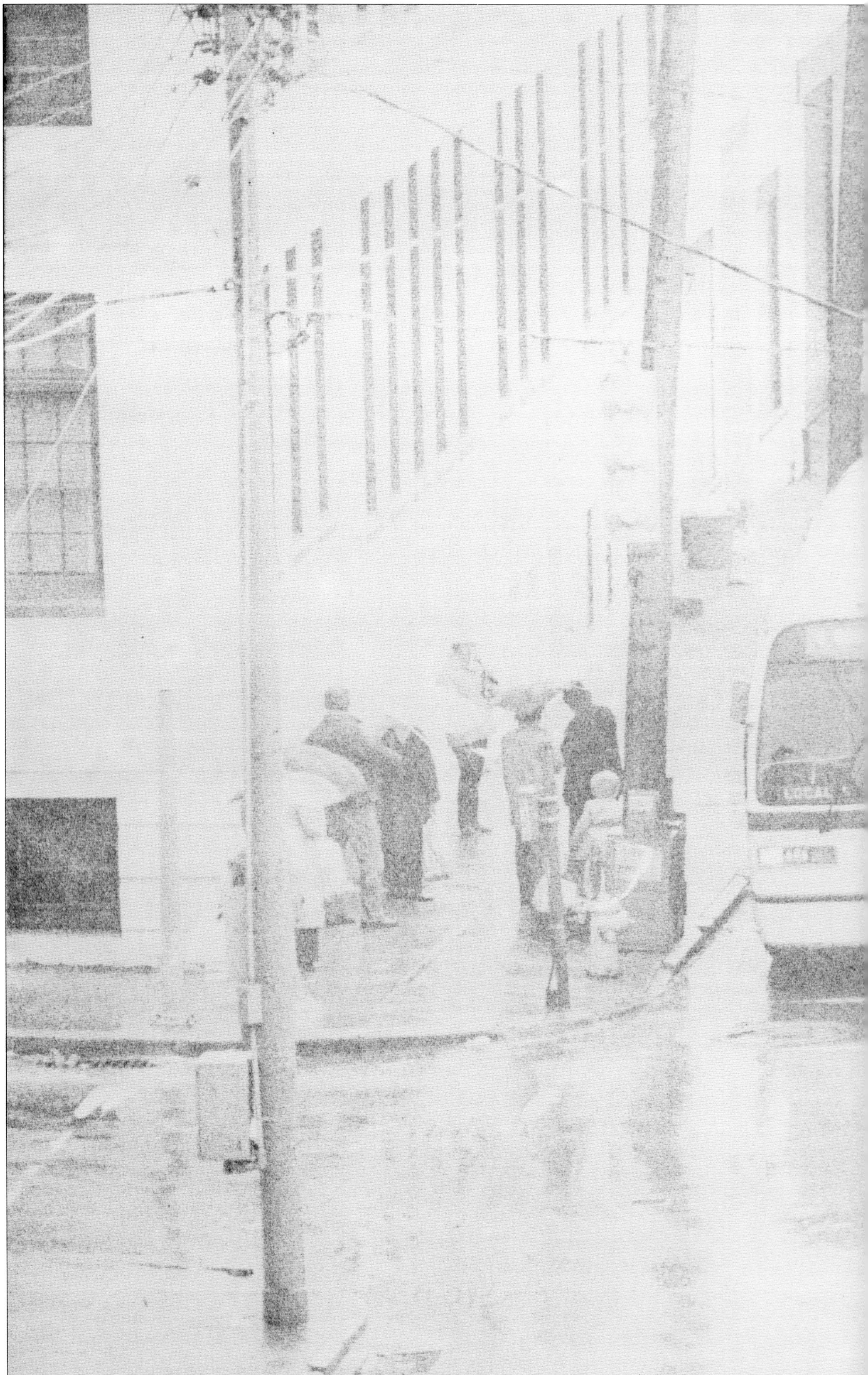

Orange Street, Wilmington, 1986

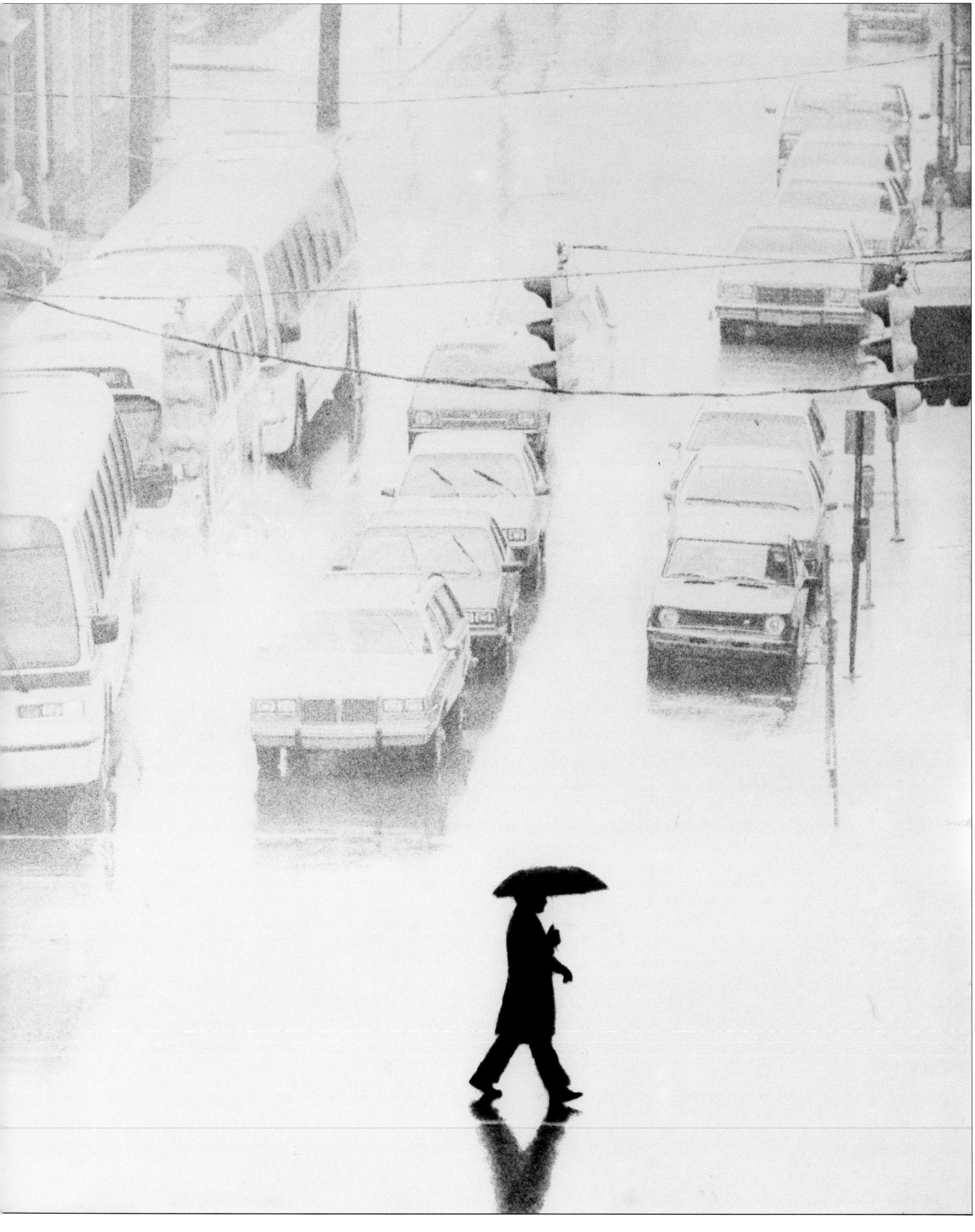

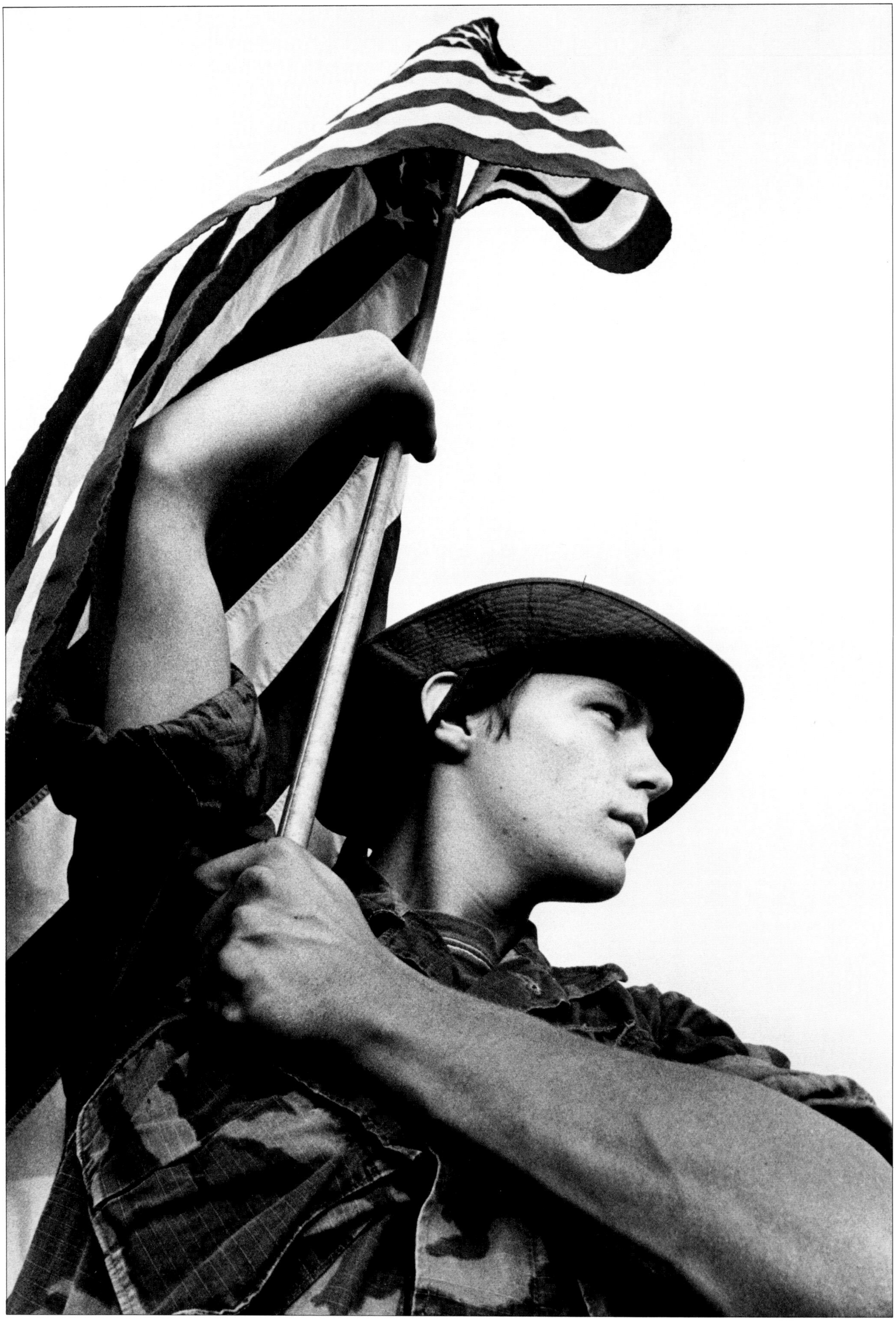

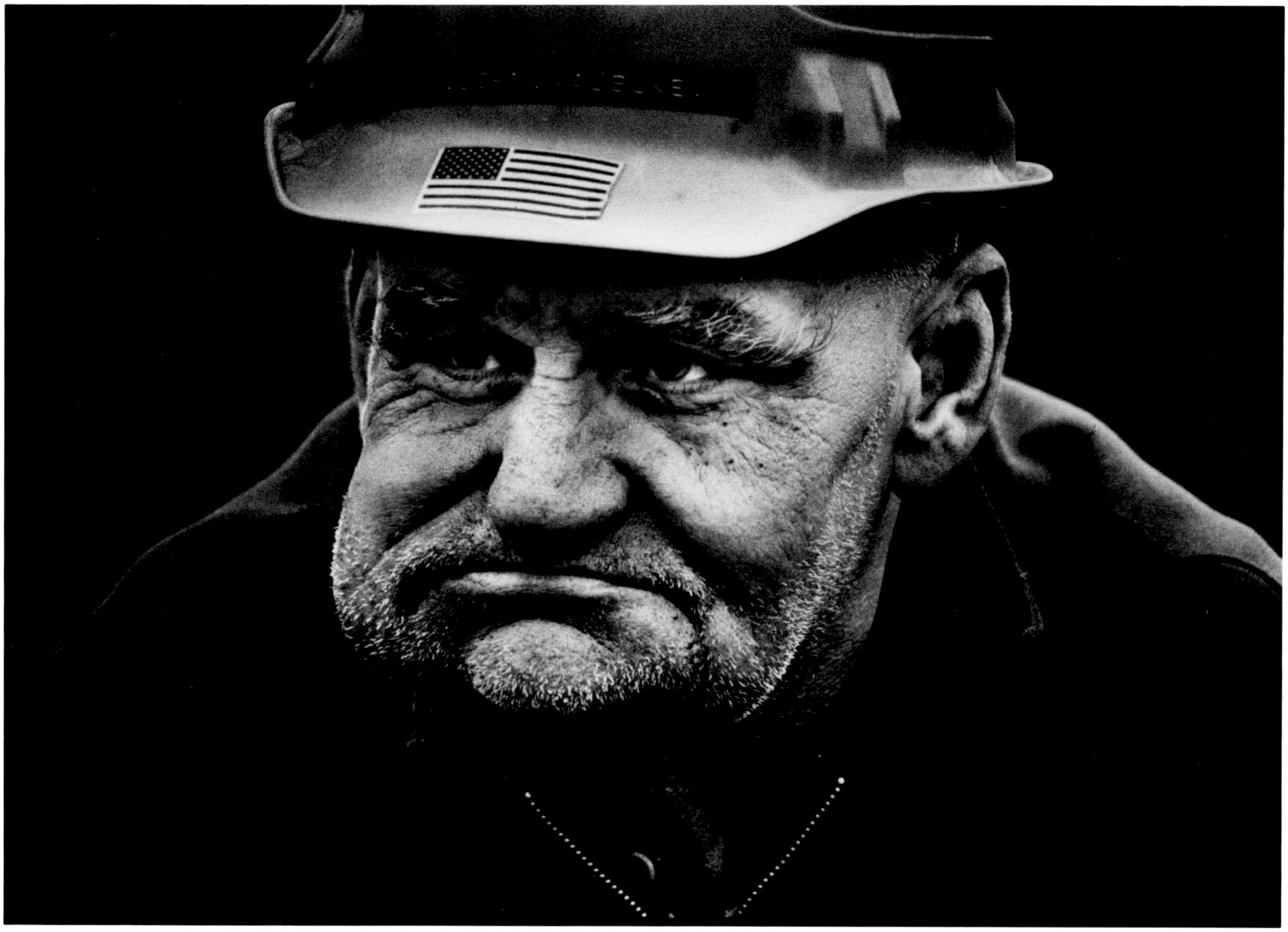

Wilmington city worker John Kulske, 1973

Sam LeCompte, pro-draft registration demonstration, Talleyville Post Office, 1982

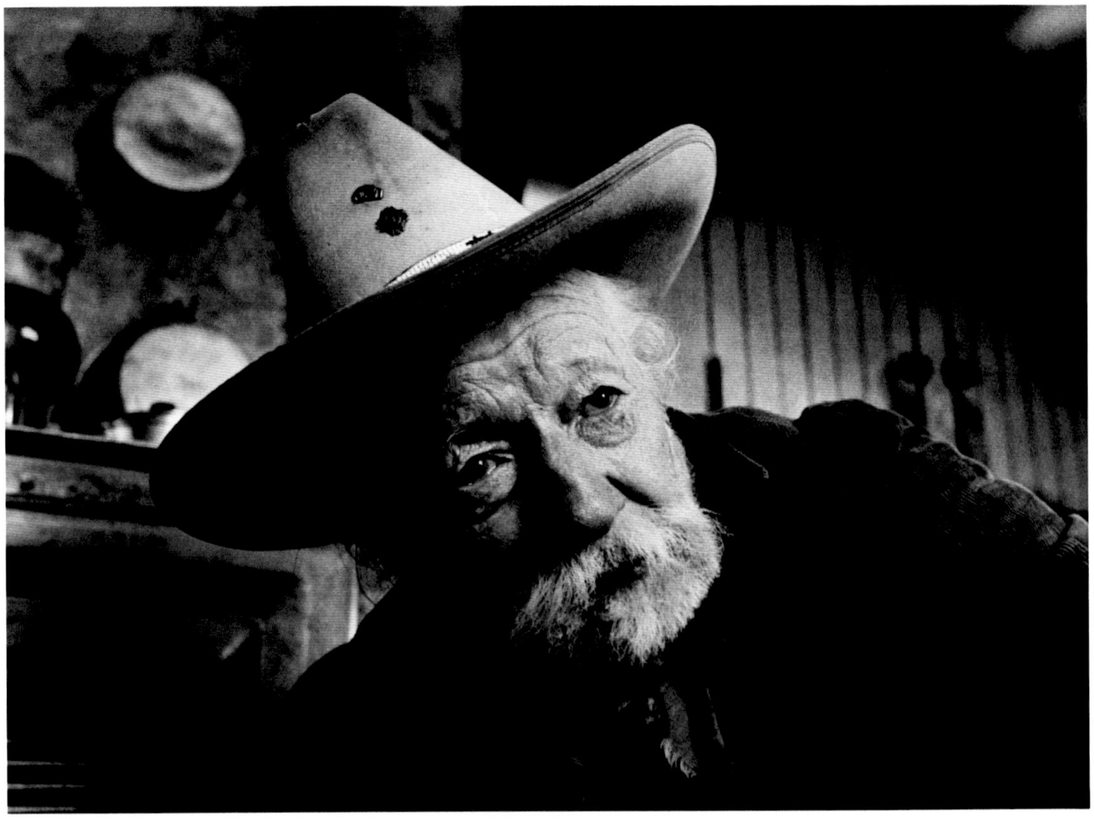

Rodeo Earl, Elkton, Maryland, 1976

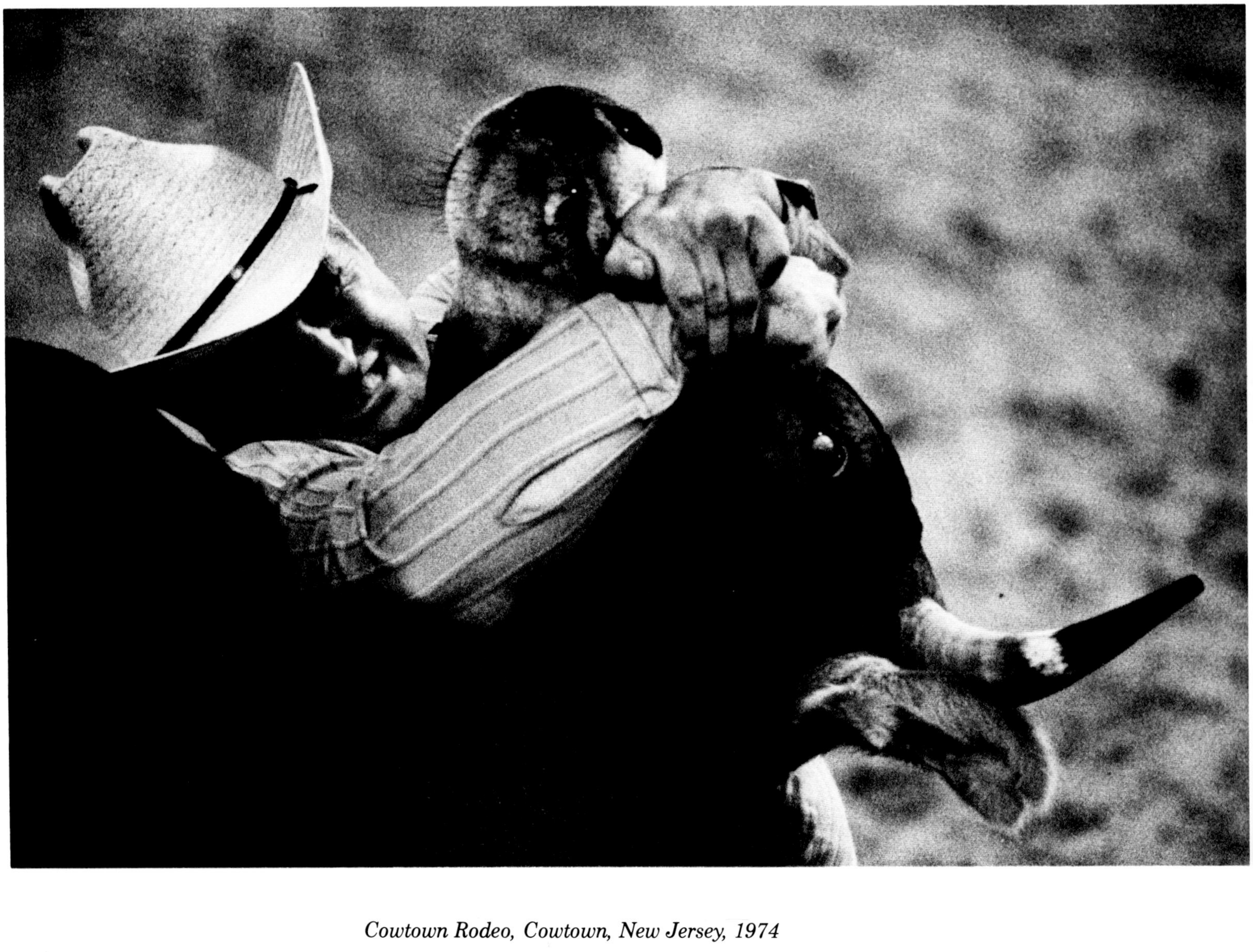

Cowtown Rodeo, Cowtown, New Jersey, 1974

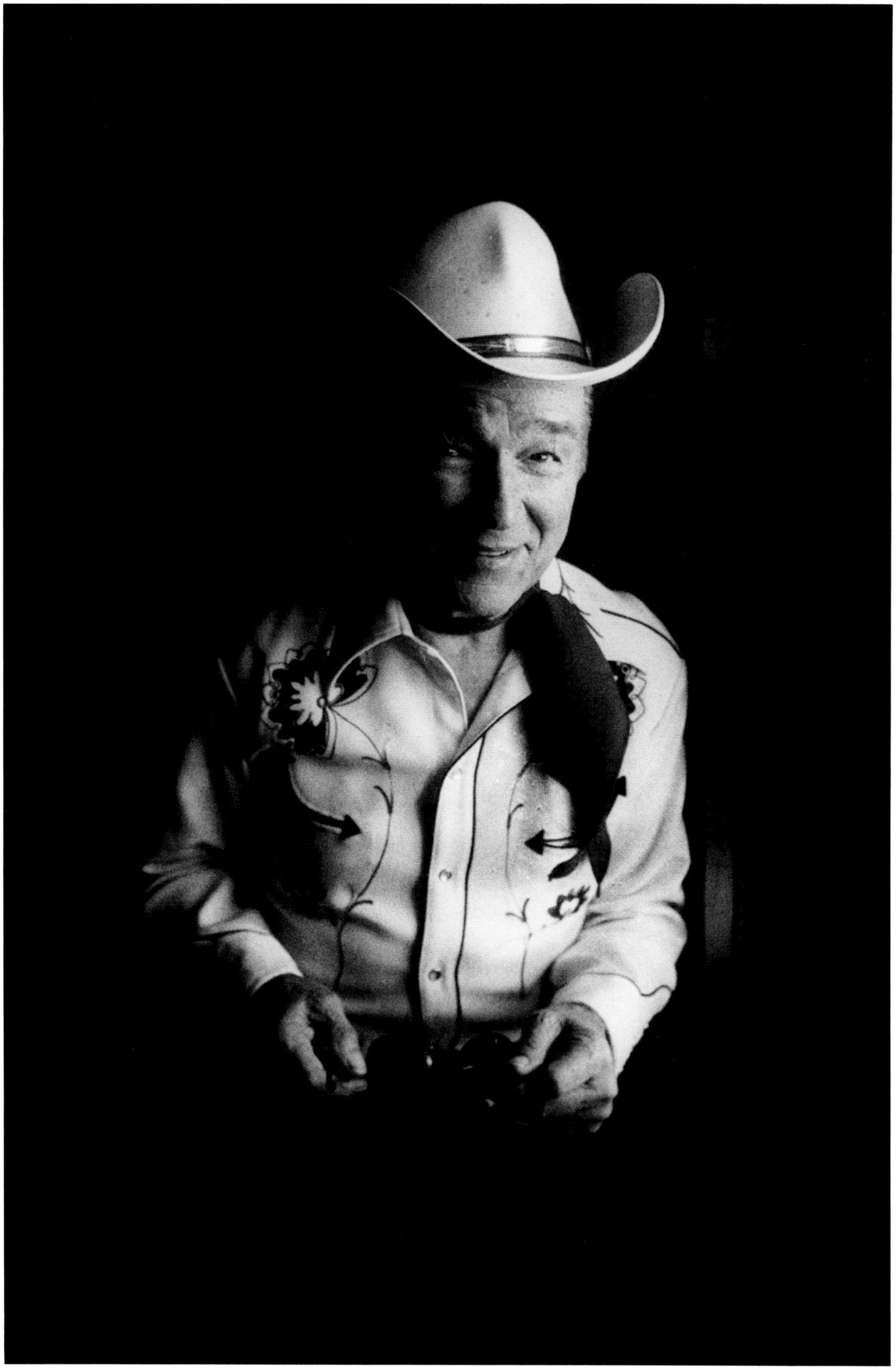

Roy Rogers, Roy Rogers Restaurant, Newark, Delaware, 1983

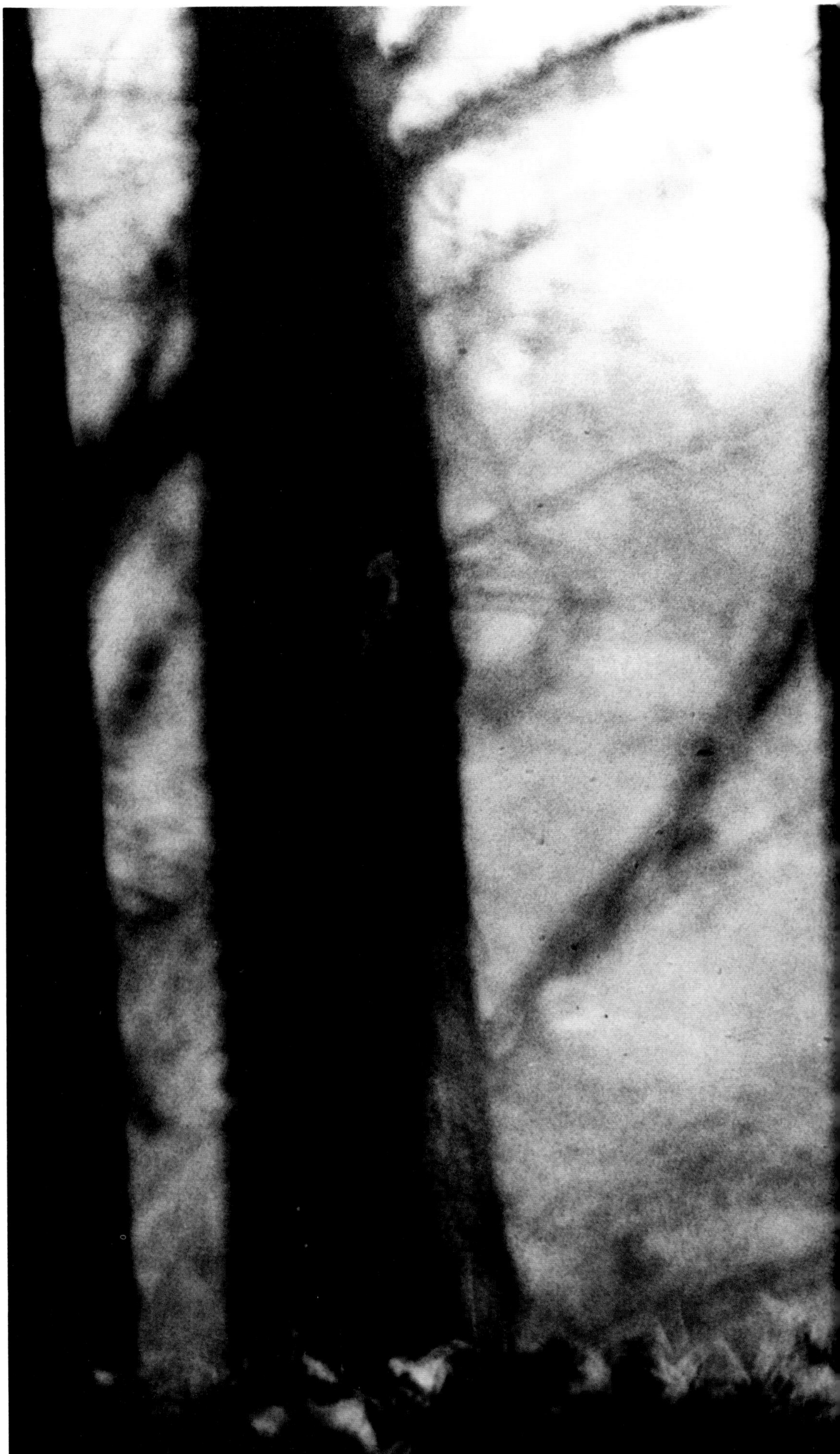

Elk Neck State Park, Cecil County, Maryland, 1987

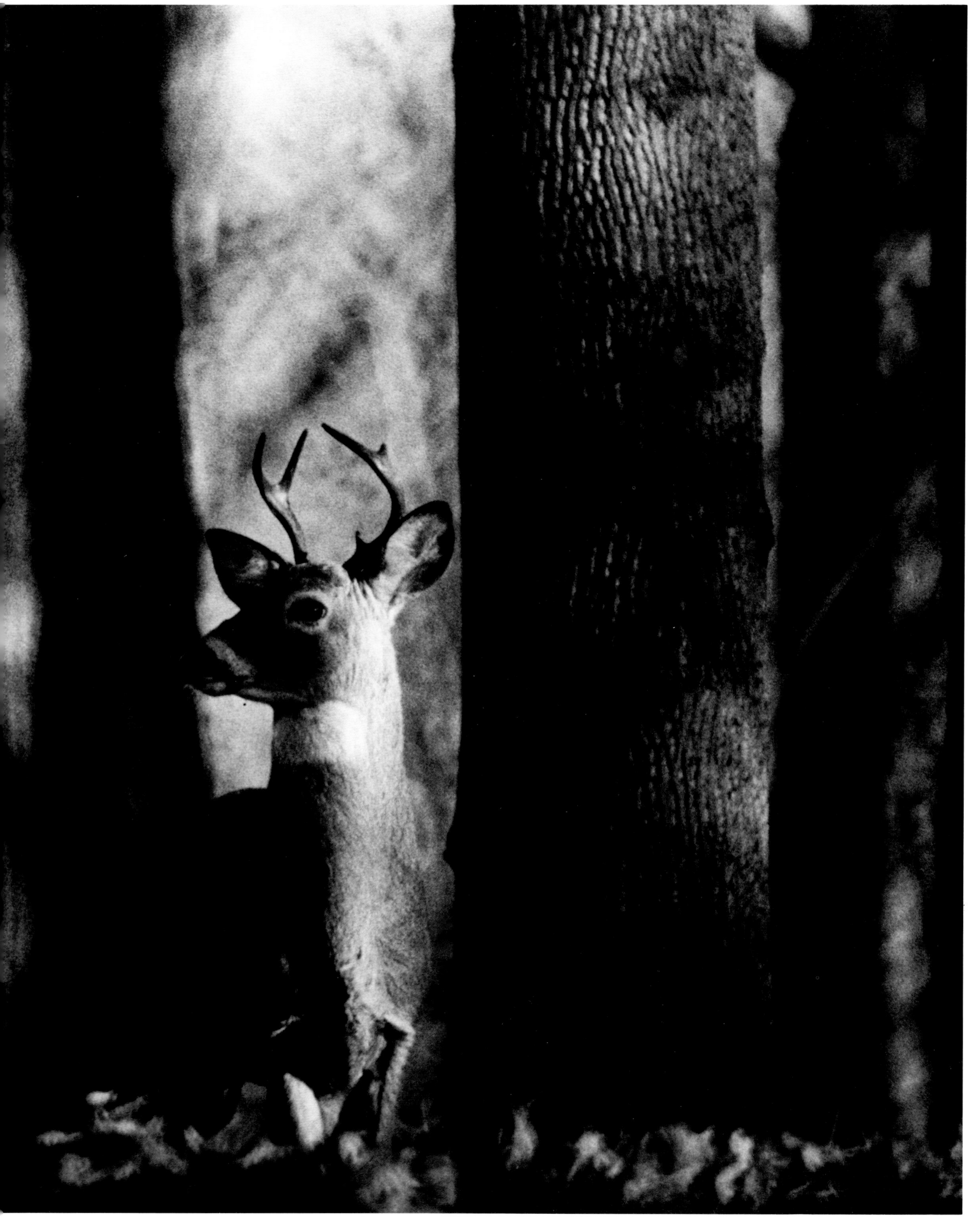

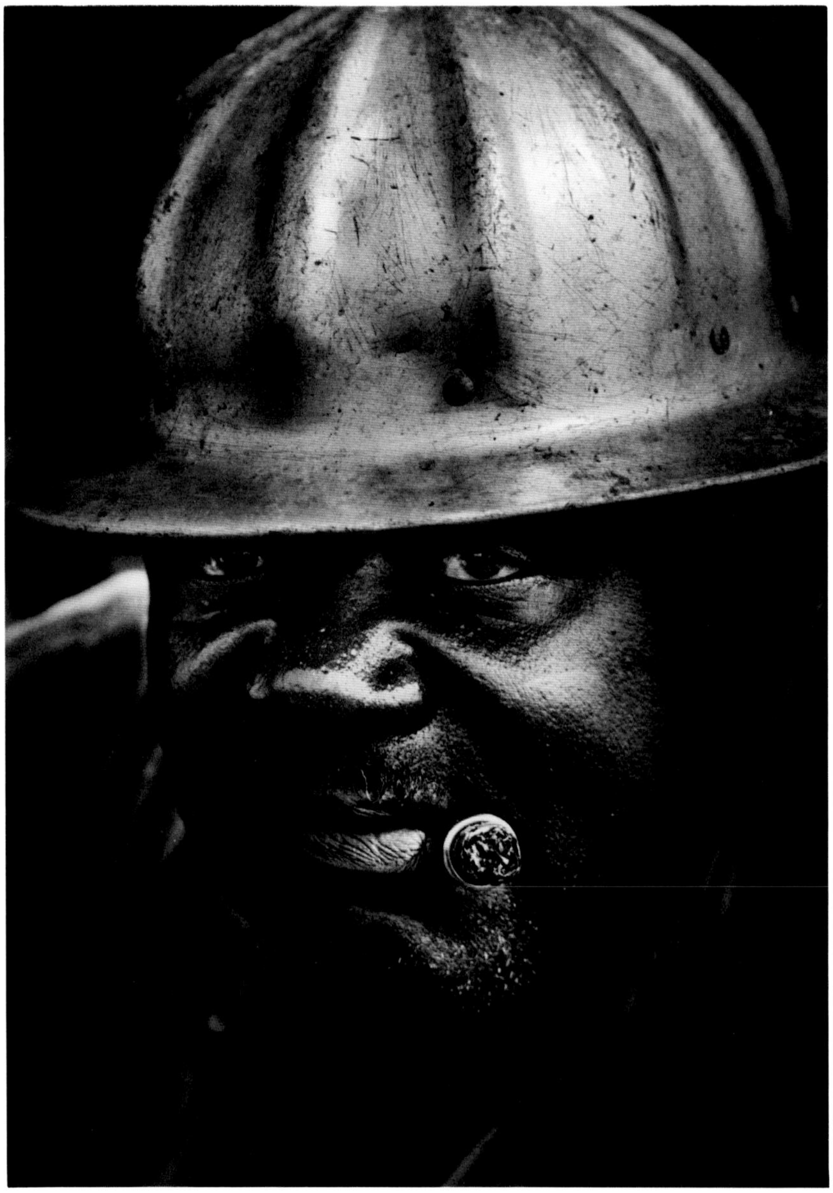

Offshore rigger in search of the 18th century wreck of the H.M.S. De Braak, *Lewes, 1969*

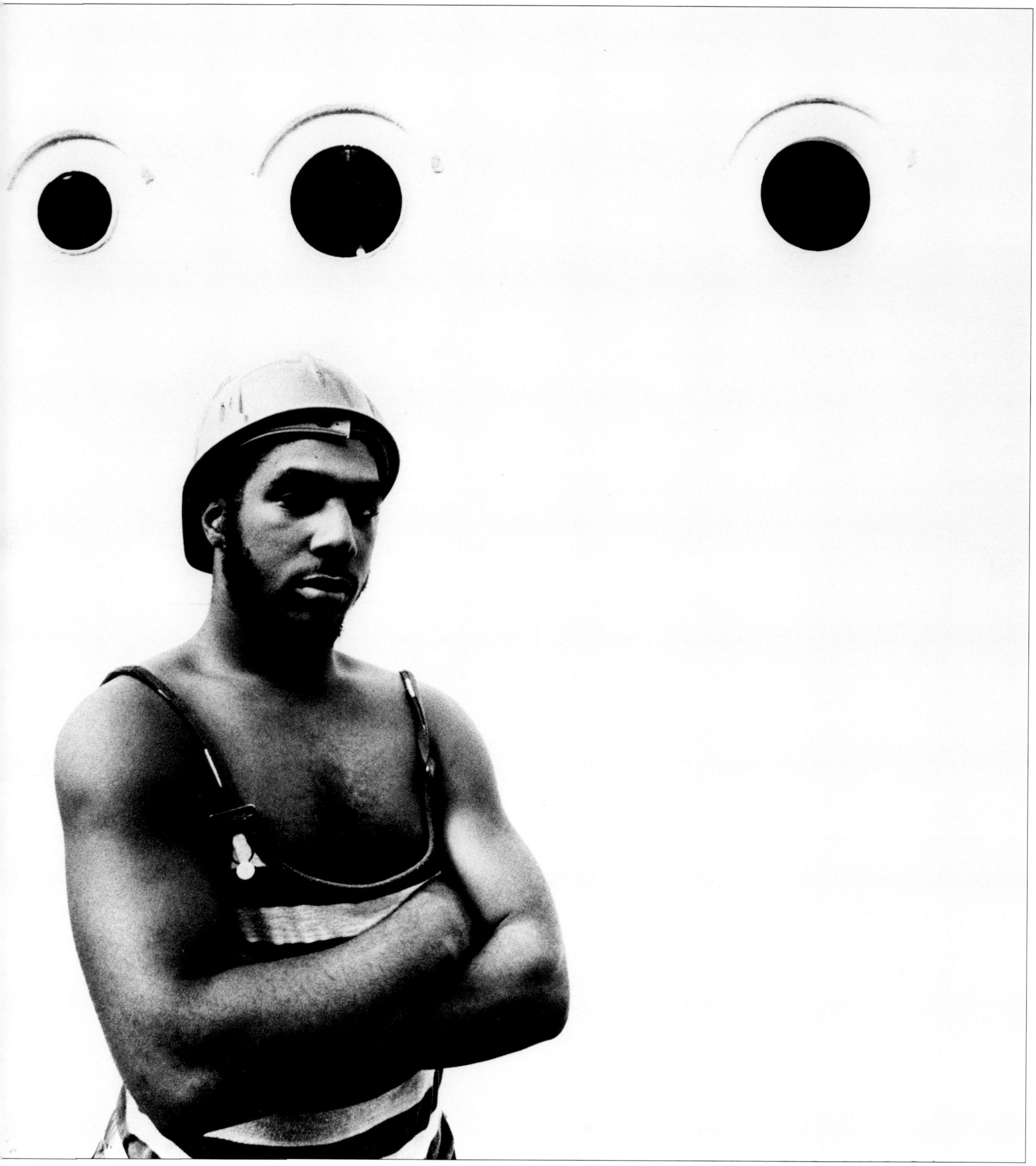

Longshoreman, Port of Wilmington, 1973

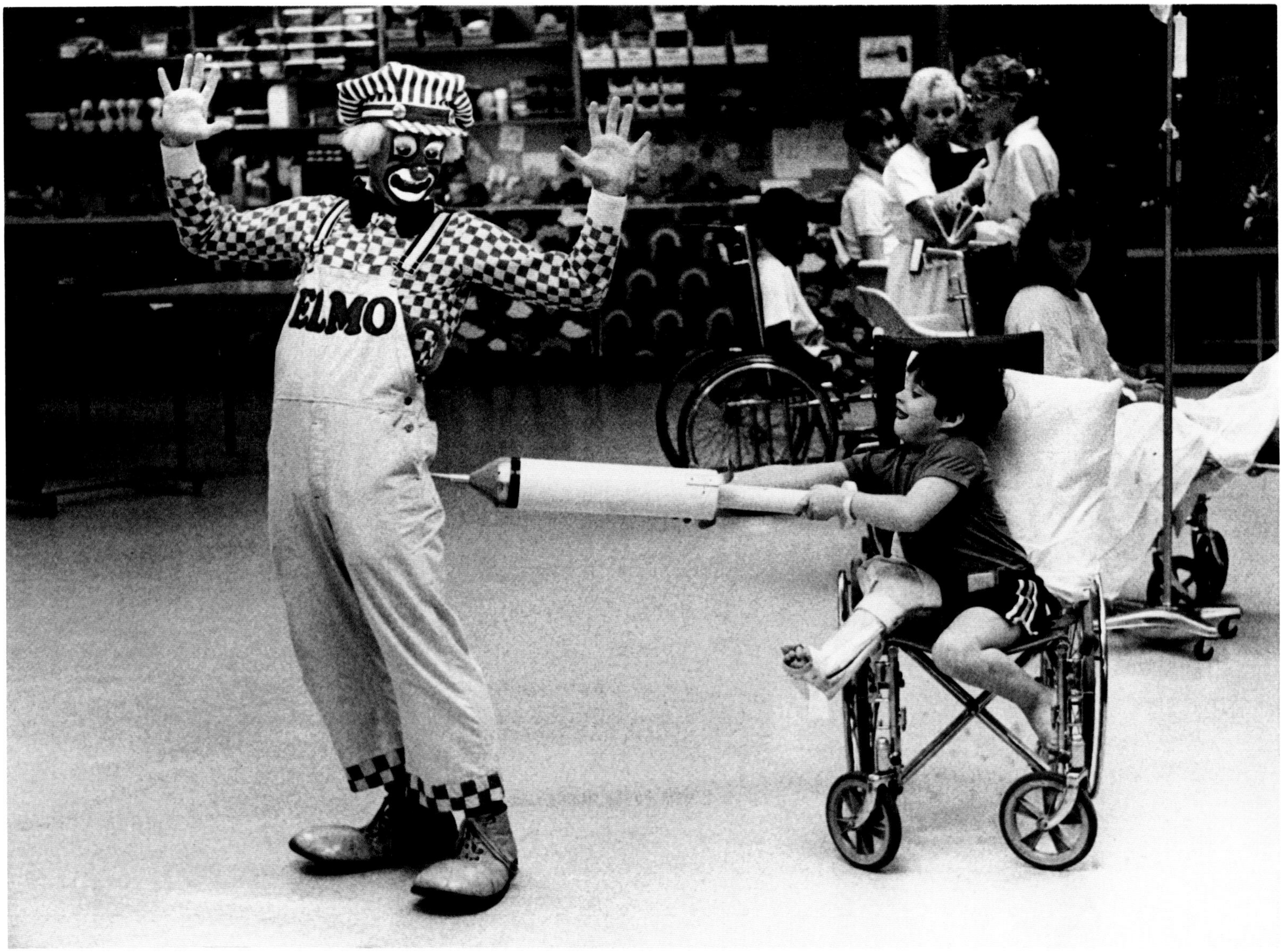

Clyde Beatty Cole Brothers' Elmo and Jason Williams, A.I. du Pont Institute, Wilmington, 1986

Alberta Grove laughs with a Clyde Beatty Cole Brothers clown, Methodist Country House, Greenville, 1987

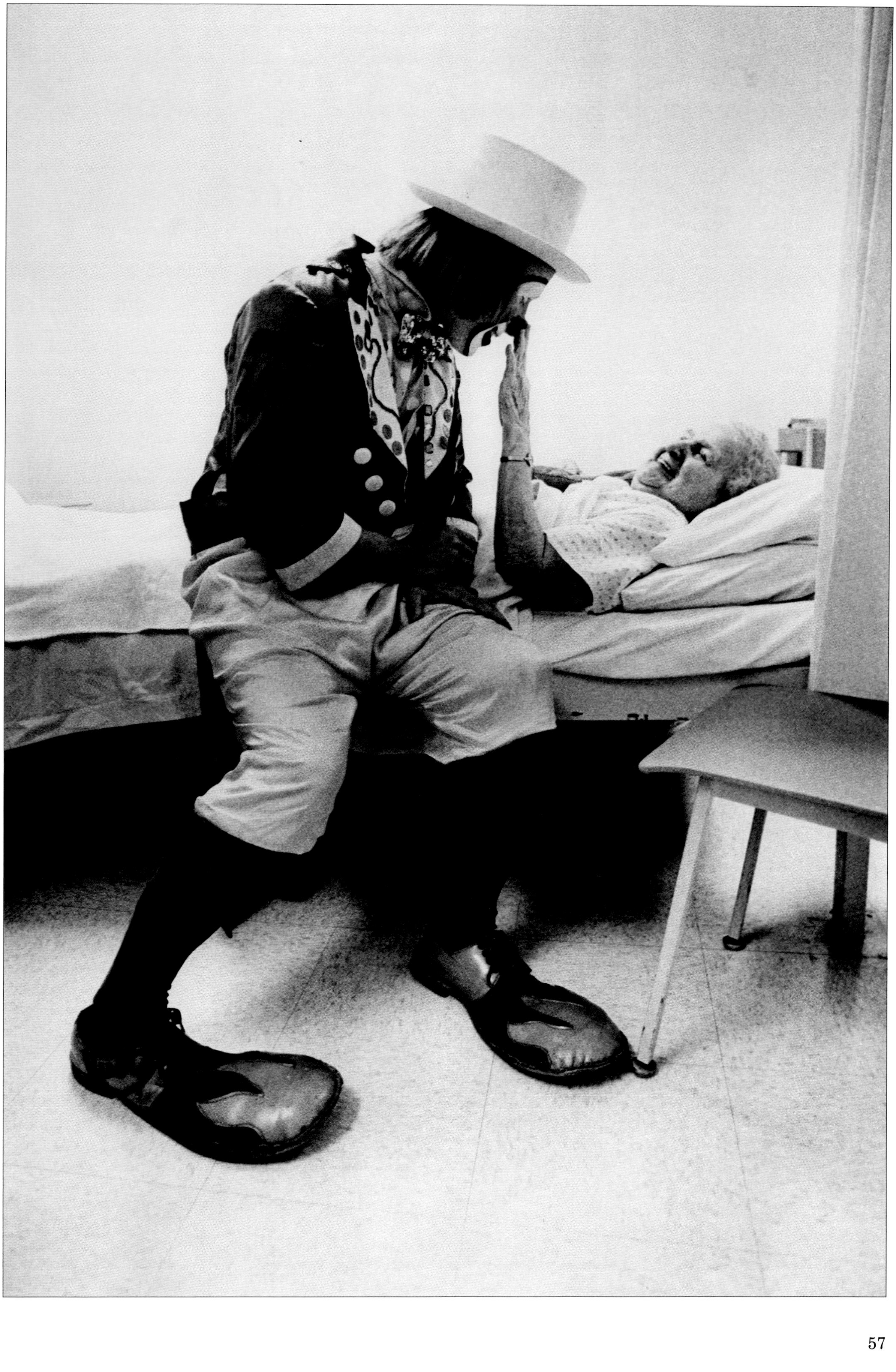

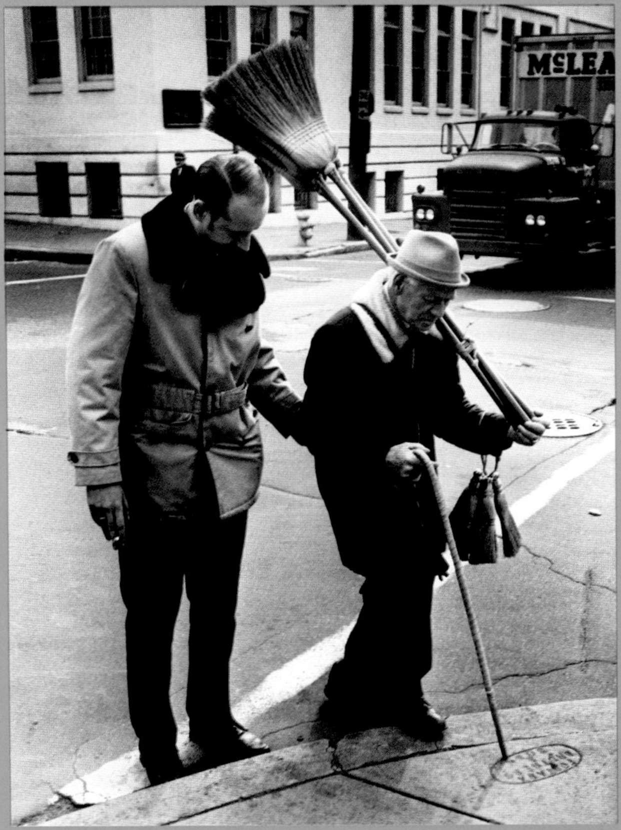

Jake the Broom Man

1975

Until his death in 1975, Jake the Broom Man was as much a fixture in Wilmington as the statue of Caesar Rodney. Jacob Isaac Woodward walked the streets for 60 years selling brooms, rugs, and dust pans. His wares were made by friends at the Delaware Commission for the Blind. Jake was blind too. He lost his sight at age 8 when flying glass from an oil lamp cut and infected his eyes. Yet he knew the city well thanks to the rap of his cane. "I know every street in the city," Jake told me. "You can't loose me in Wilmington."

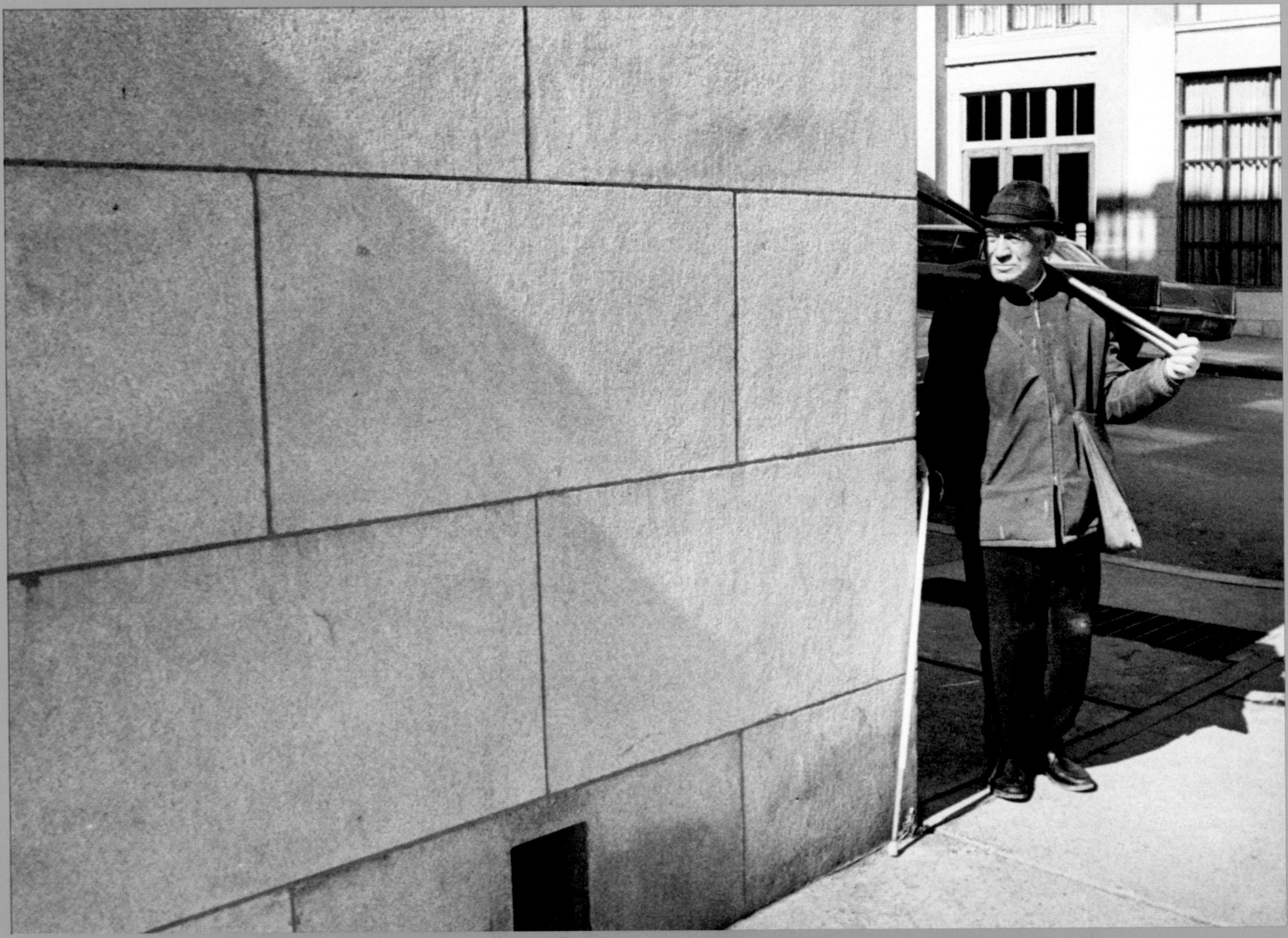

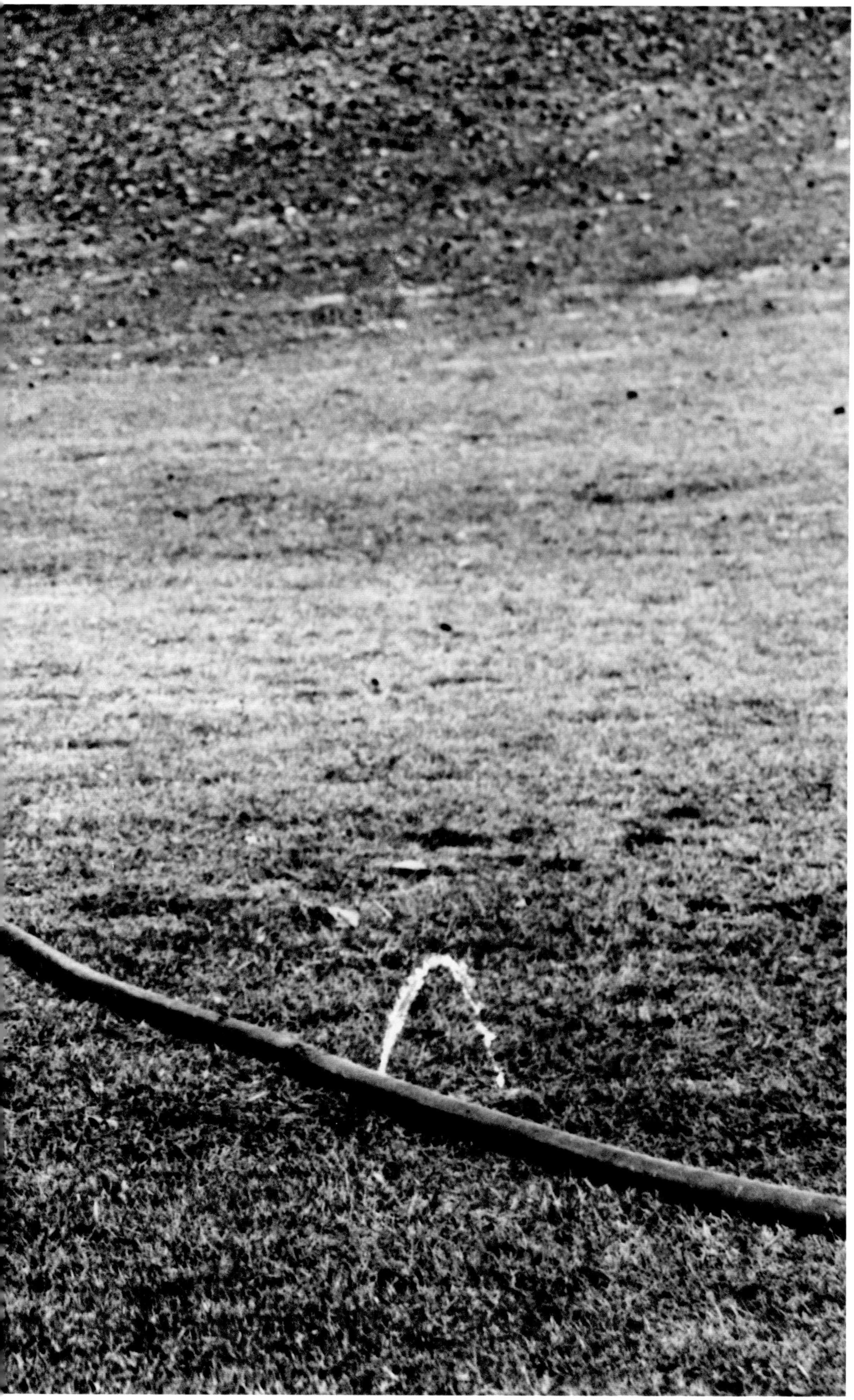

Winterthur Museum
Fire Company, 1970

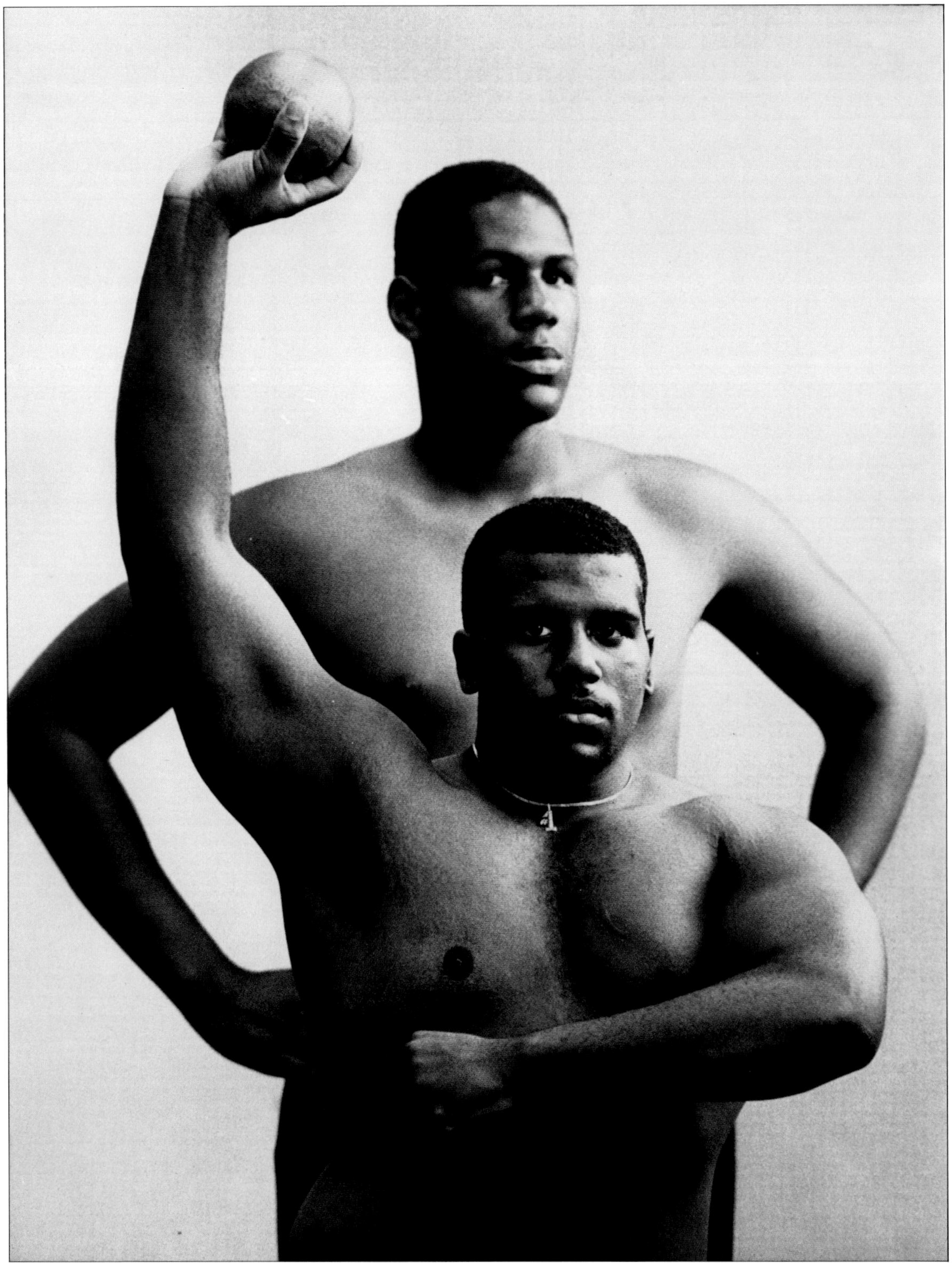

Jim Croner, bottom, and Eric Edwards, Wilmington High School, 1987

Harry Spencer, Jr., Wilmington, 1984

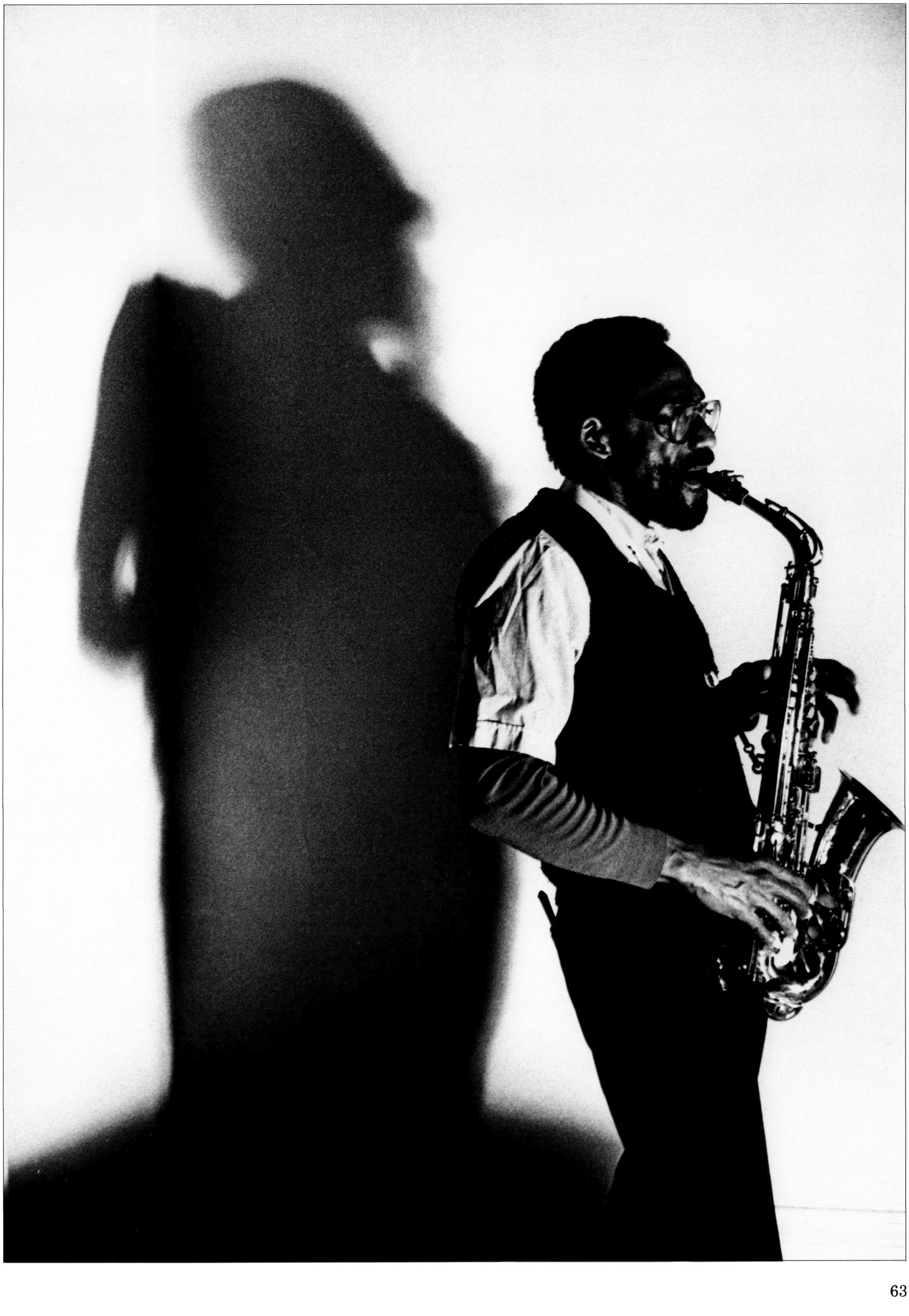

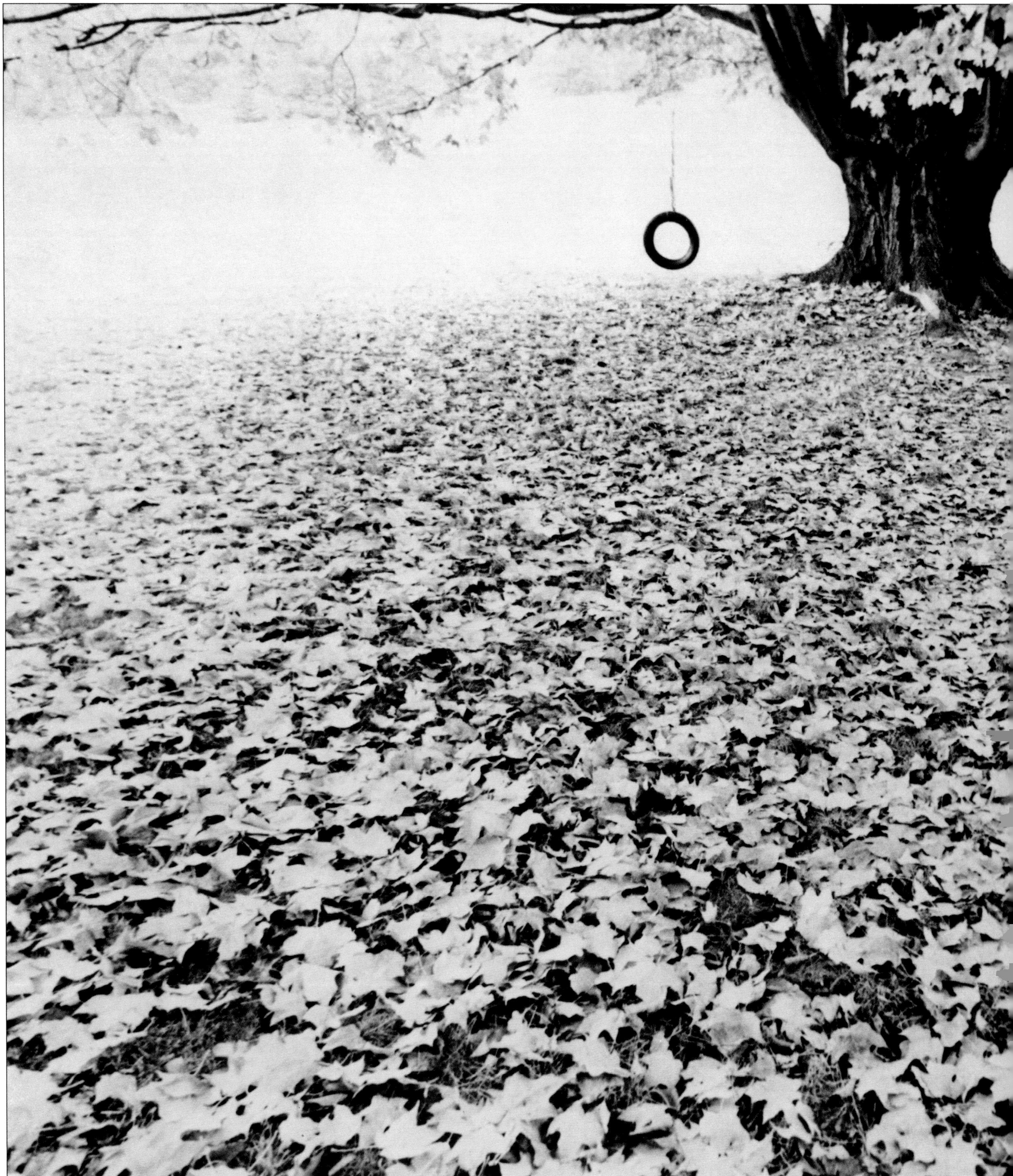

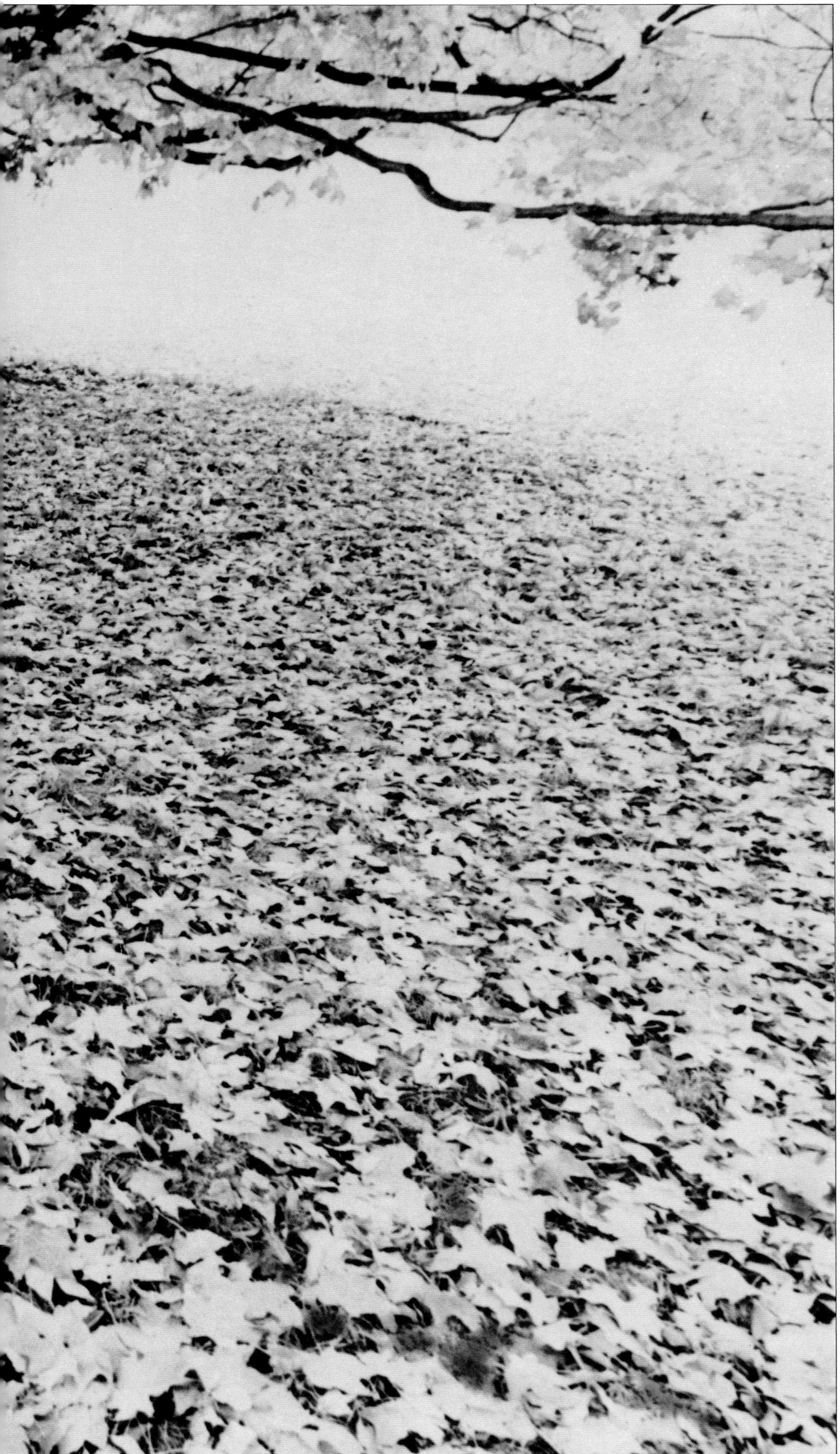

Greenville, 1975

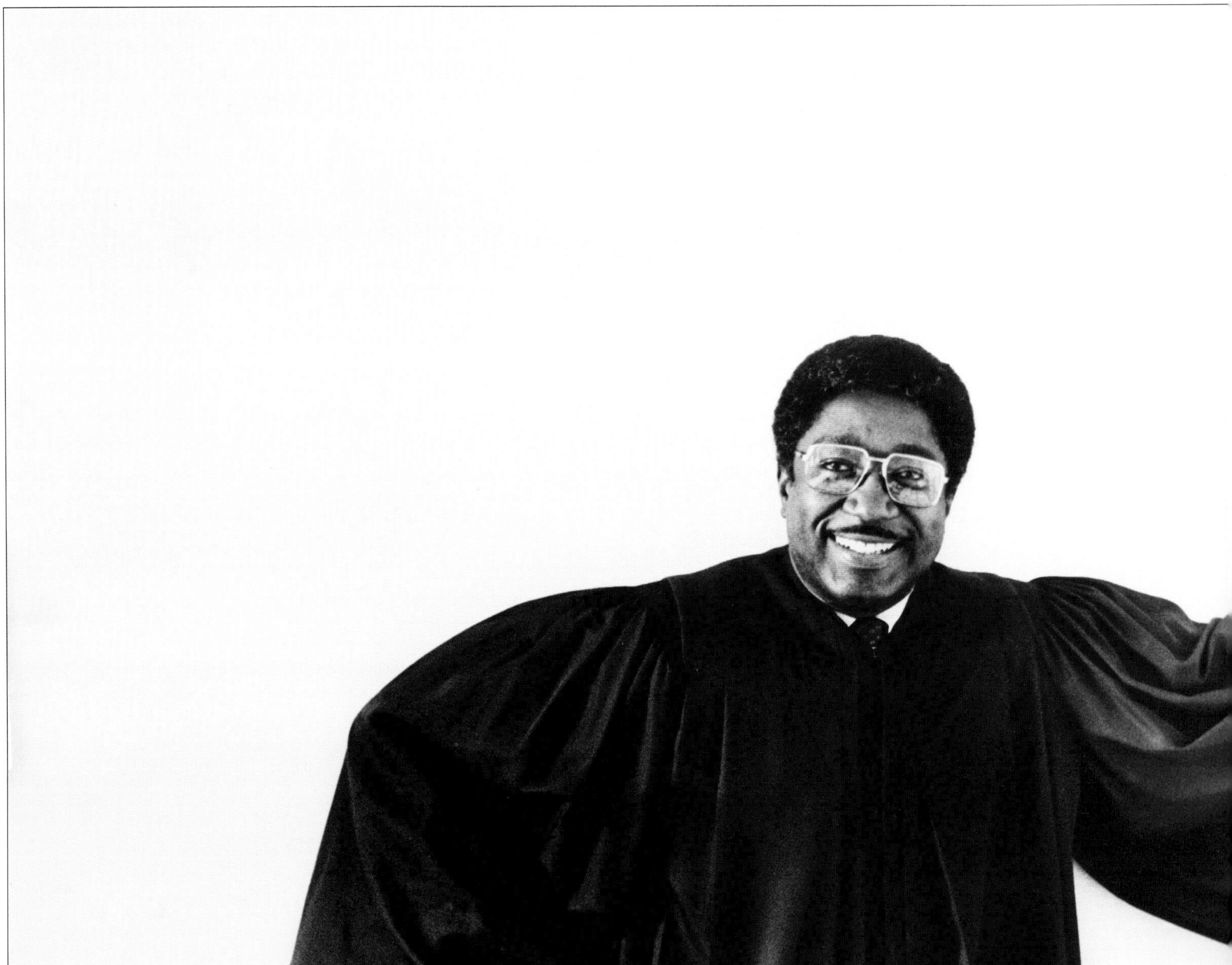

Delaware Superior Court Judge Joshua Martin, Wilmington, 1987

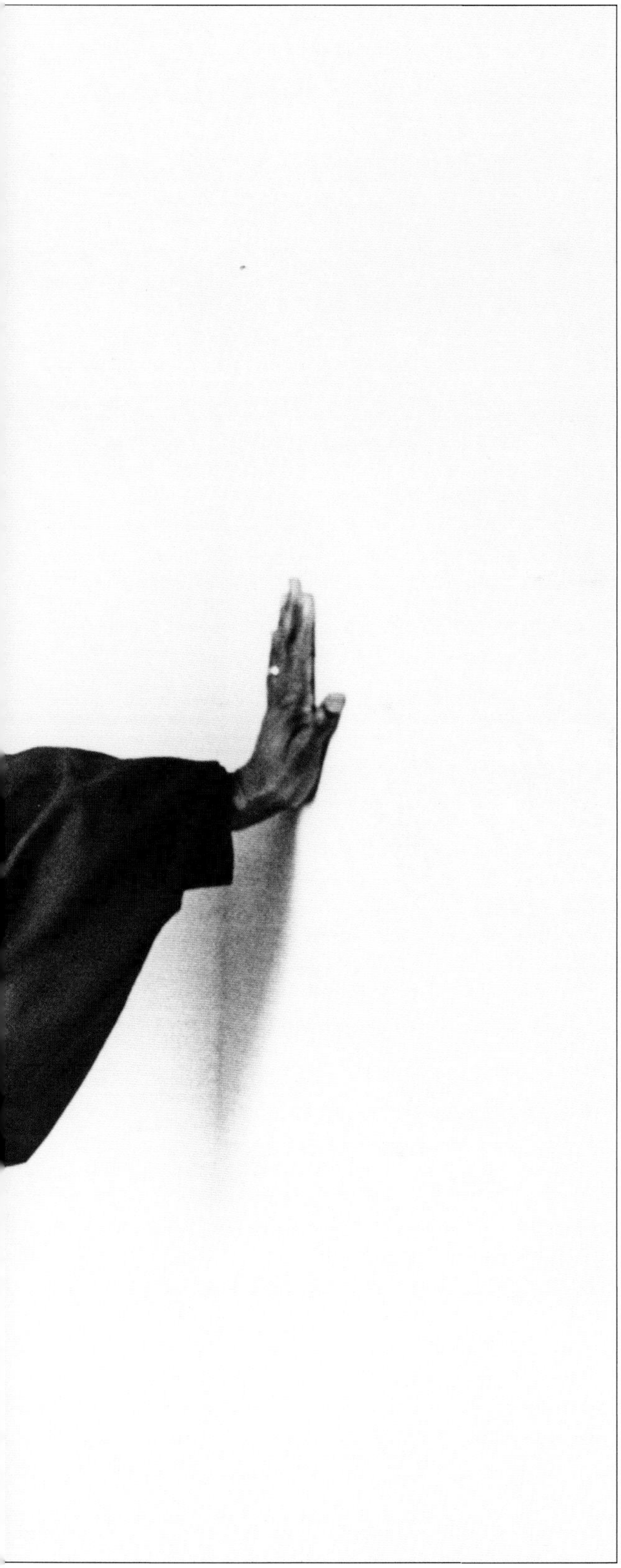

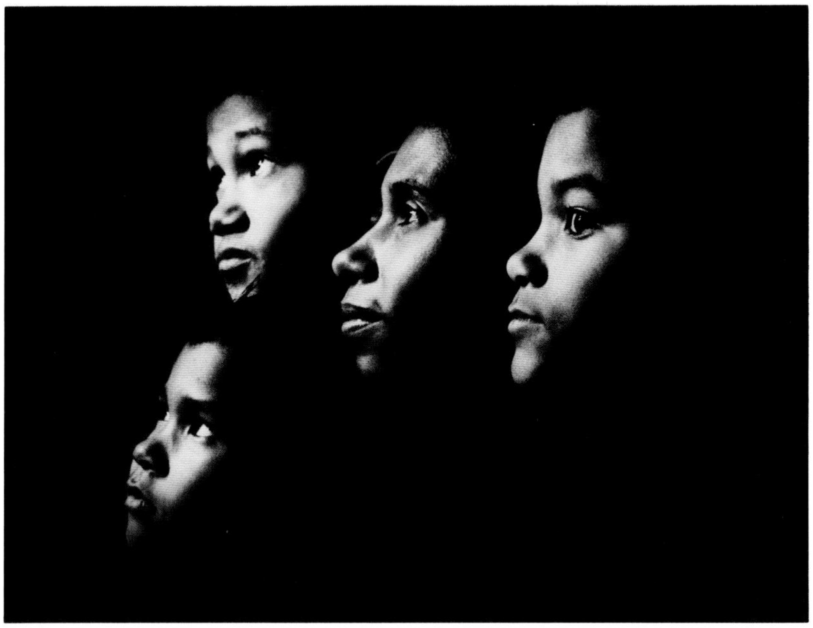

Community leader Arva Jackson and family, Wilmington, 1969

Etchings of Time

Photographing an old man in Wilmington in 1971 I realized how much the starkness of the background drew attention to the lines and contours of his face. I decided to take a series of photographs against white backgrounds. My subjects were people I met and talked to on the street – people of outstanding spirit. I still look for faces that show the etchings of time.

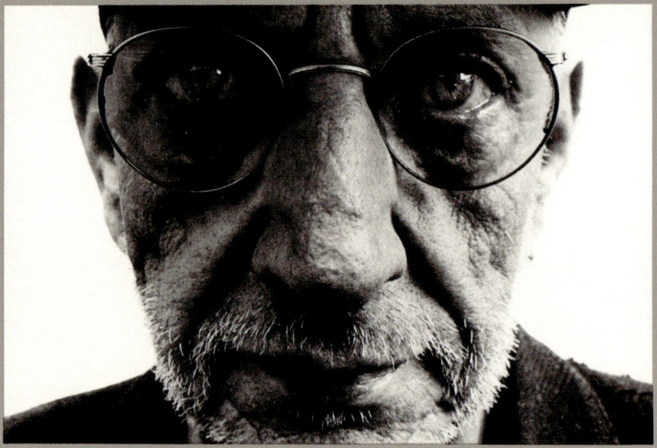

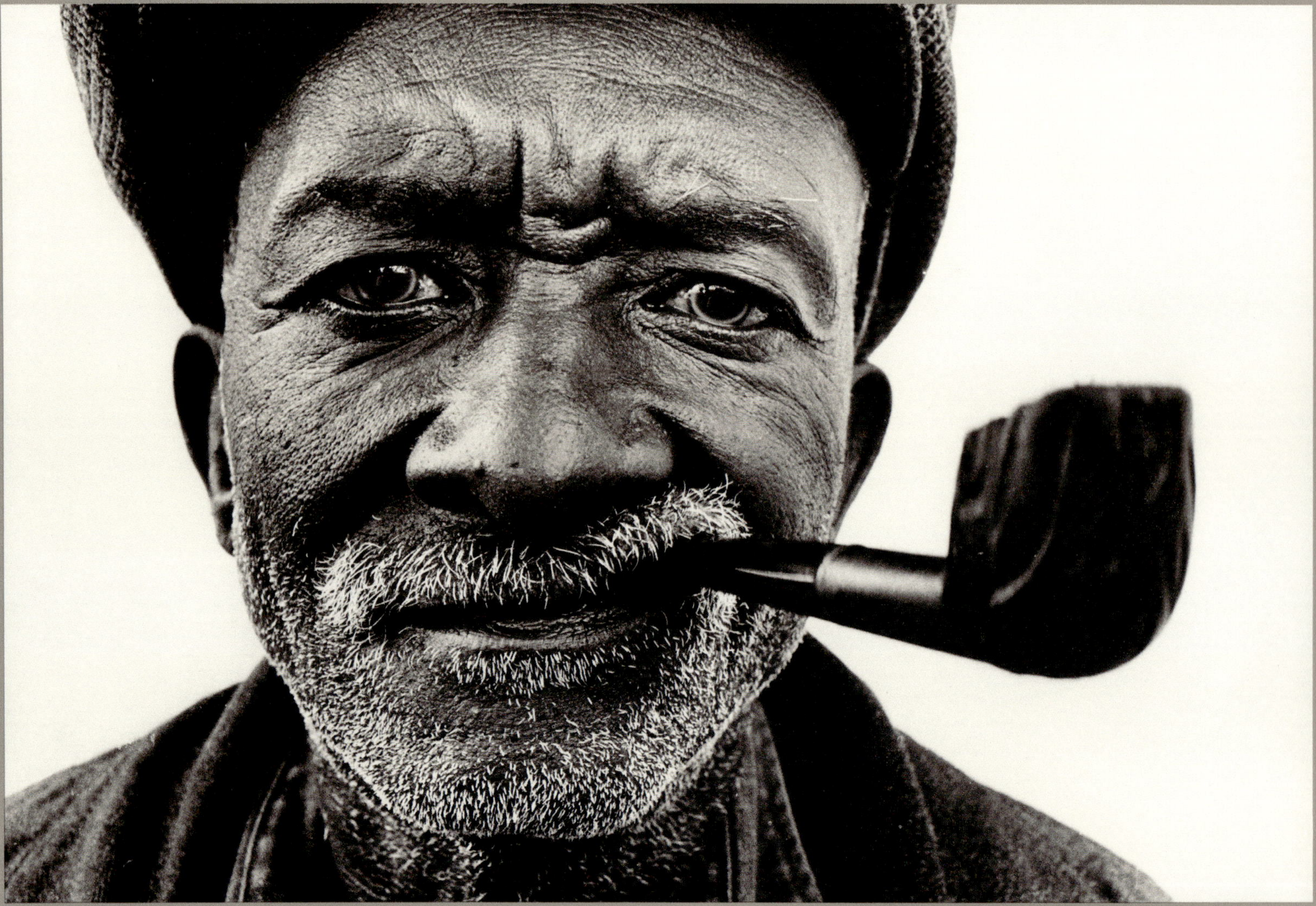

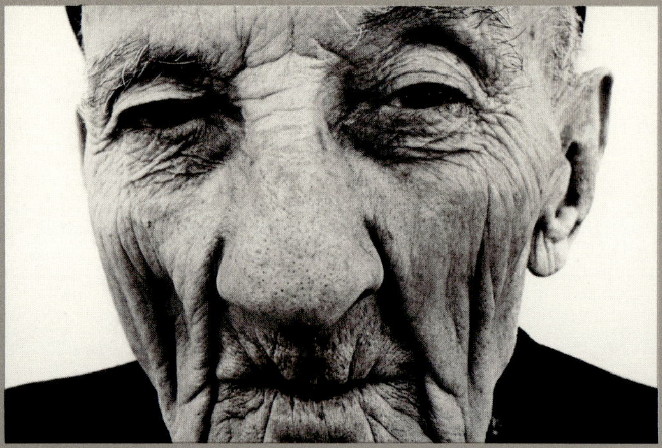

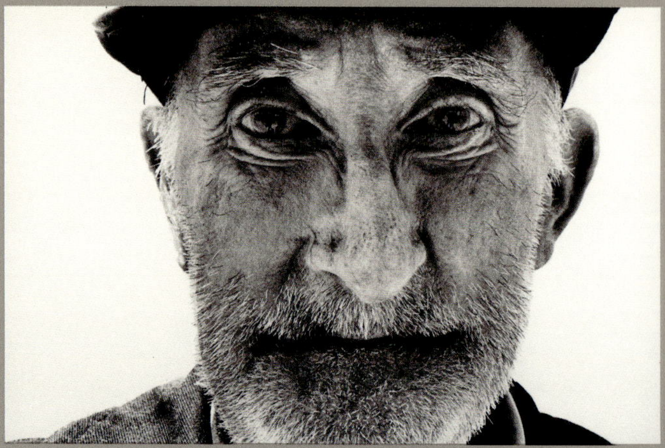

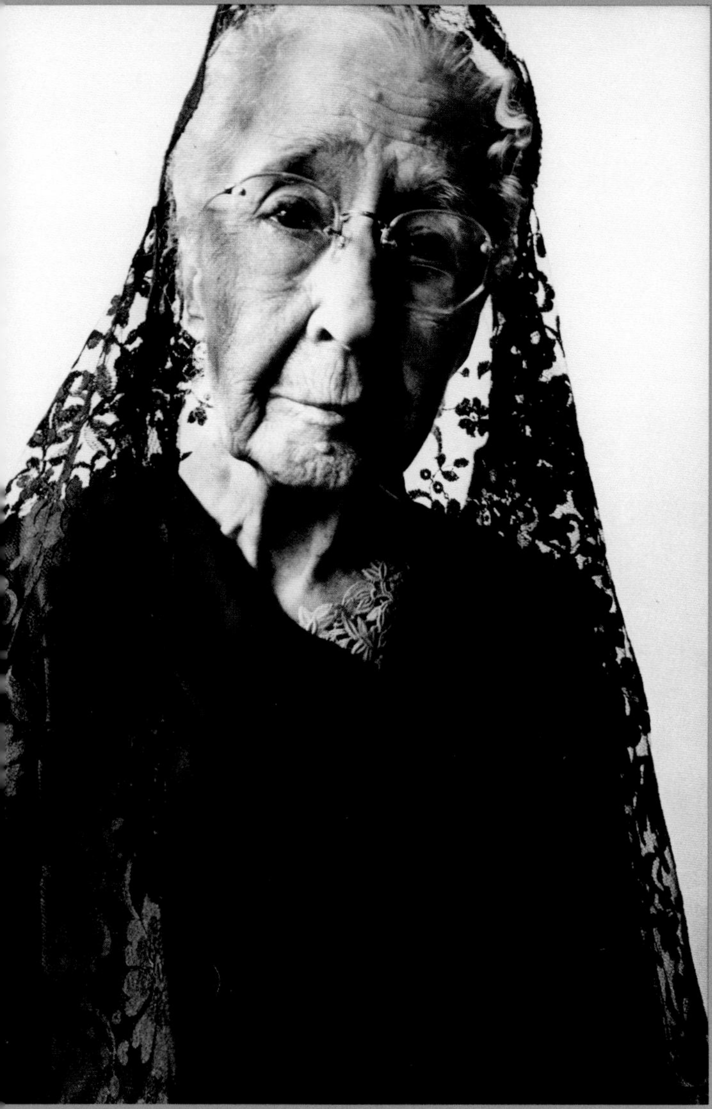
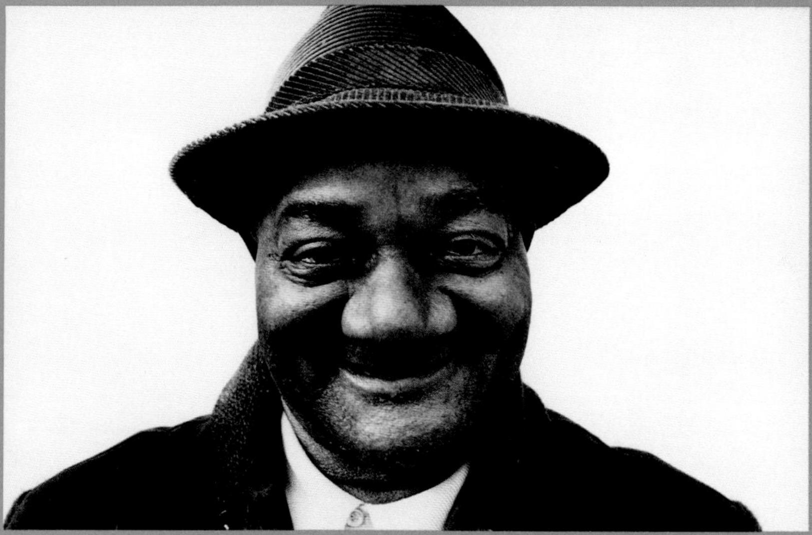
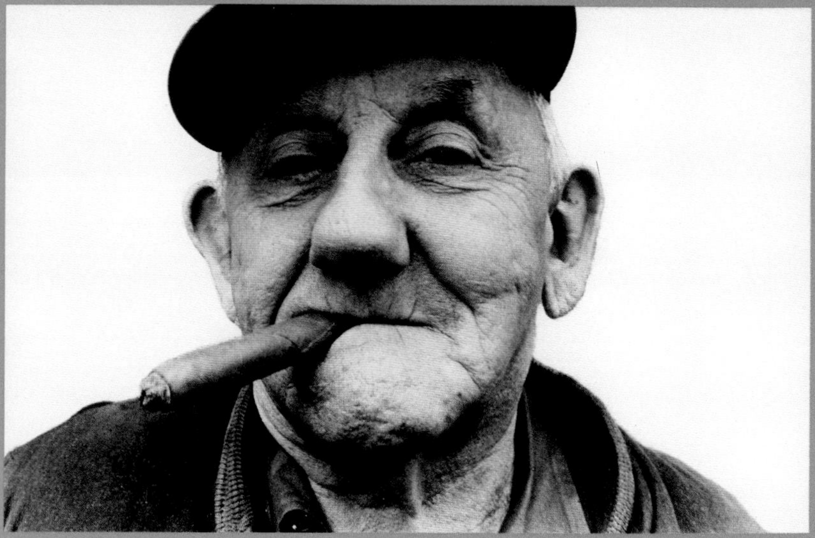
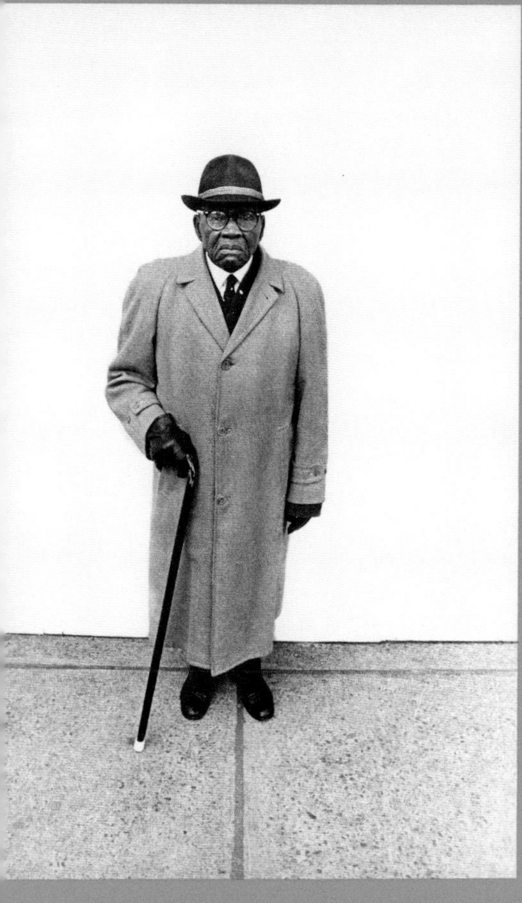
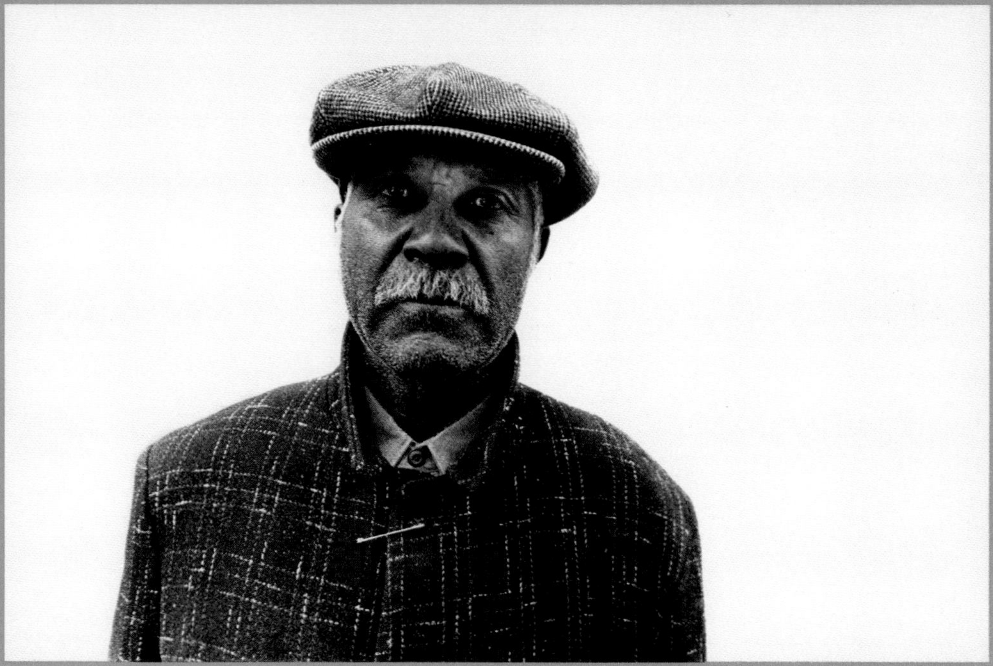

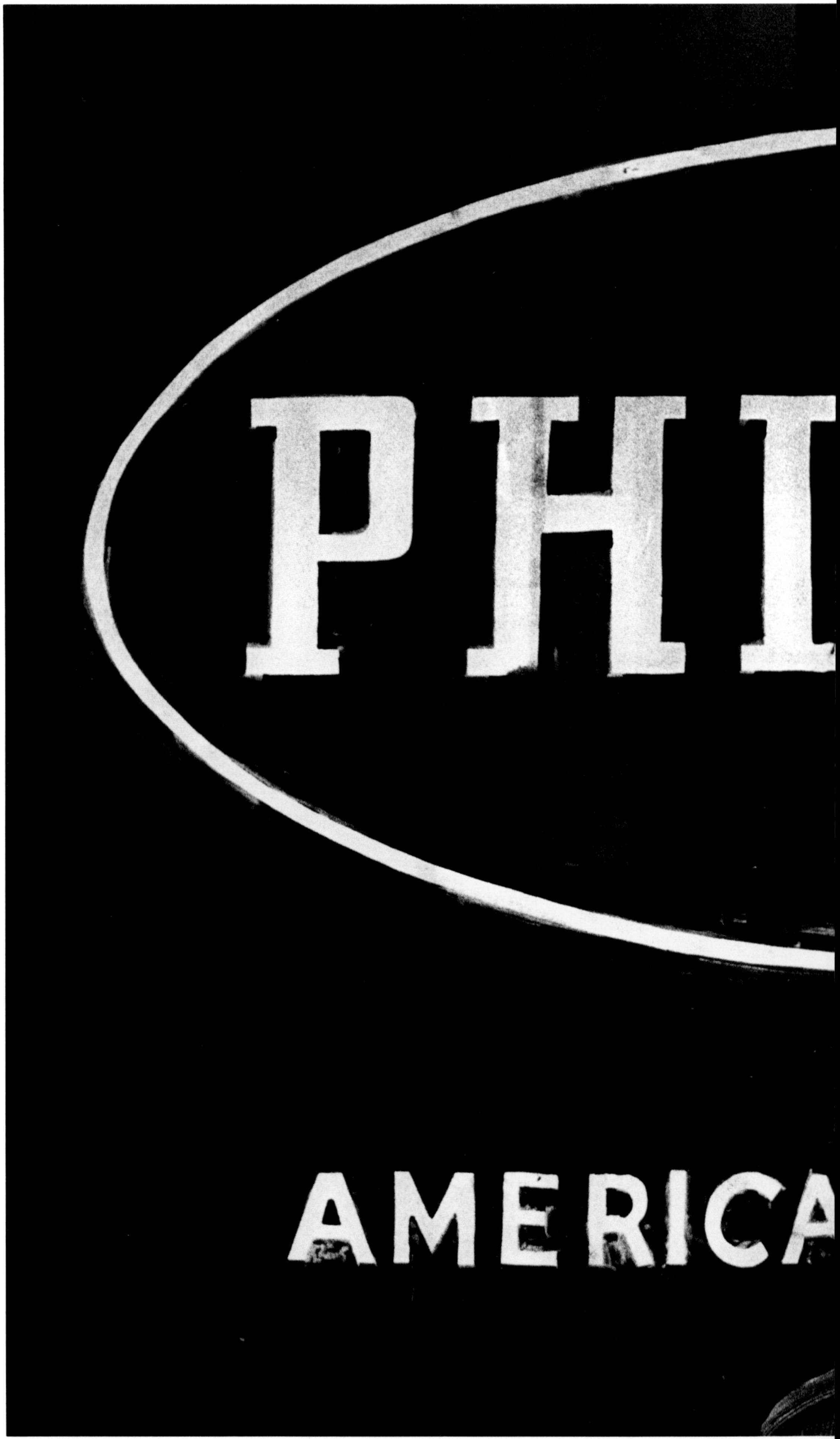

Cigar store, Market Street, Wilmington, 1973

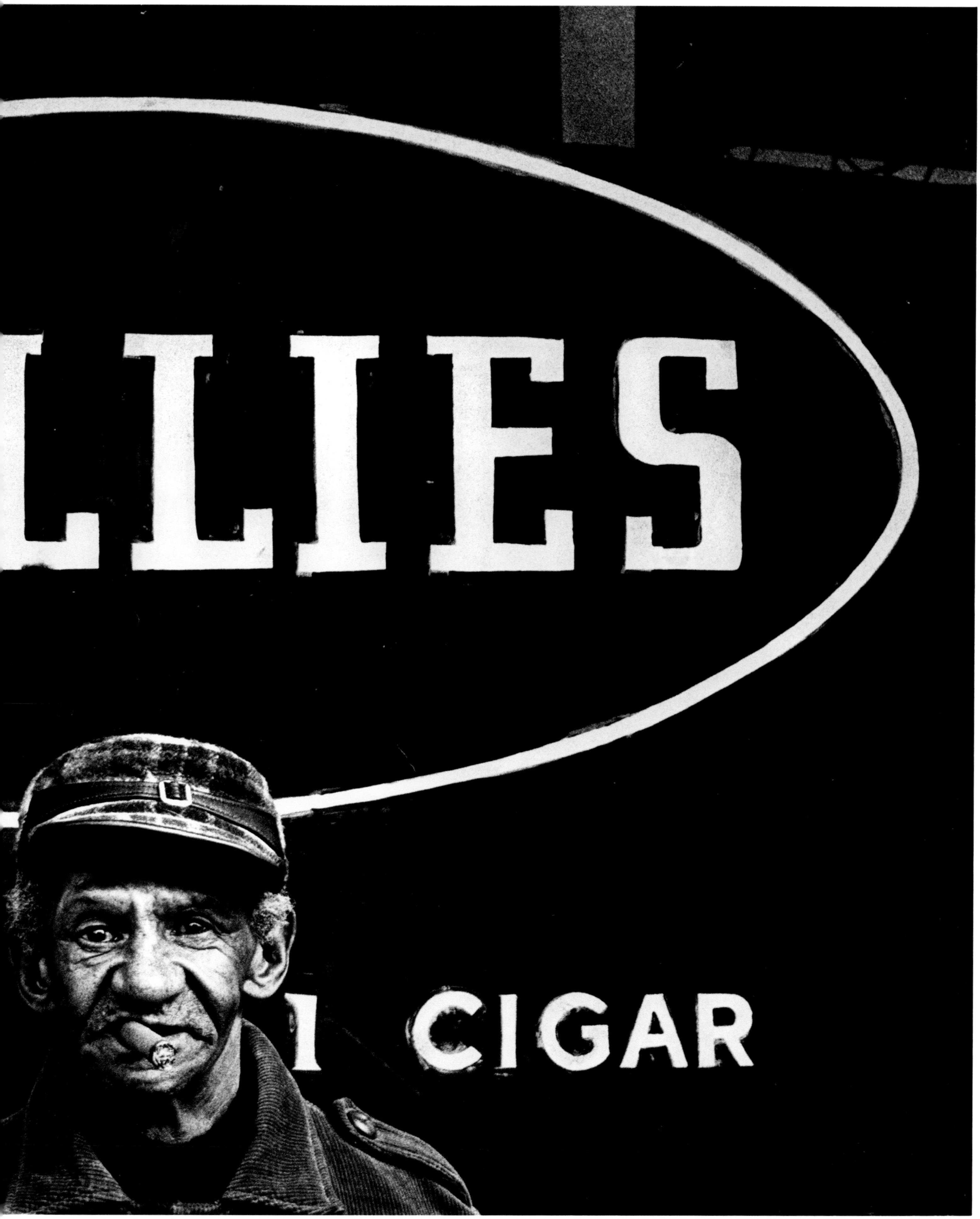
LLIES
I CIGAR

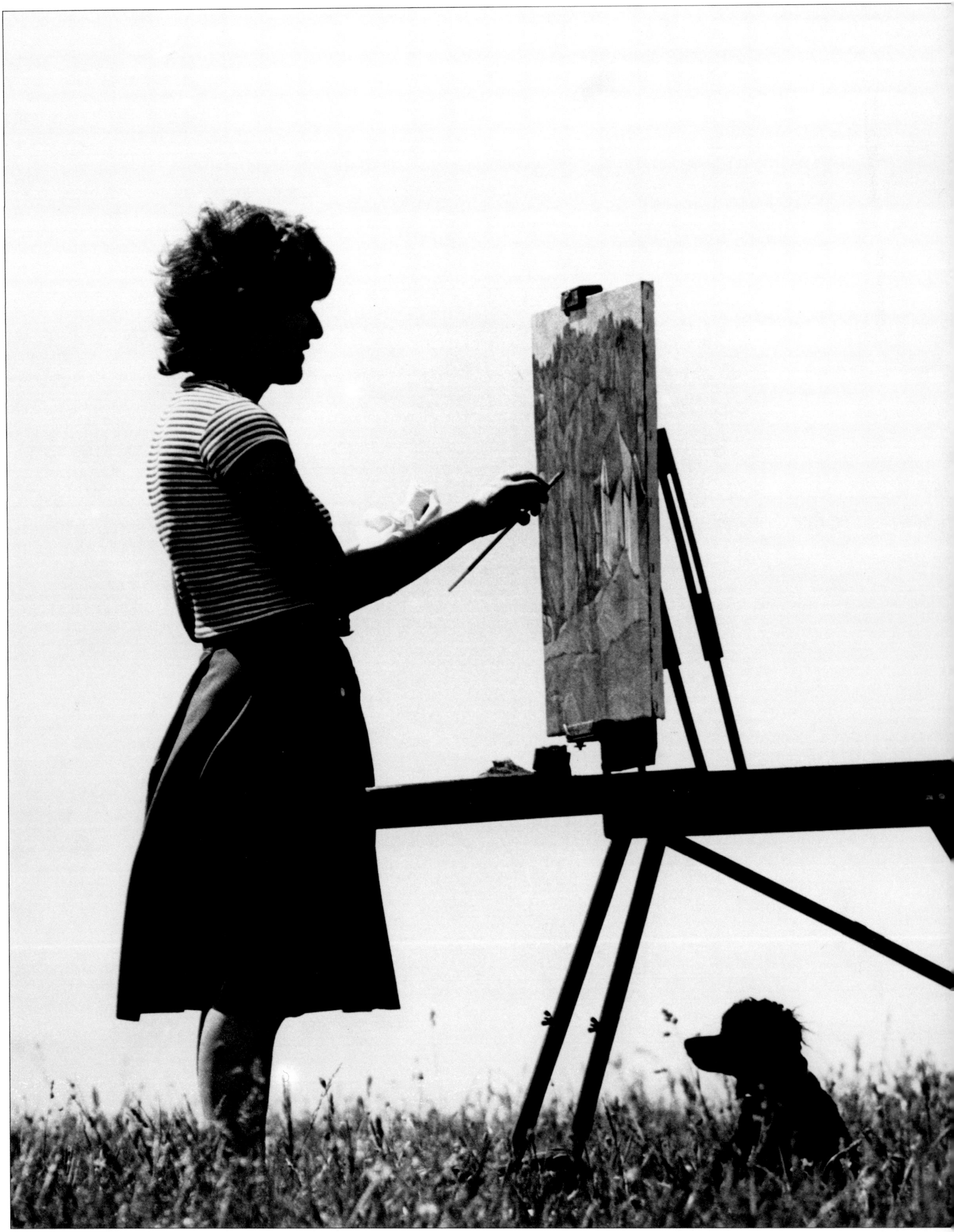

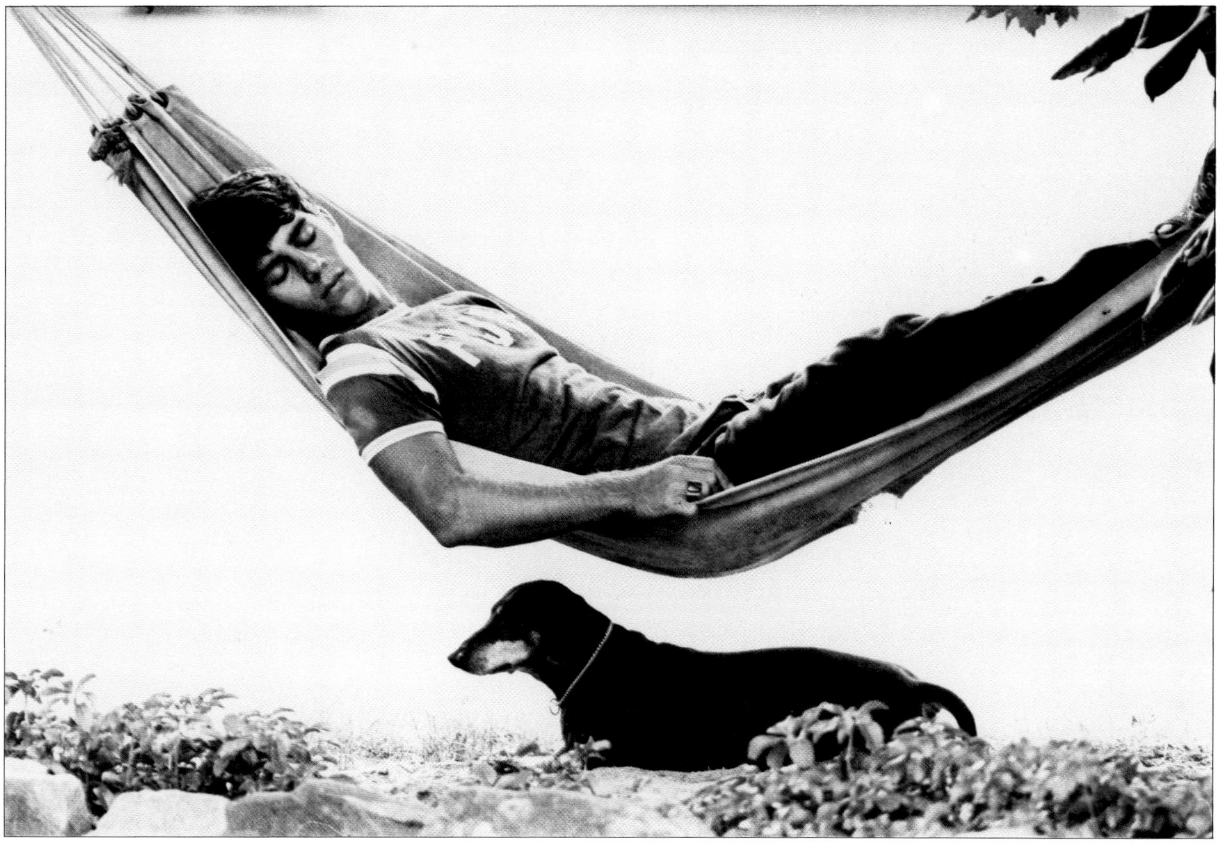

Wilmington, 1971

Marilyn Bauman and Tiff,
Brandywine Creek State Park, 1985

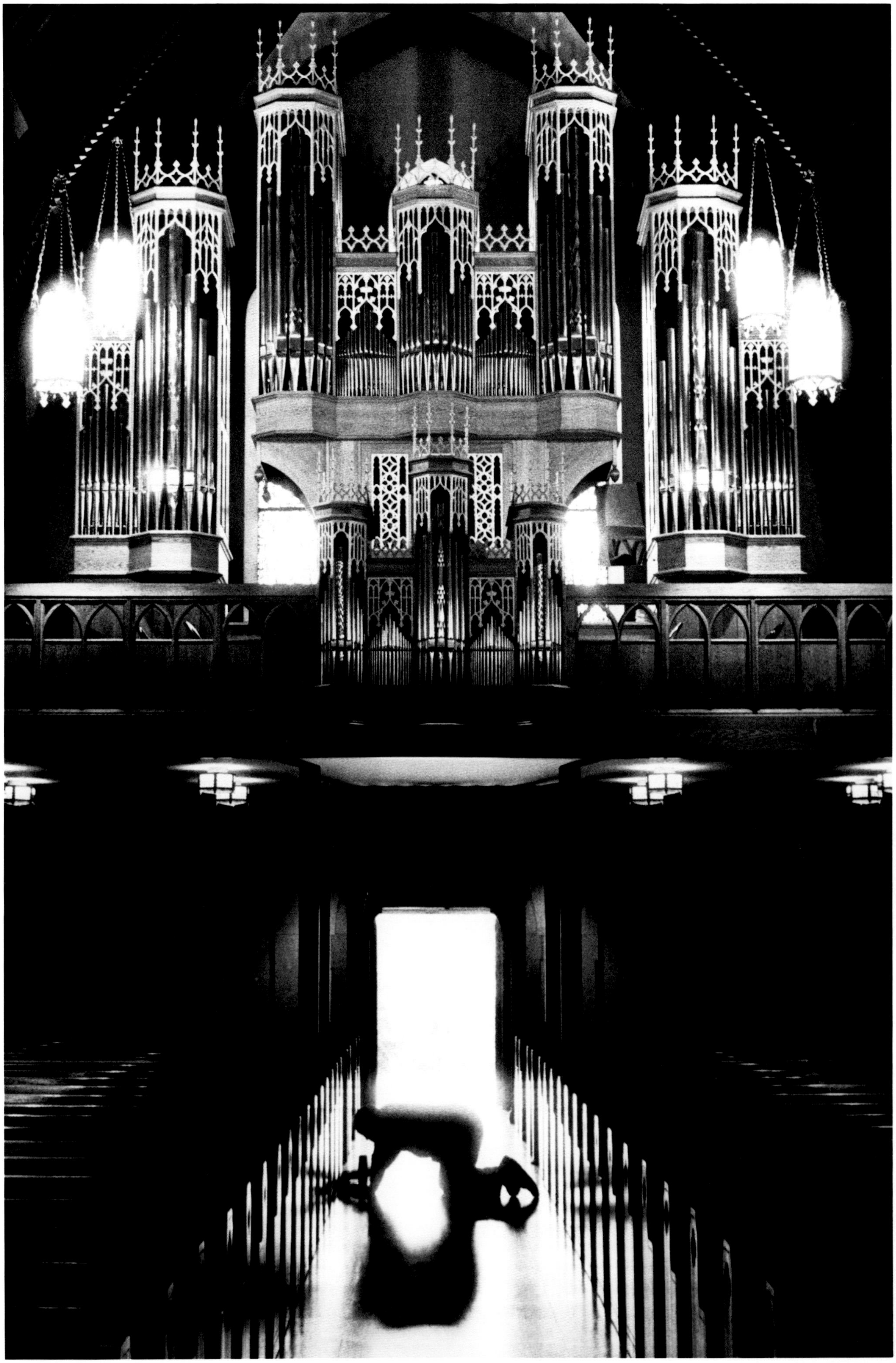

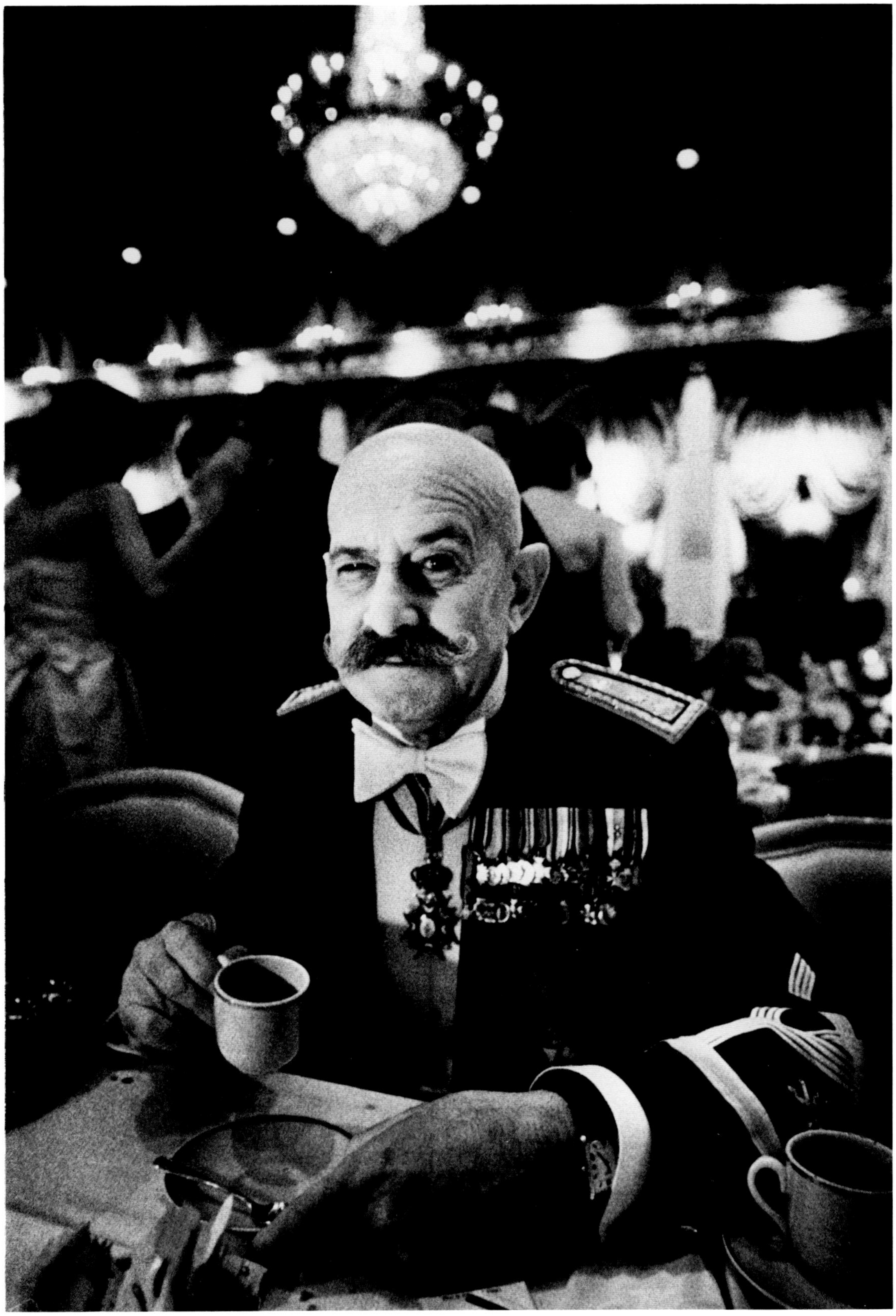

Debutante ball, New York City, 1981

Francis James, Cathedral Church of St. John, Wilmington, 1987

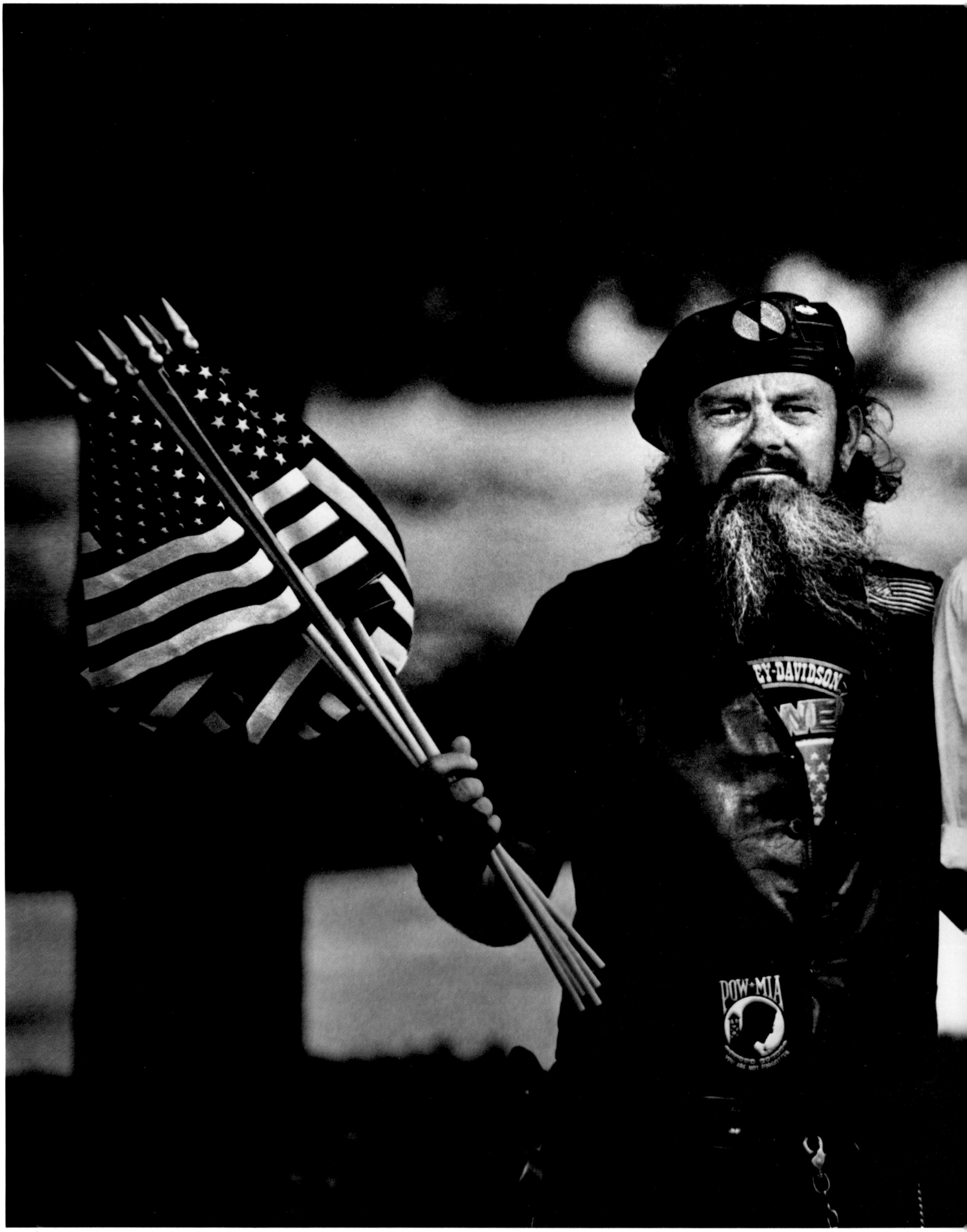
EY-DAVIDSON
POW★MIA

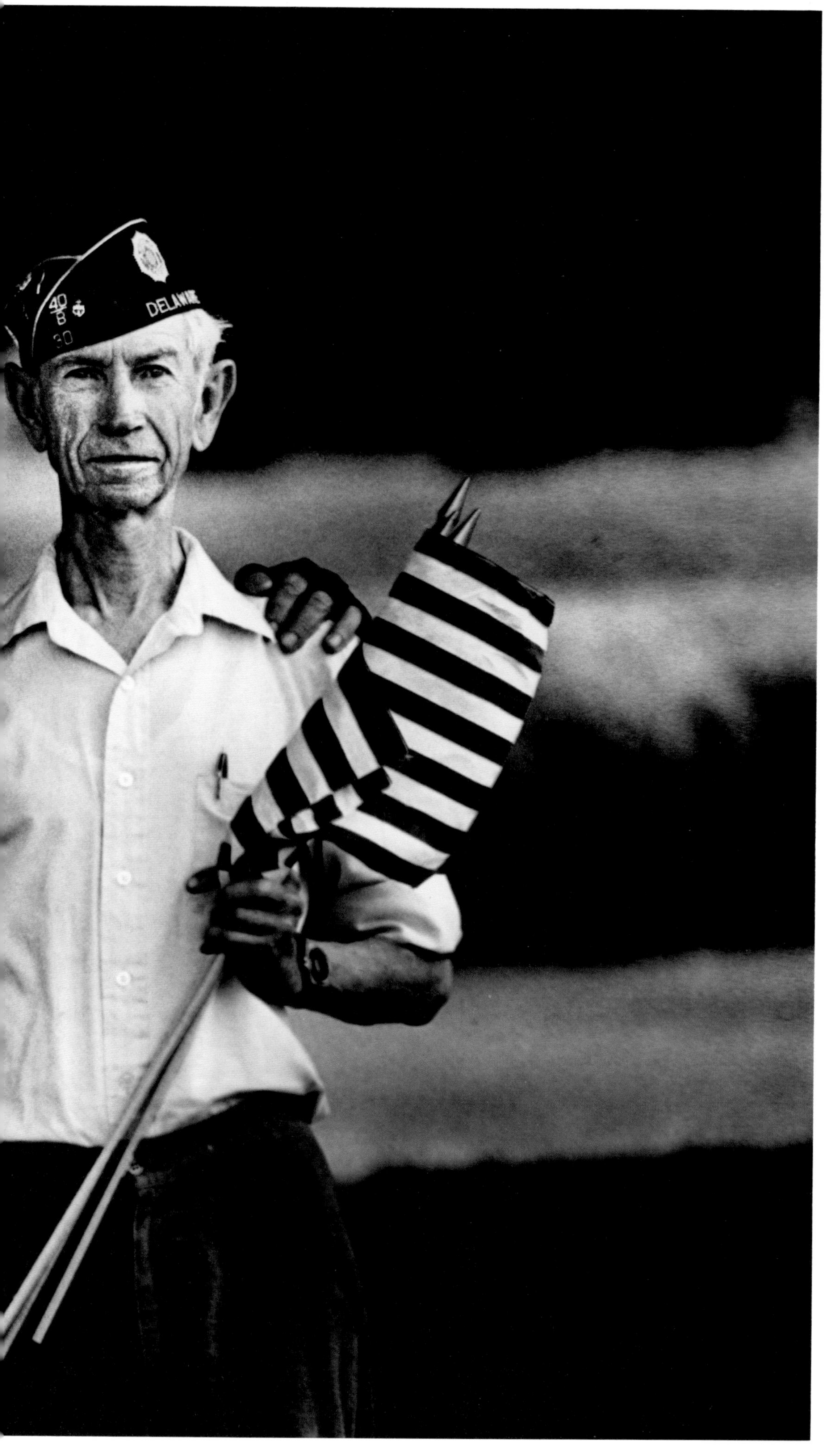

Vietnam veteran Lonnie Dillon and World War II veteran Sid Long, Gracelawn Cemetery, New Castle, 1986

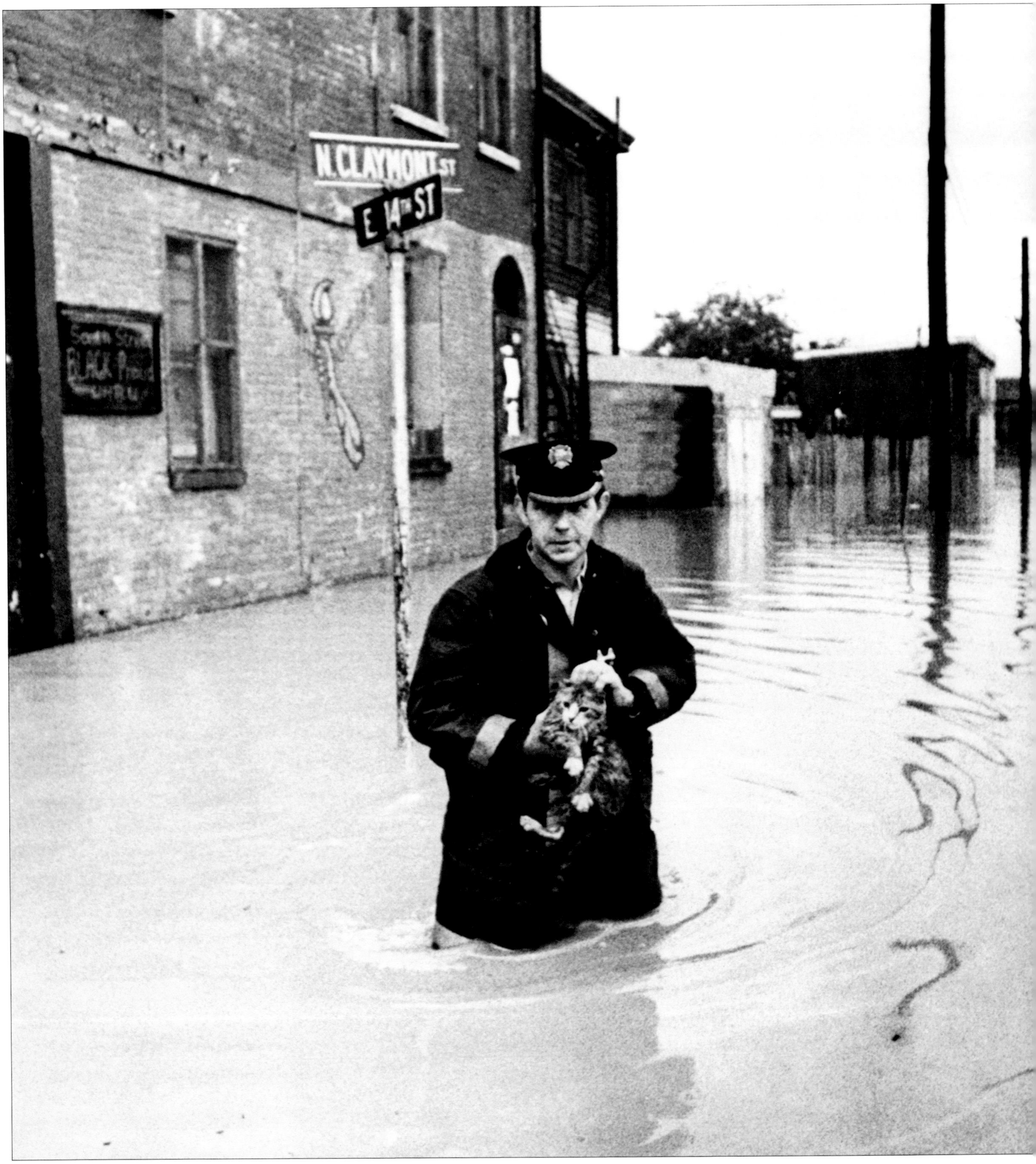
N. CLAYMONT ST
E 14TH ST

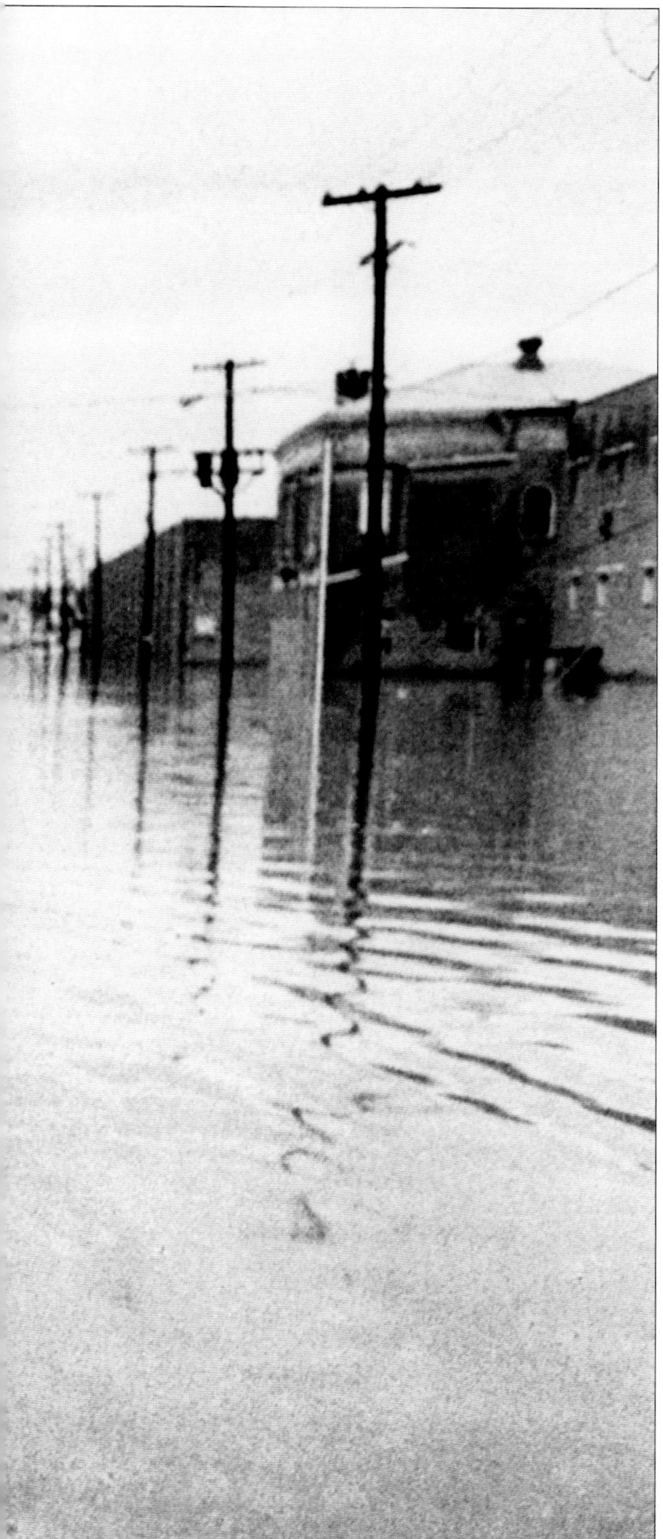

Wilmington flood, 1972

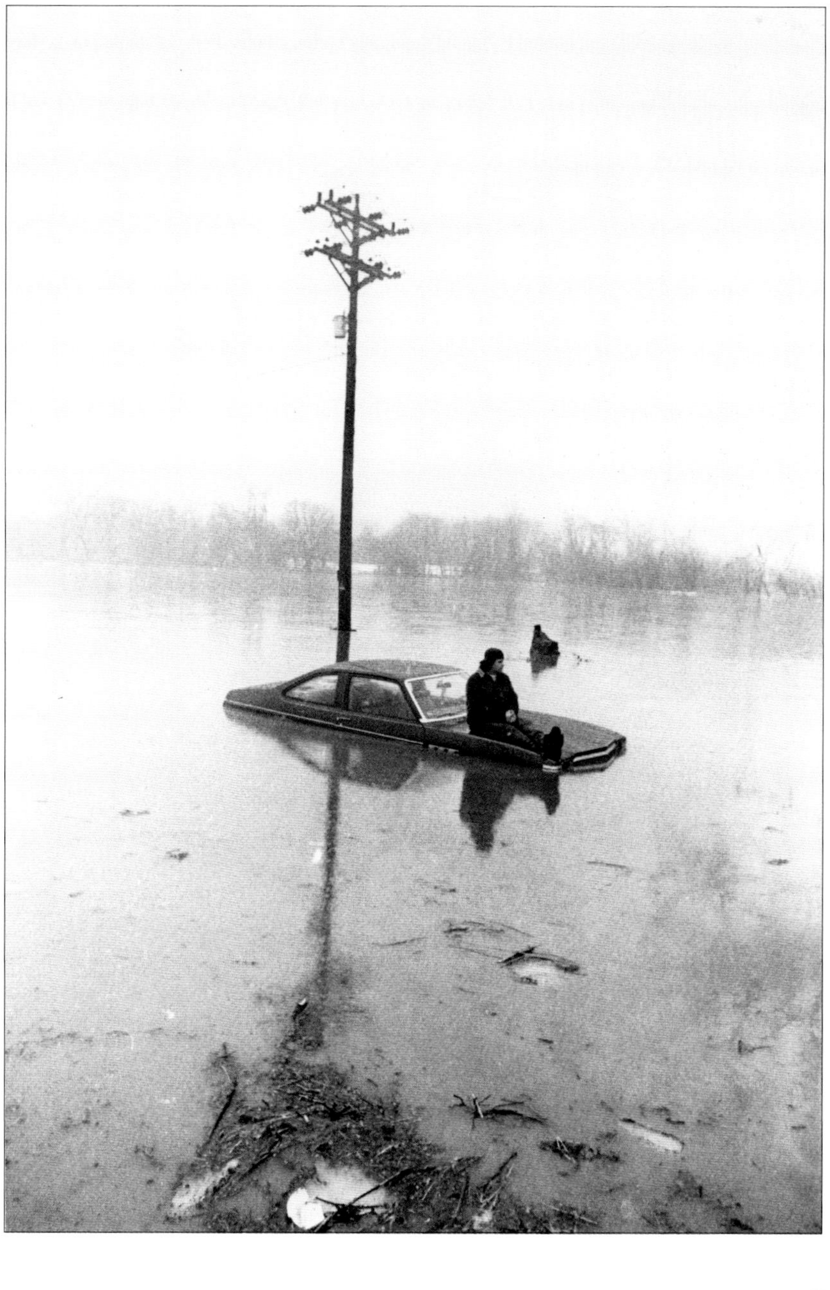

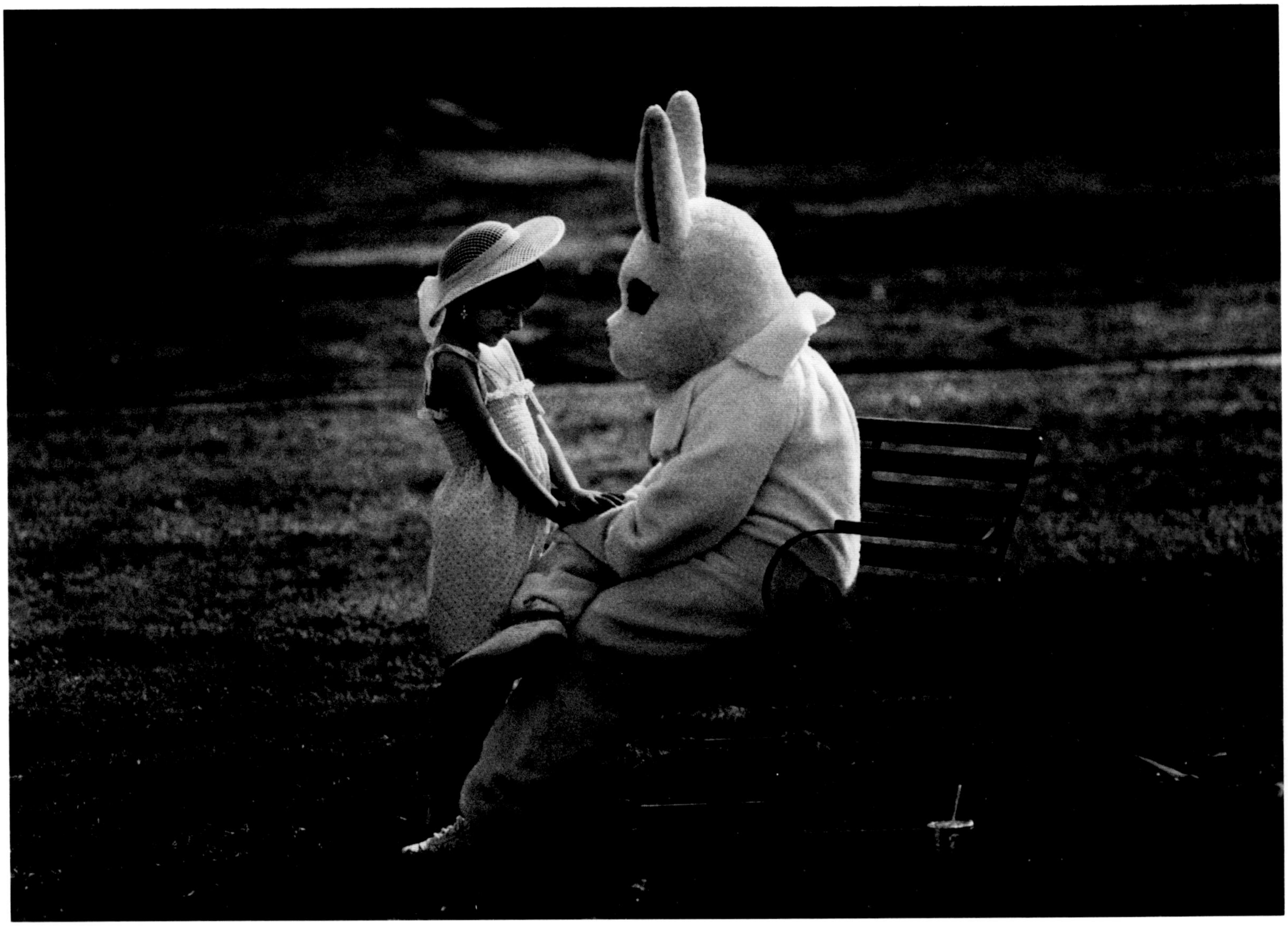

Easter Parade, New Castle, 1986

Roy V. Behlke, Christmas shopping, Wilmington, 1969

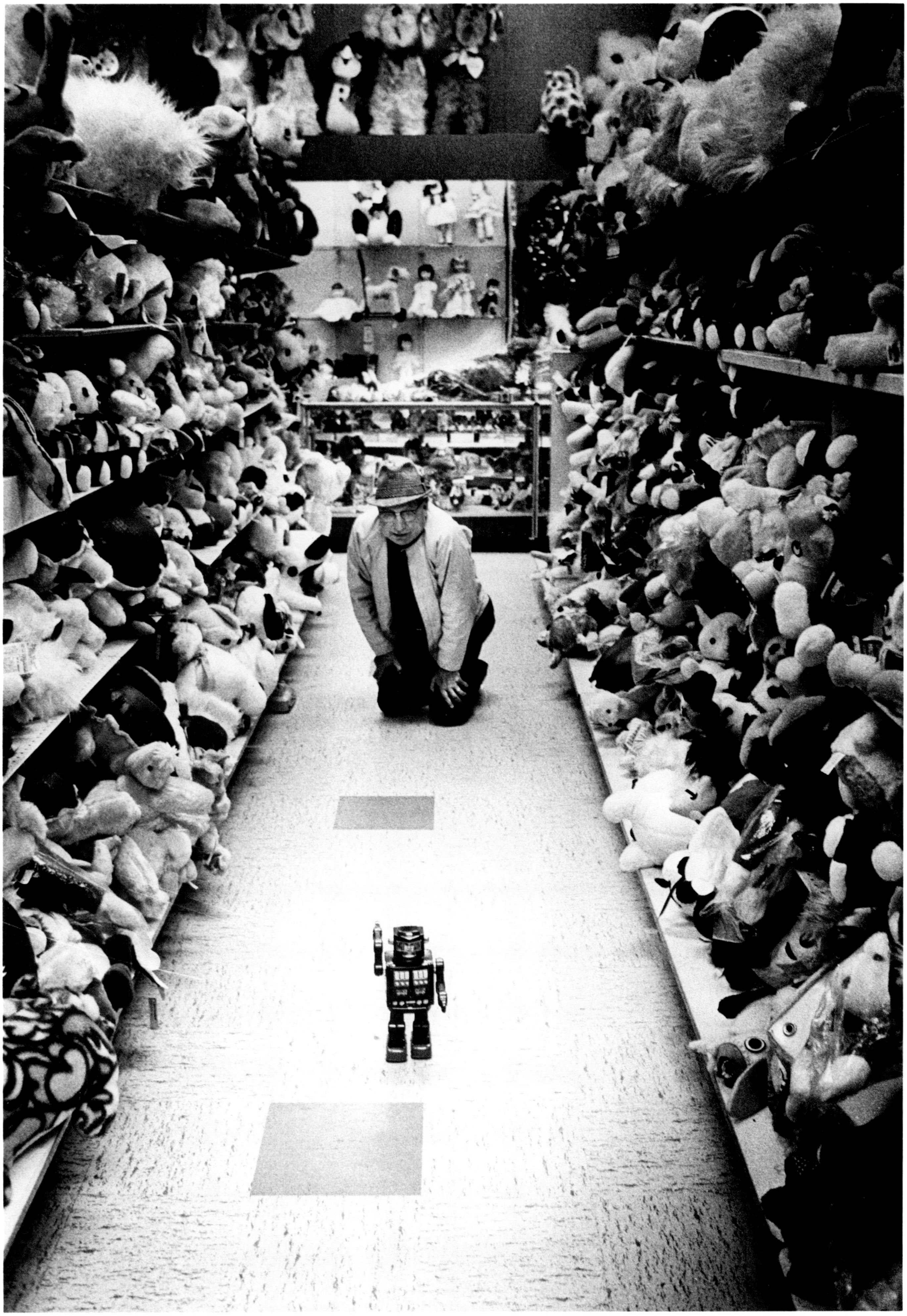

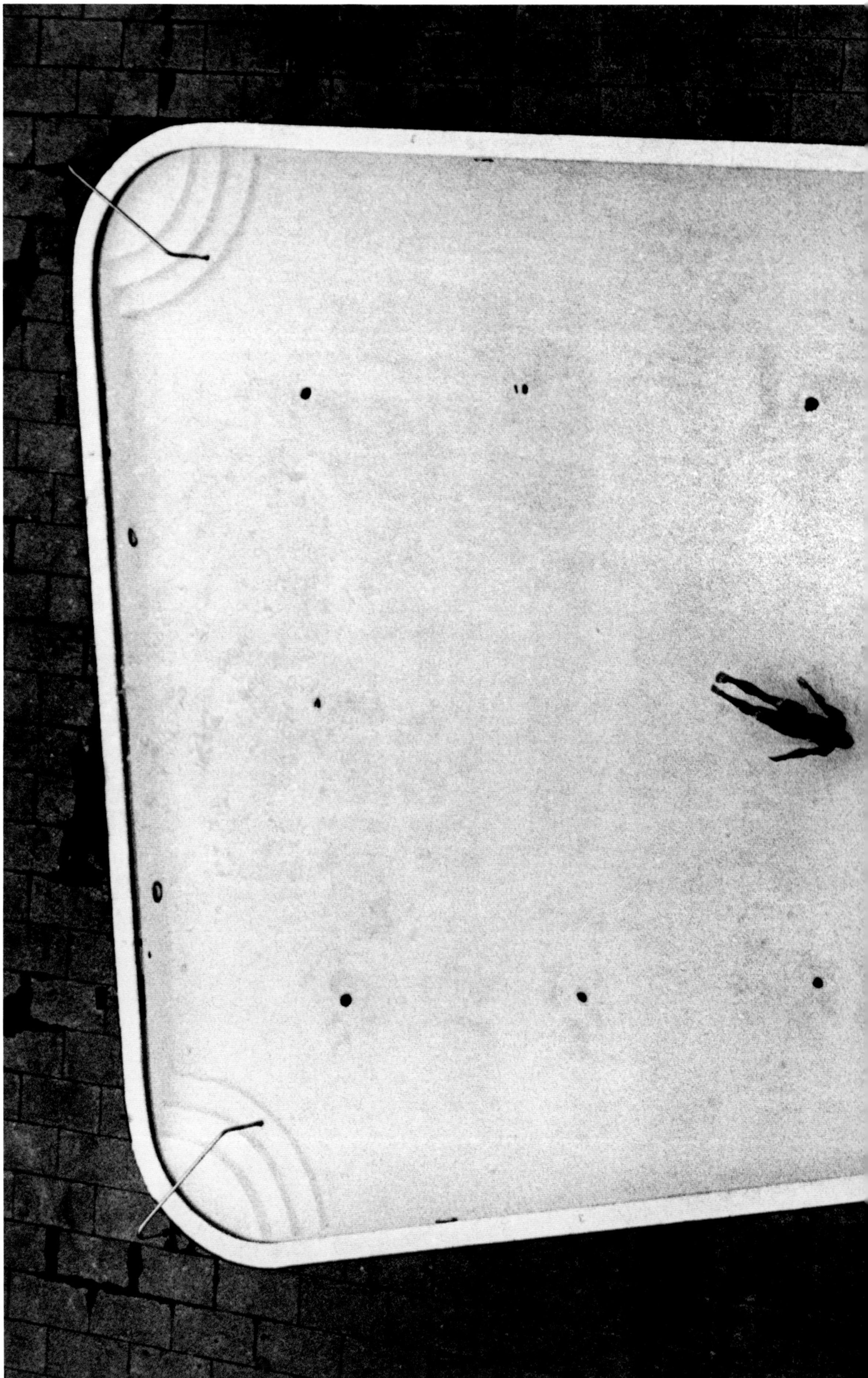

The Devon apartment building swimming pool, Wilmington, 1970

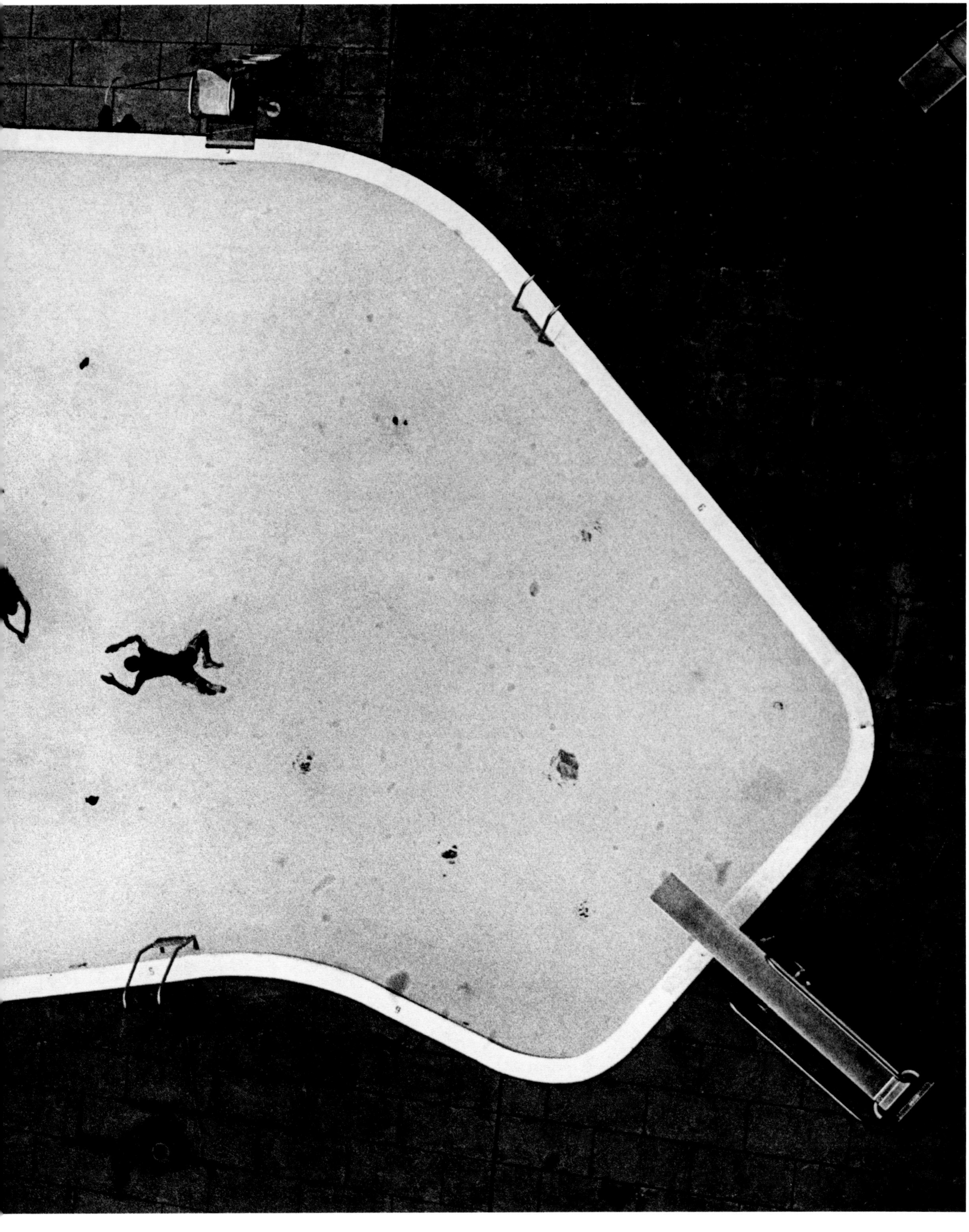

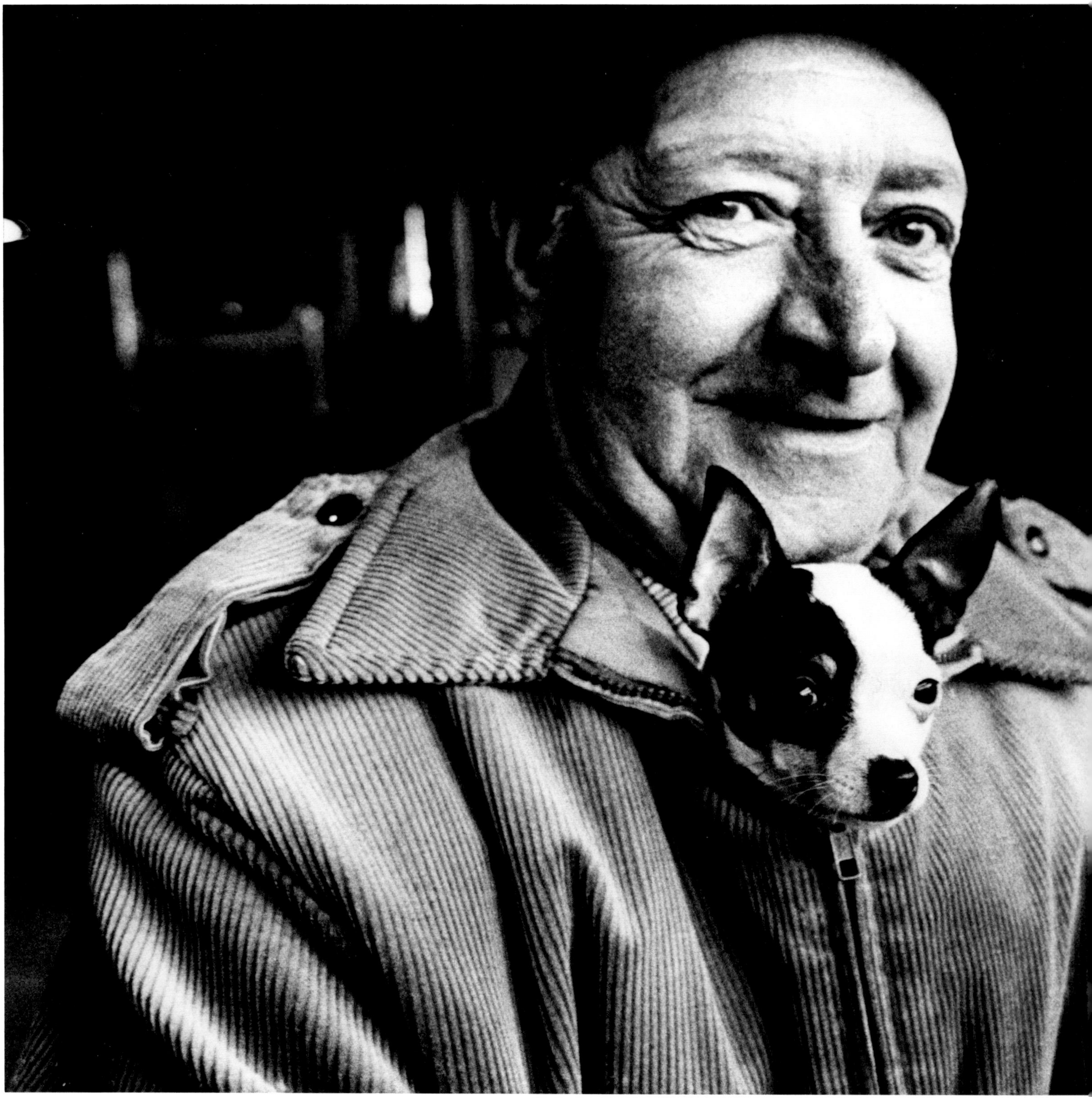

Irvin Cannon and Holly, Hummers Parade, Middletown, 1987

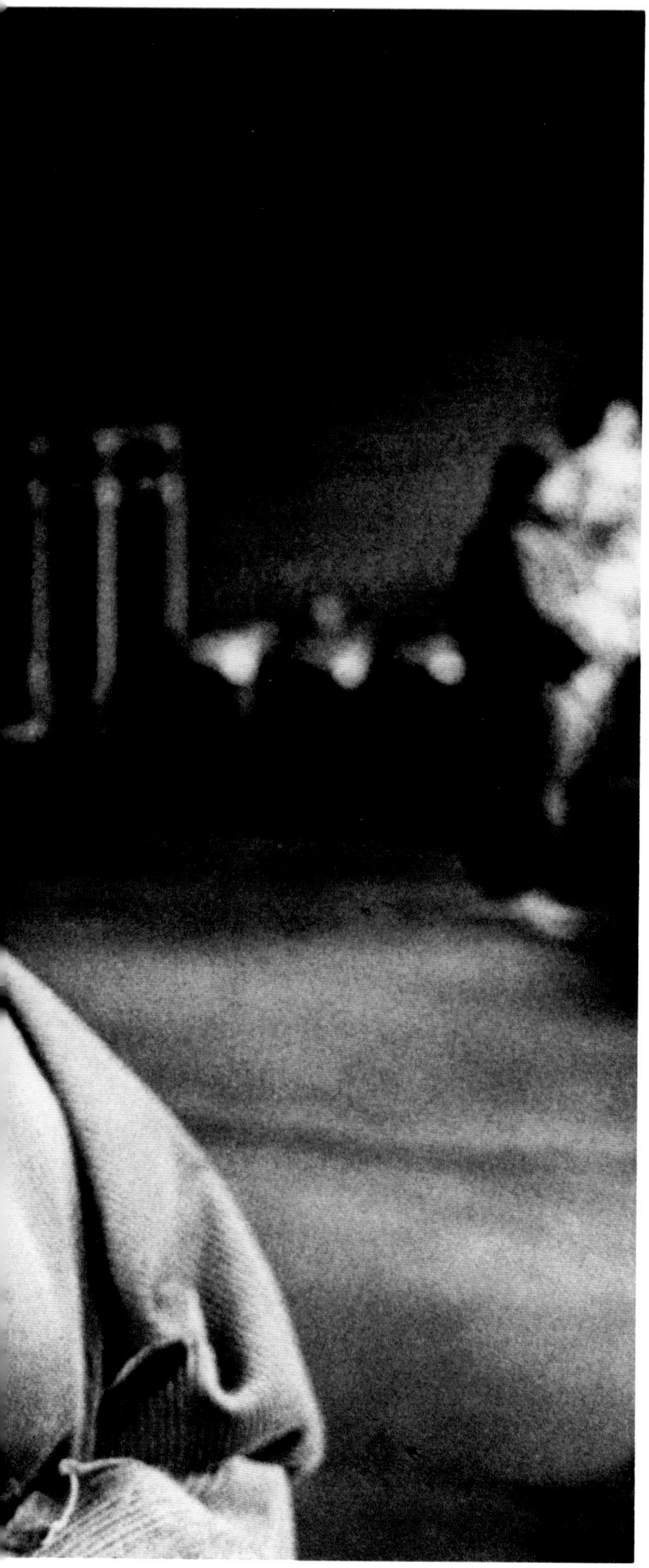

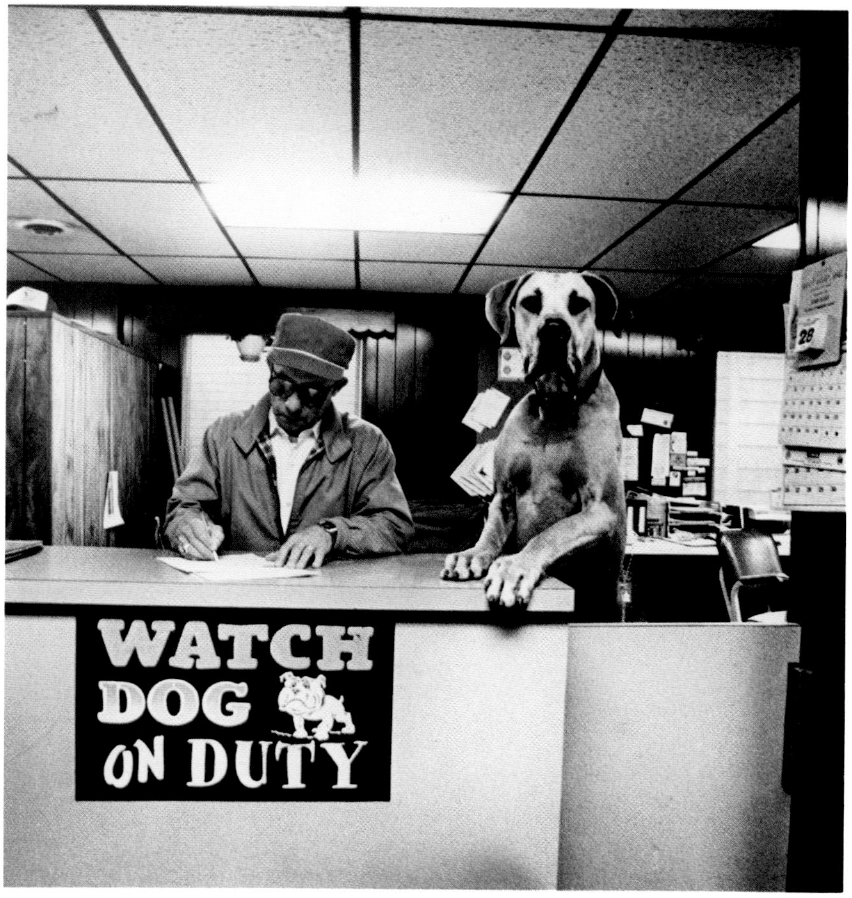

Neal Shavick and Butch, John's Body Shop, Wilmington, 1987

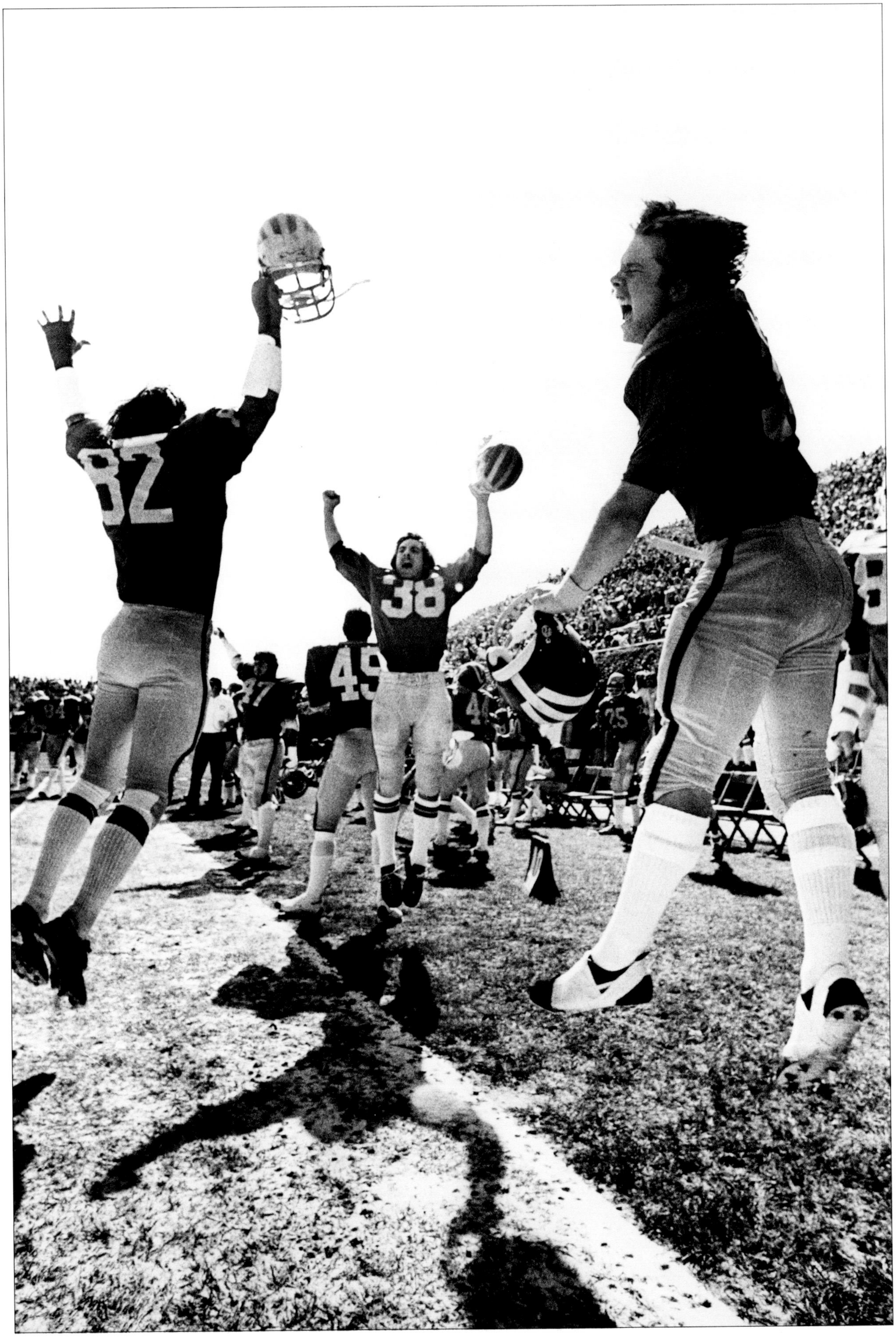

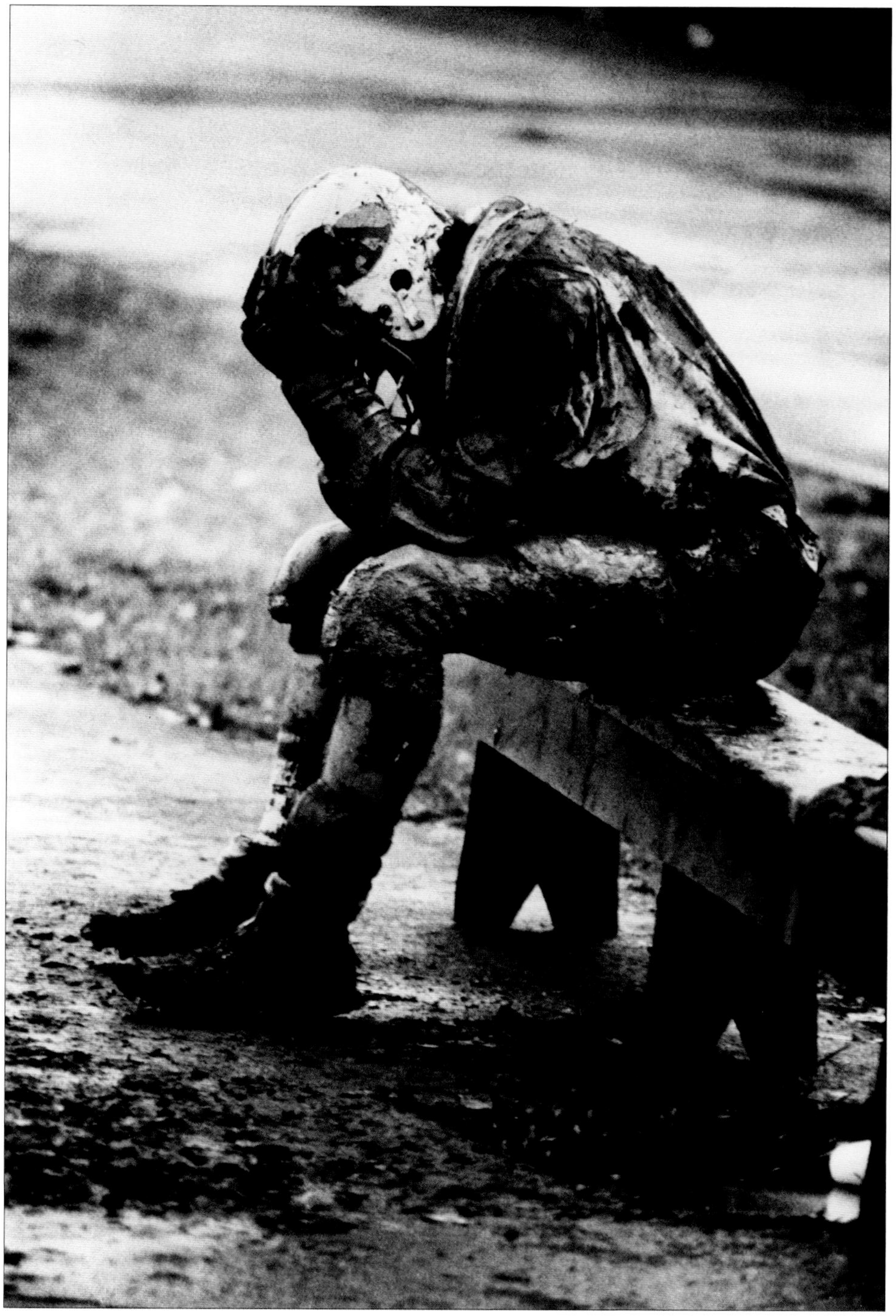

Peter Walsh, A.I. du Pont High School, 1977

University of Delaware, Newark, 1974

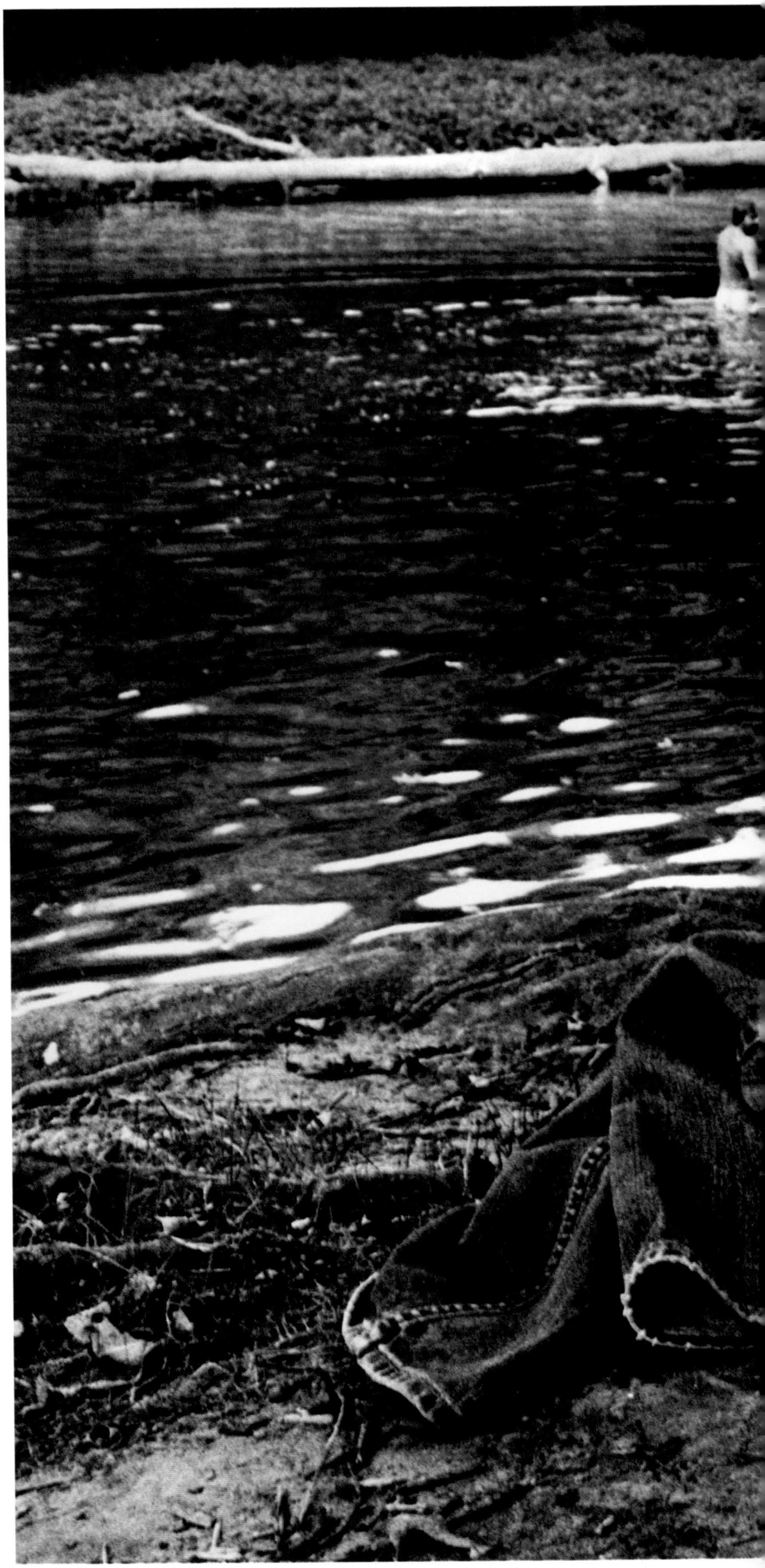

Brandywine River at Thompson's Bridge, 1974

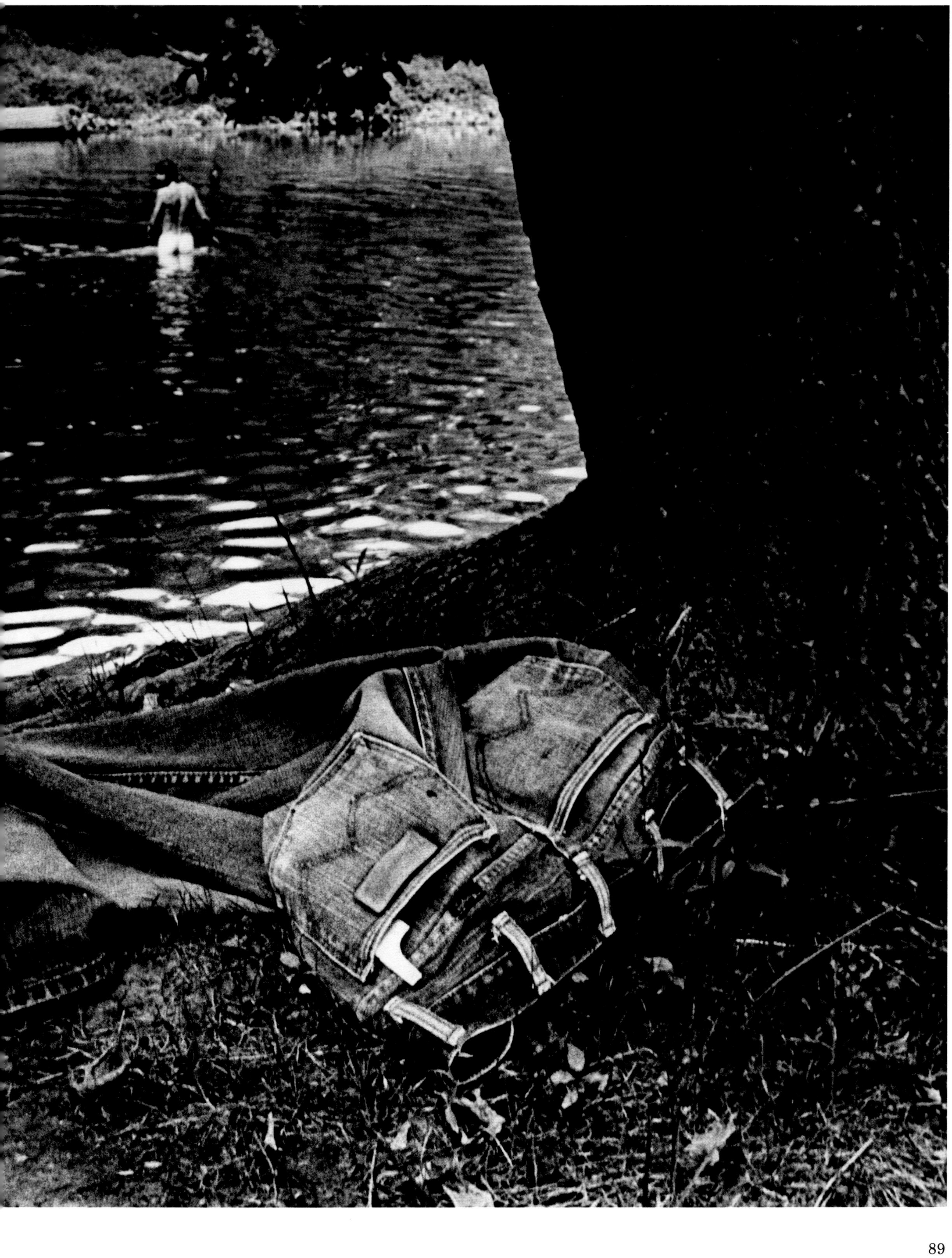

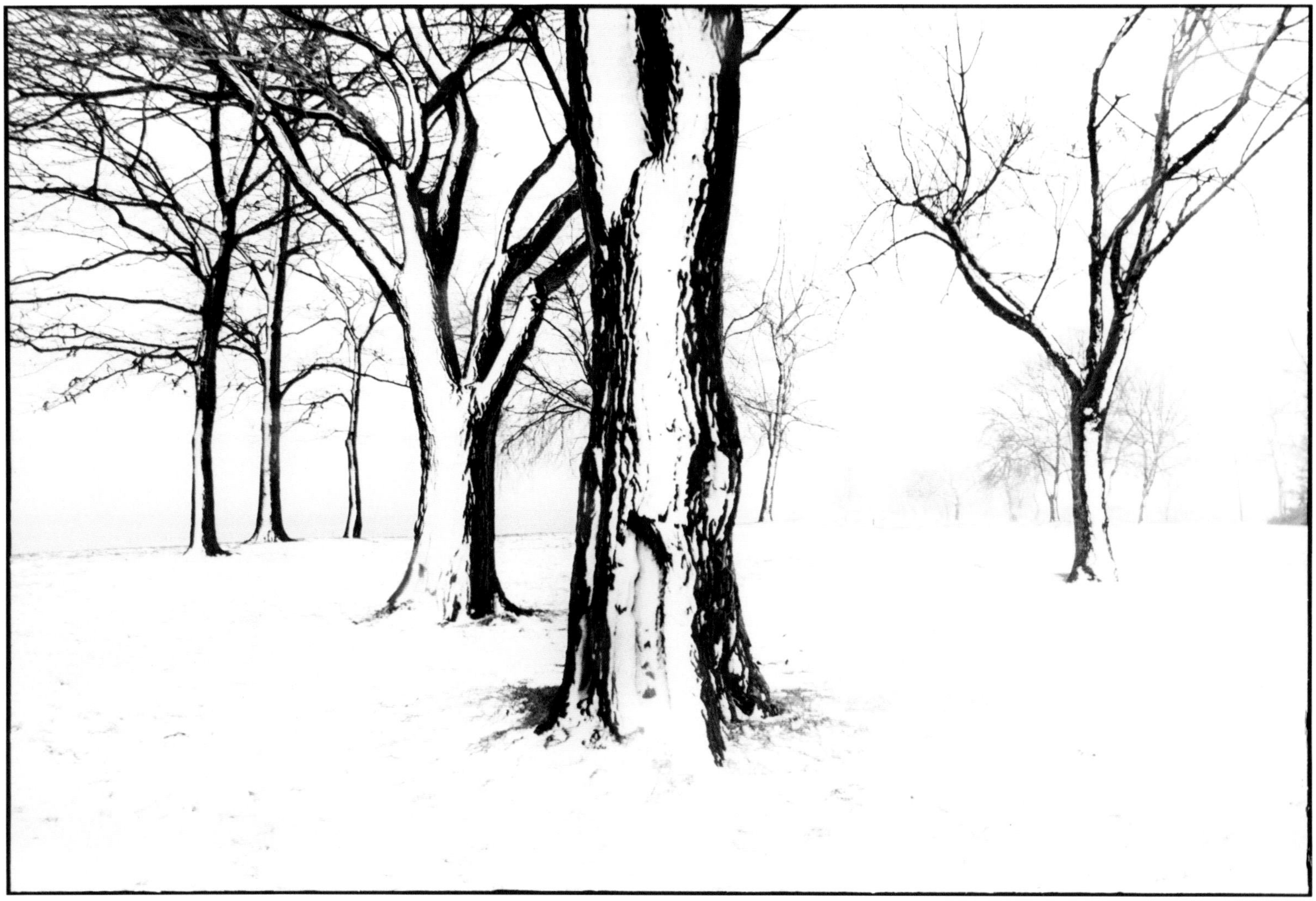

Battery Park, New Castle, 1973

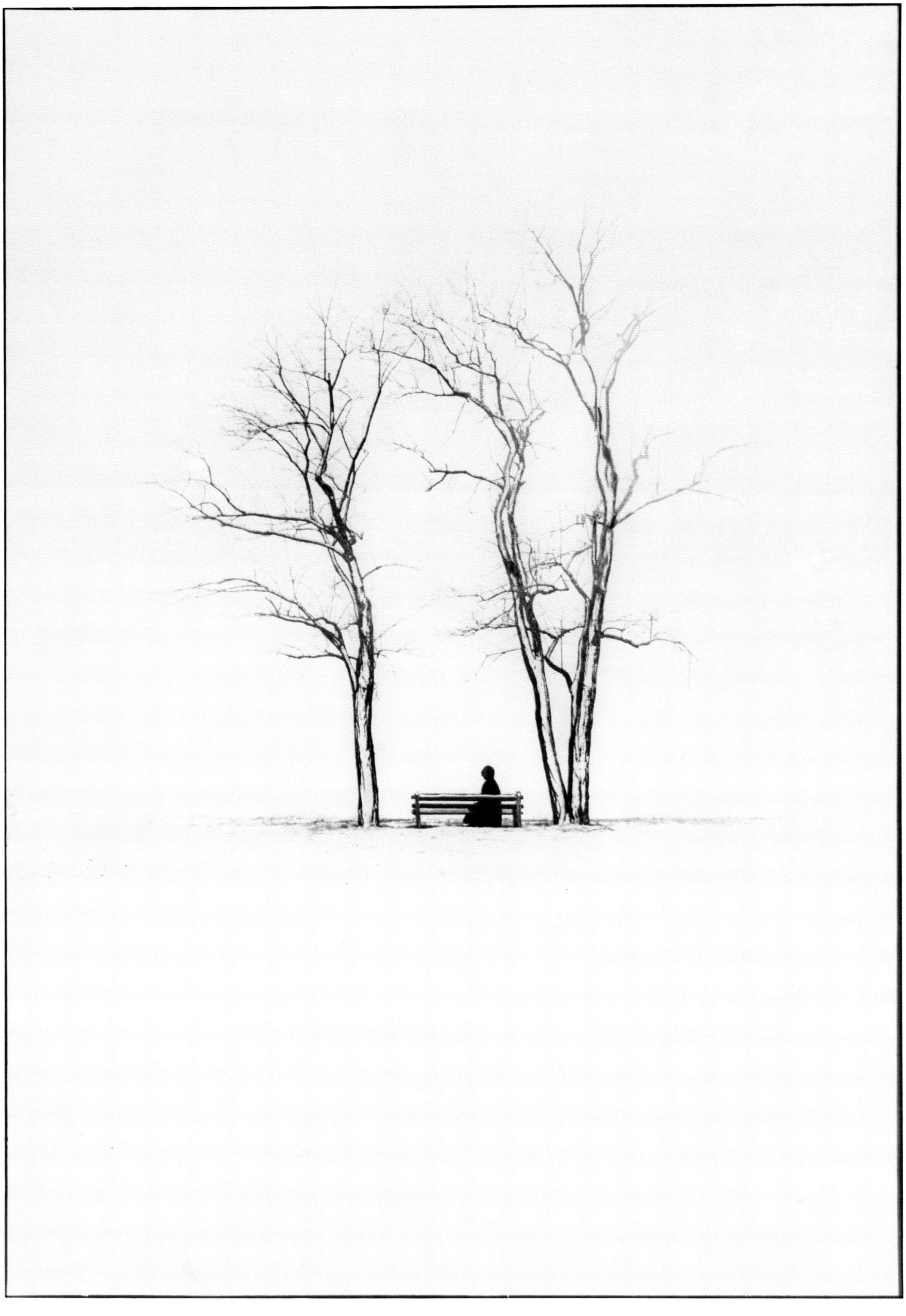

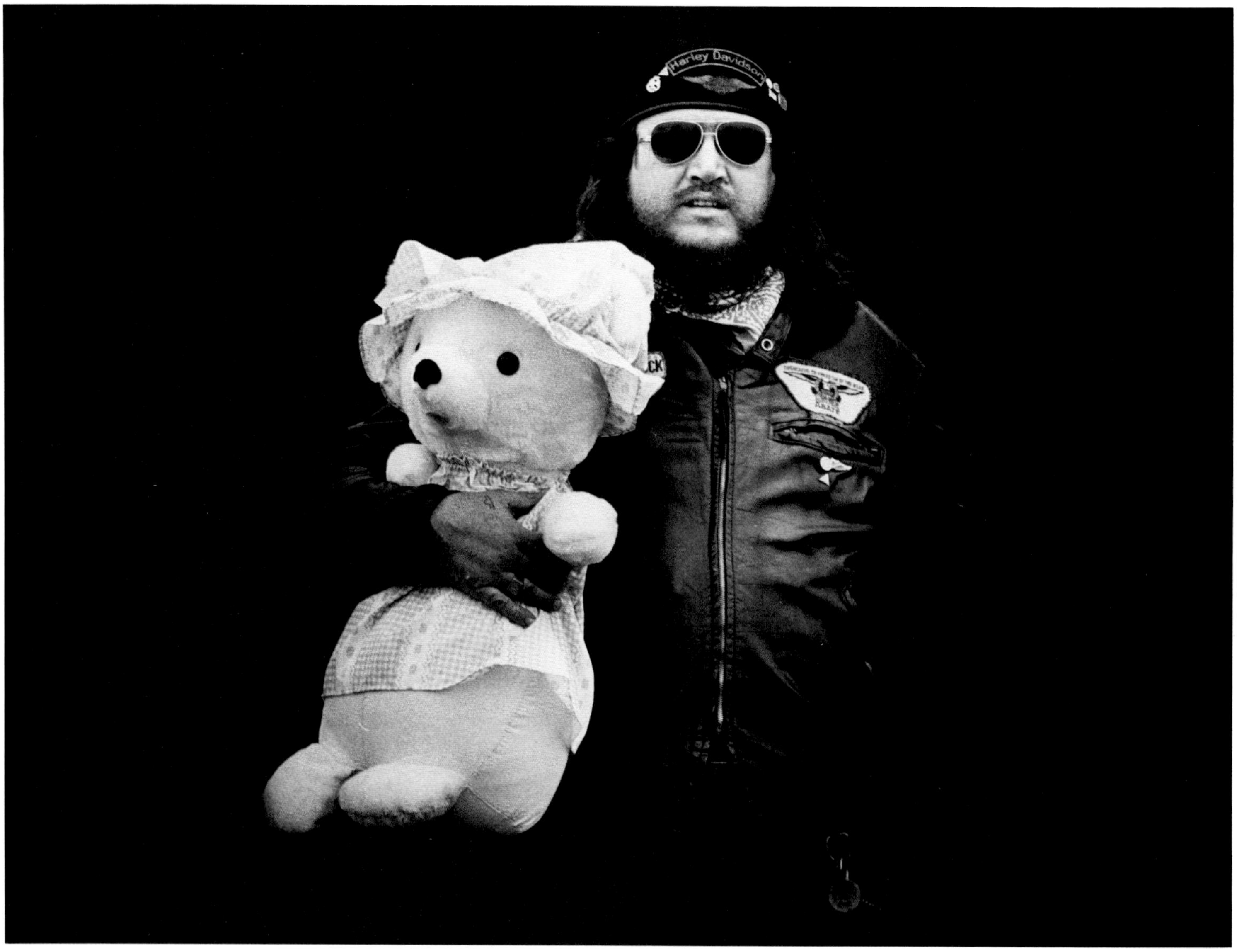

Toys for Tots, Banning Park, Wilmington, 1985

Delaware State policeman,
Greater Wilmington Airport, 1972

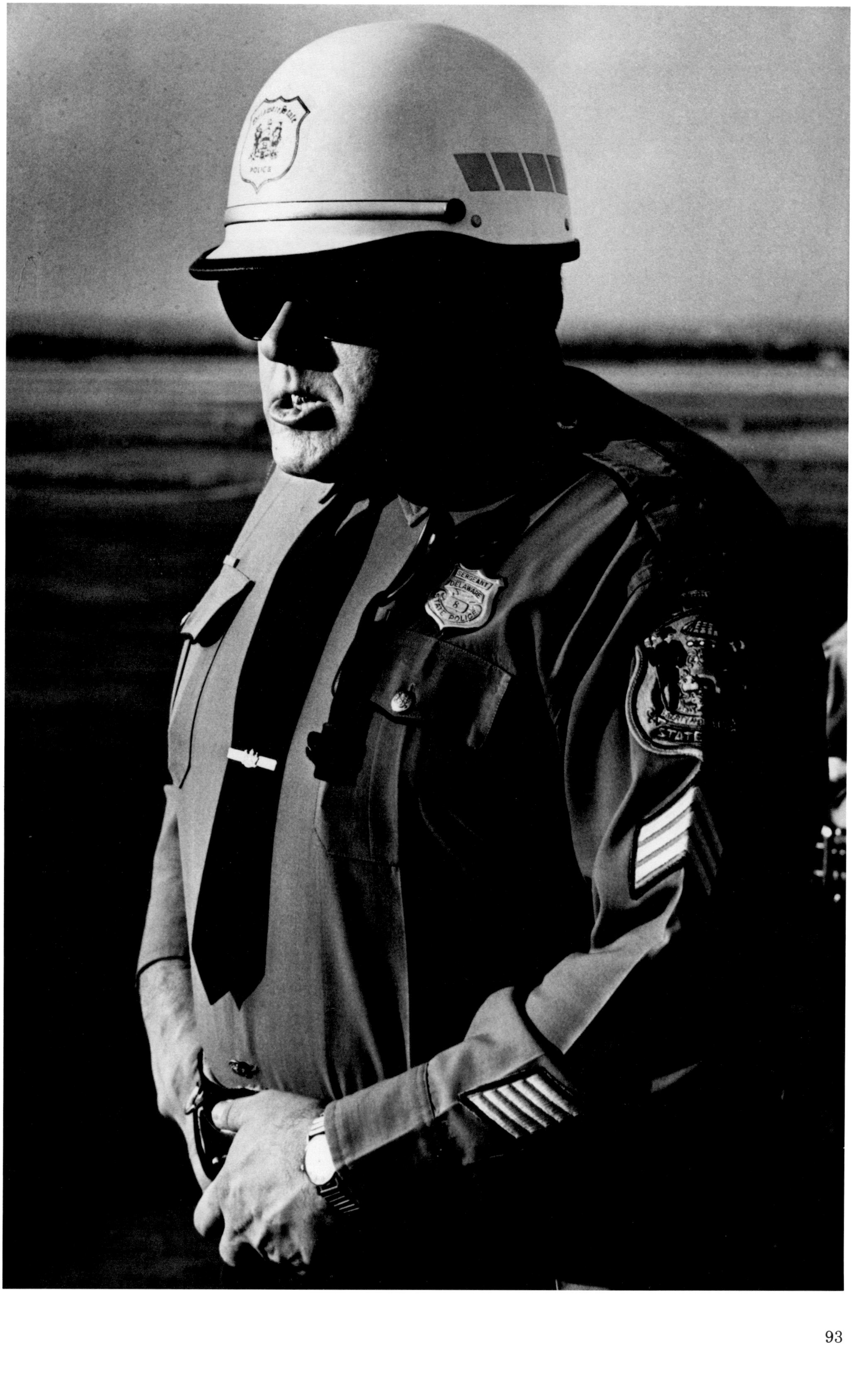
SERGEANT
DELAWARE
STATE

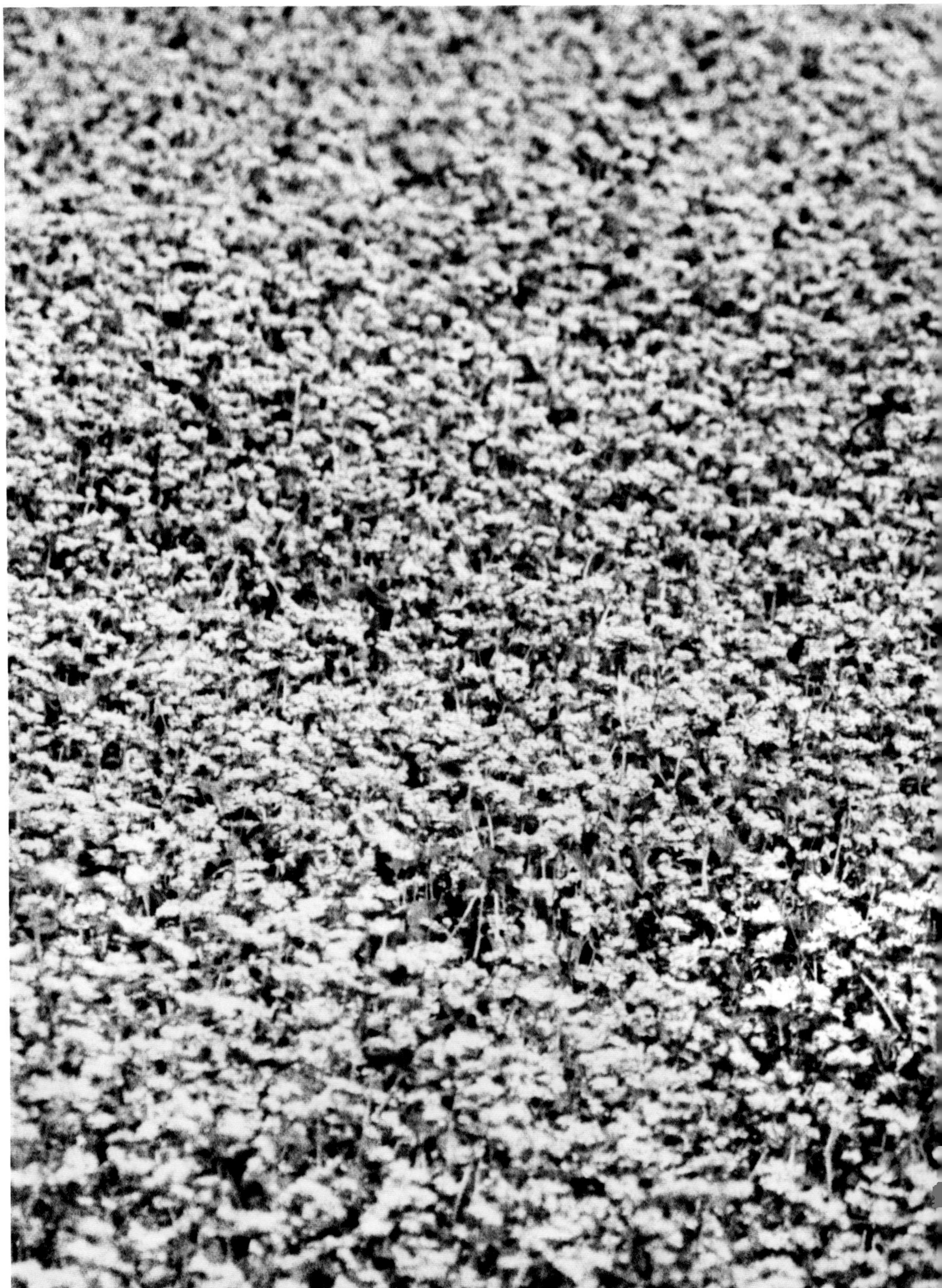

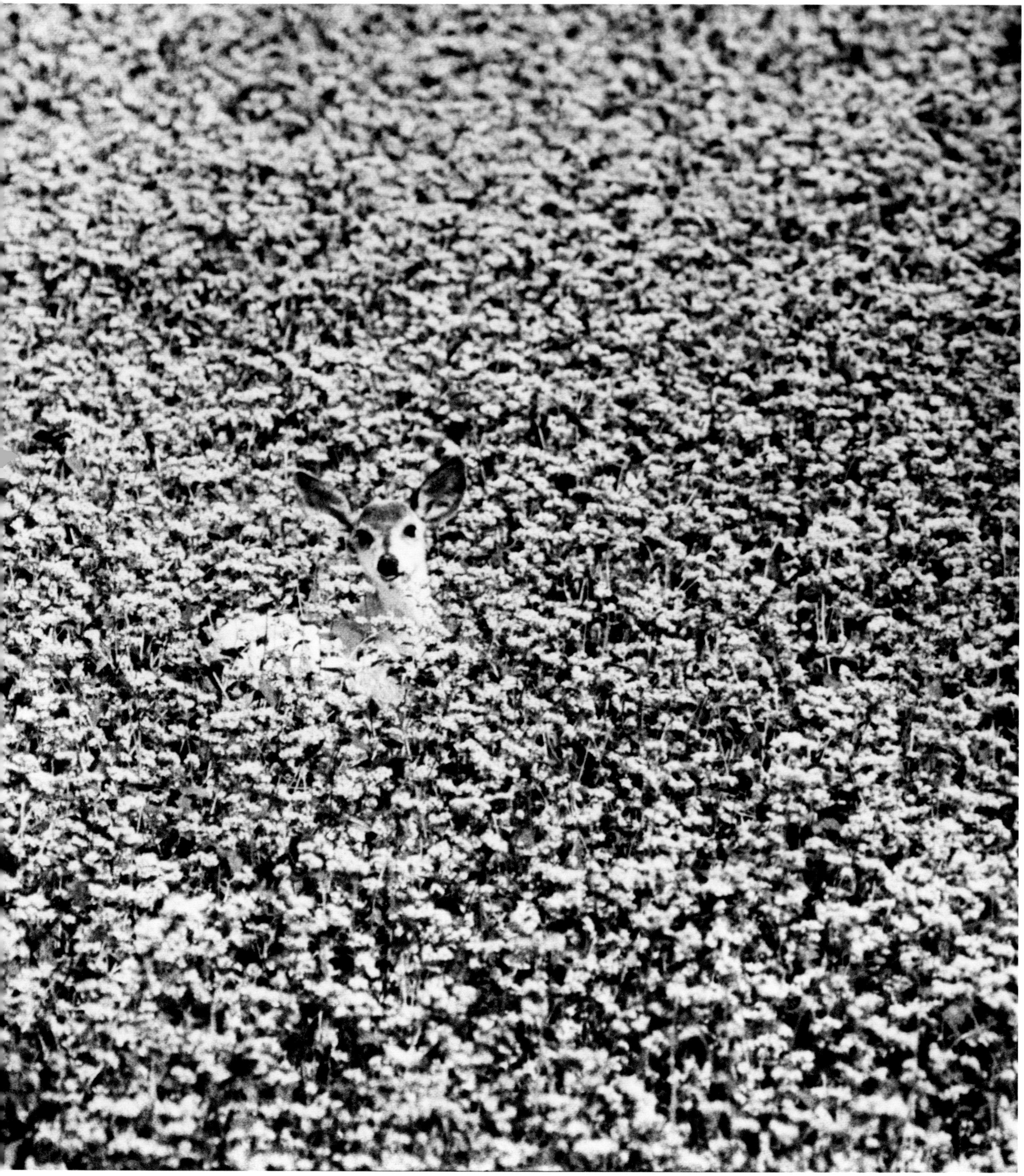

White-tailed deer, Bombay Hook National Wildlife Refuge, 1986

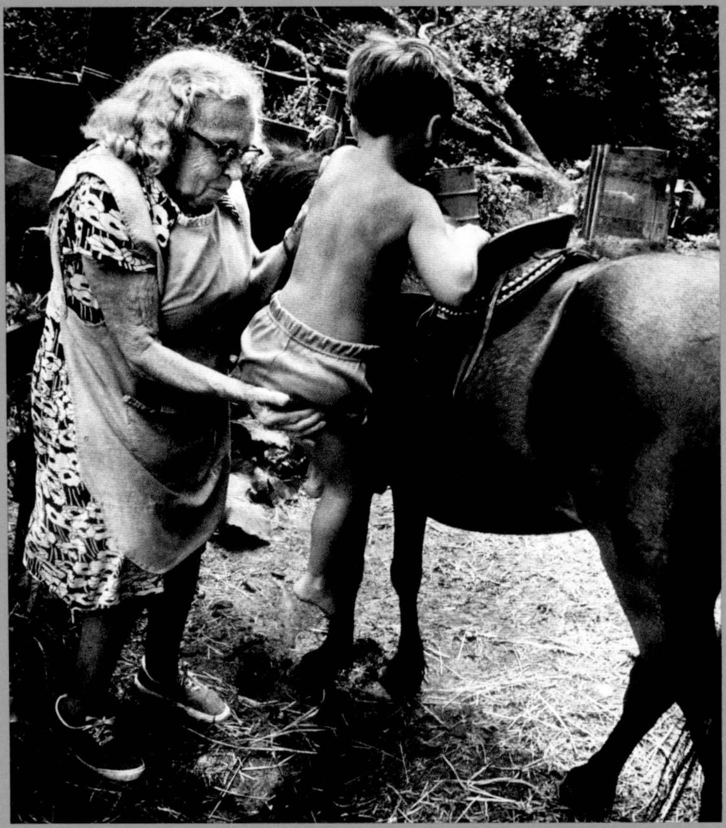

Small in the Saddle

1982

When my boys were young, I took them to a pony-riding farm partially hidden by trees off Paper Mill Road near Newark. Many years later, in the early 1980s, I decided to do a photo story on the owner, 80-year-old Gladys Spencer. Spending several days with her was a wonderful experience. She lovingly cared for her 14 ponies, mostly Shetlands, and delighted the children with long rides. "That's really why we stay in business – for the young people," she said, and boosted Ronney Schorah into the saddle.

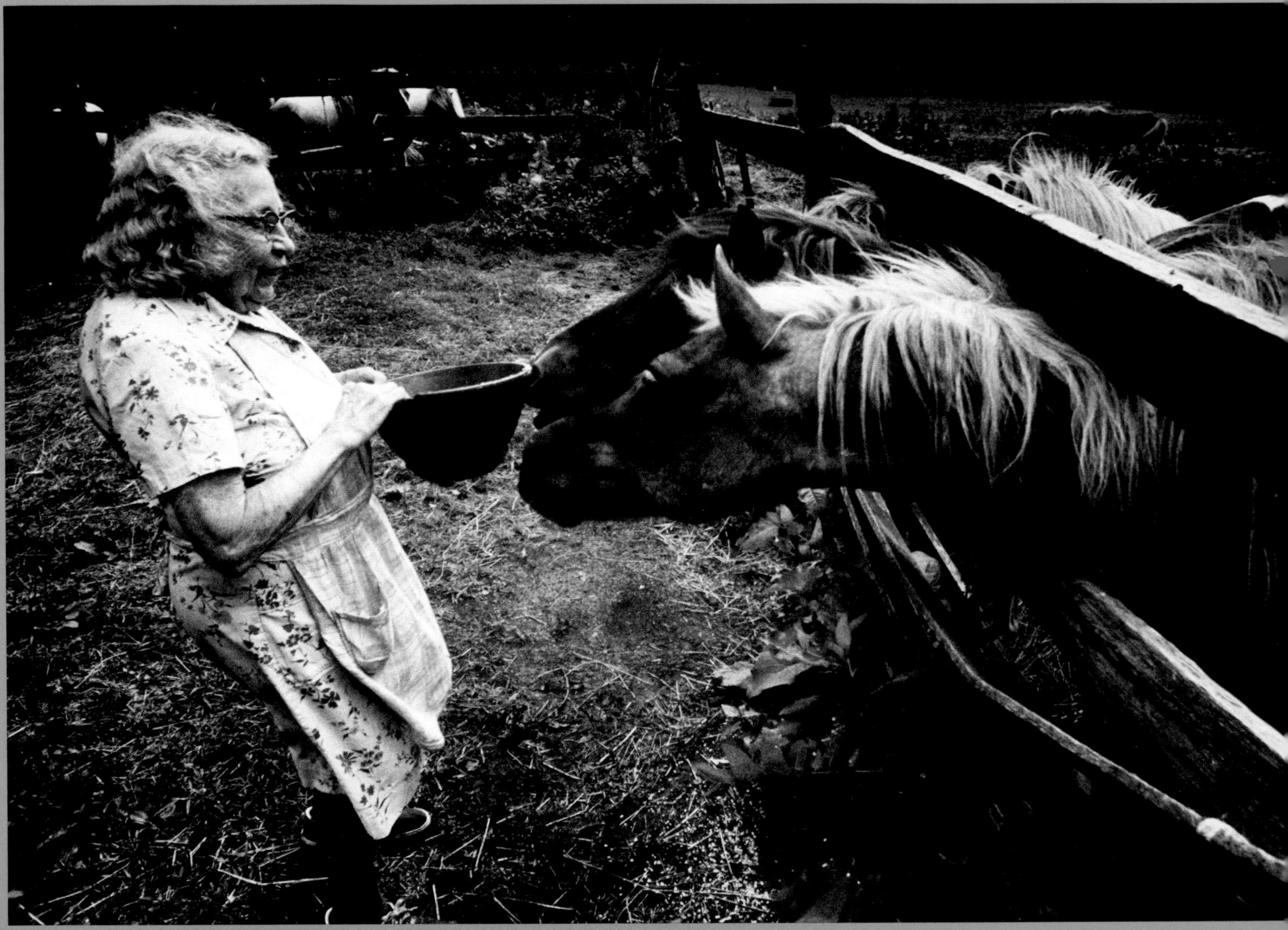

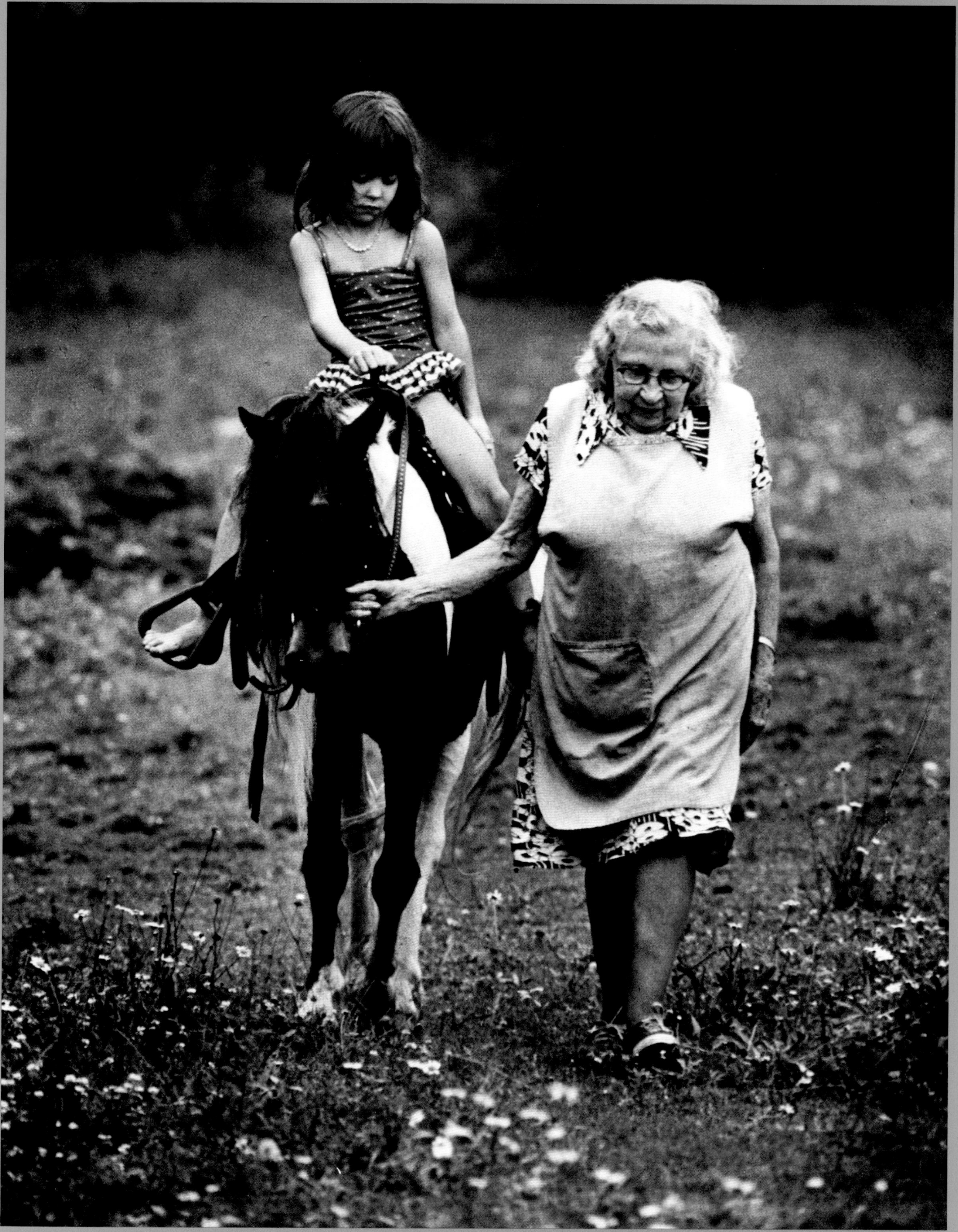

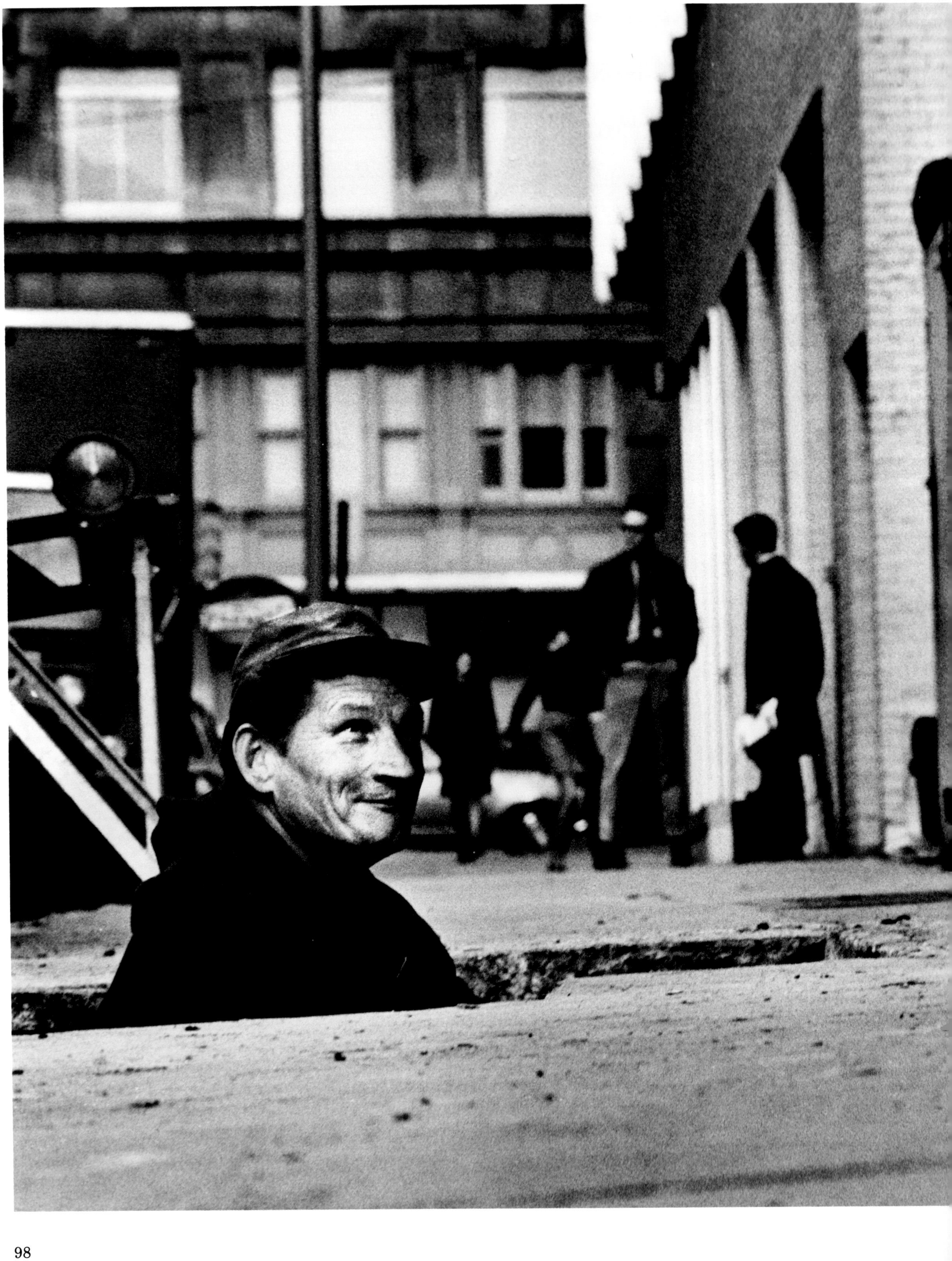

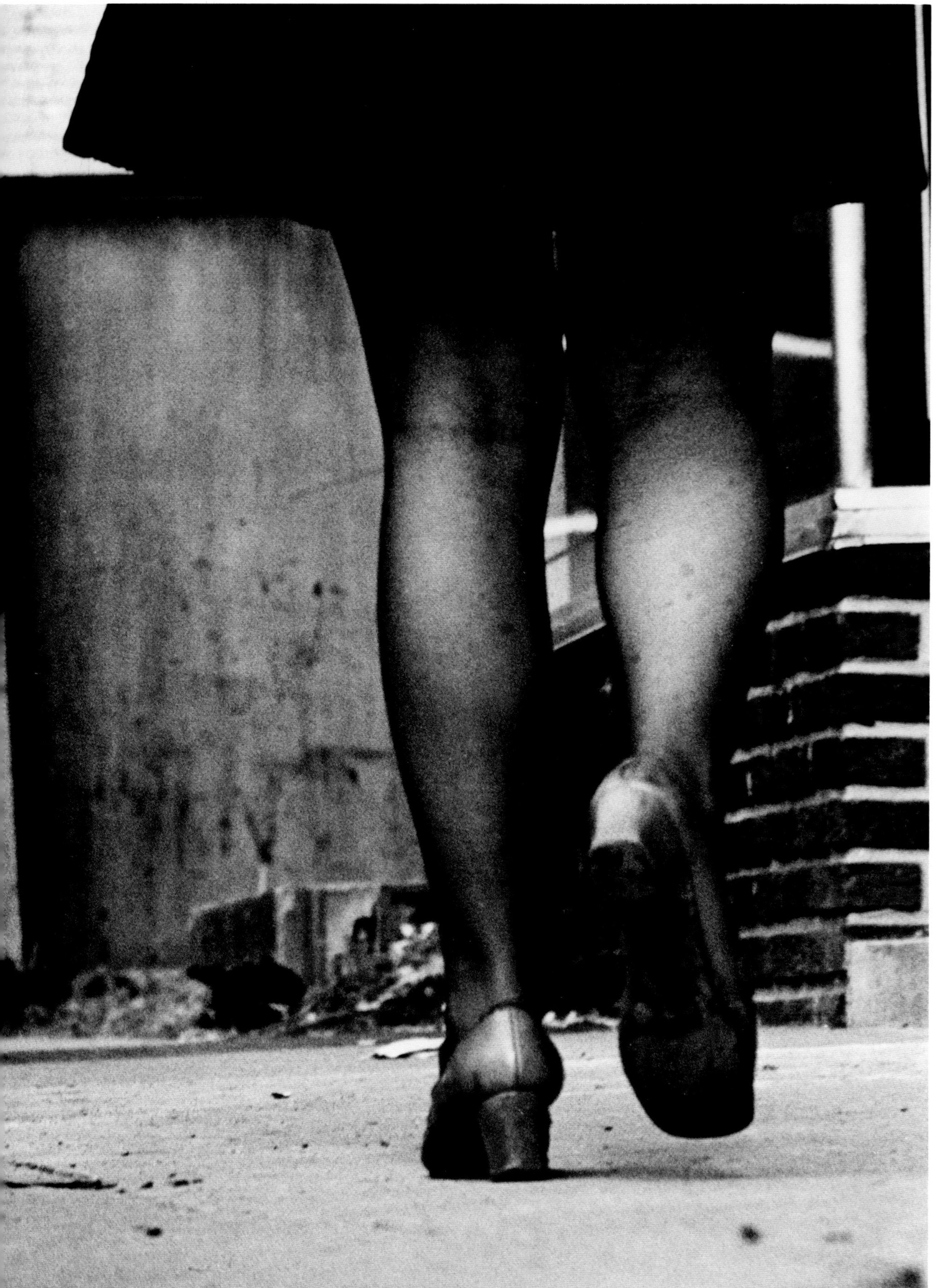

Construction worker,
Wilmington, 1970

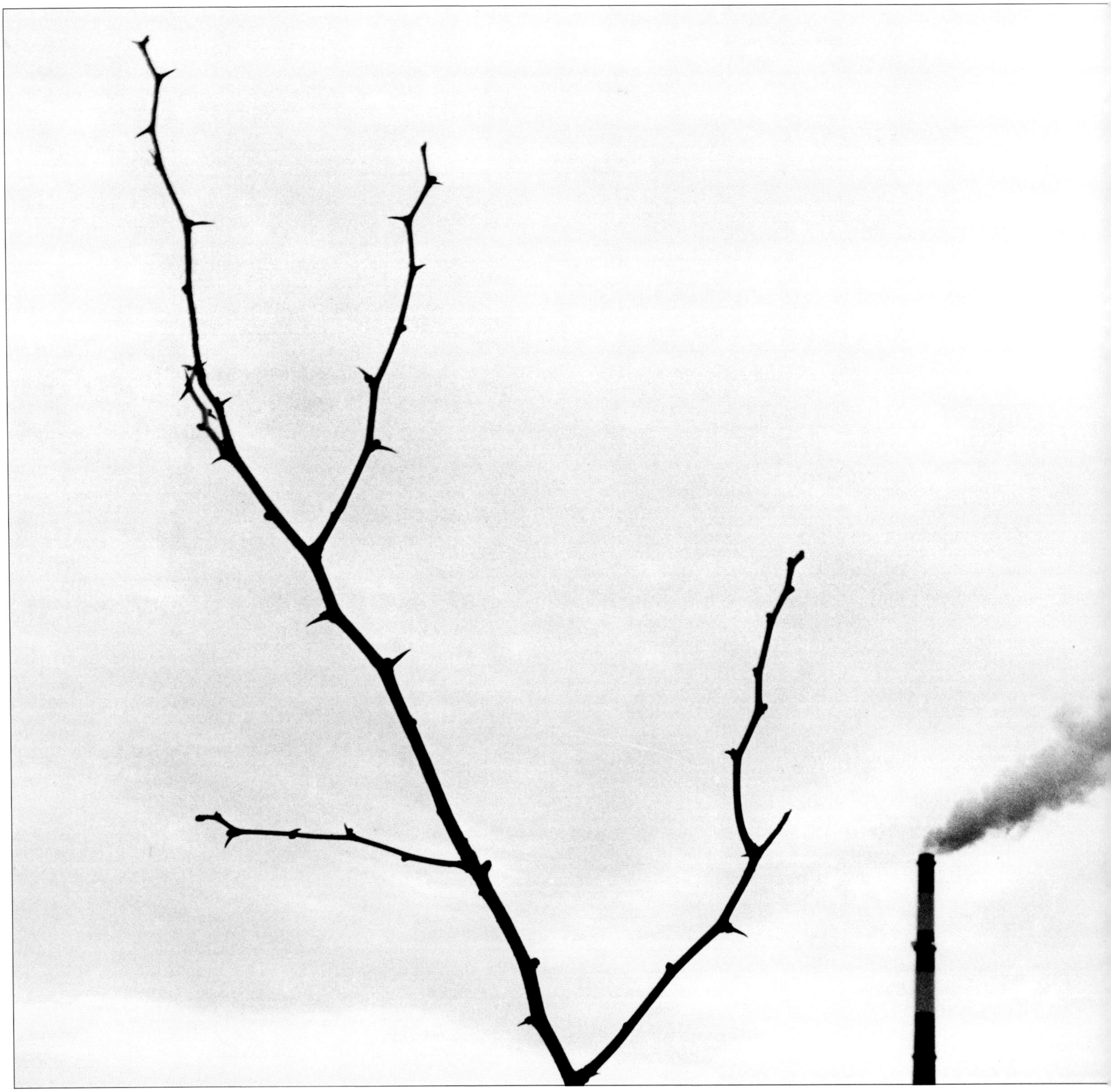

Power plant, Route 9, 1972

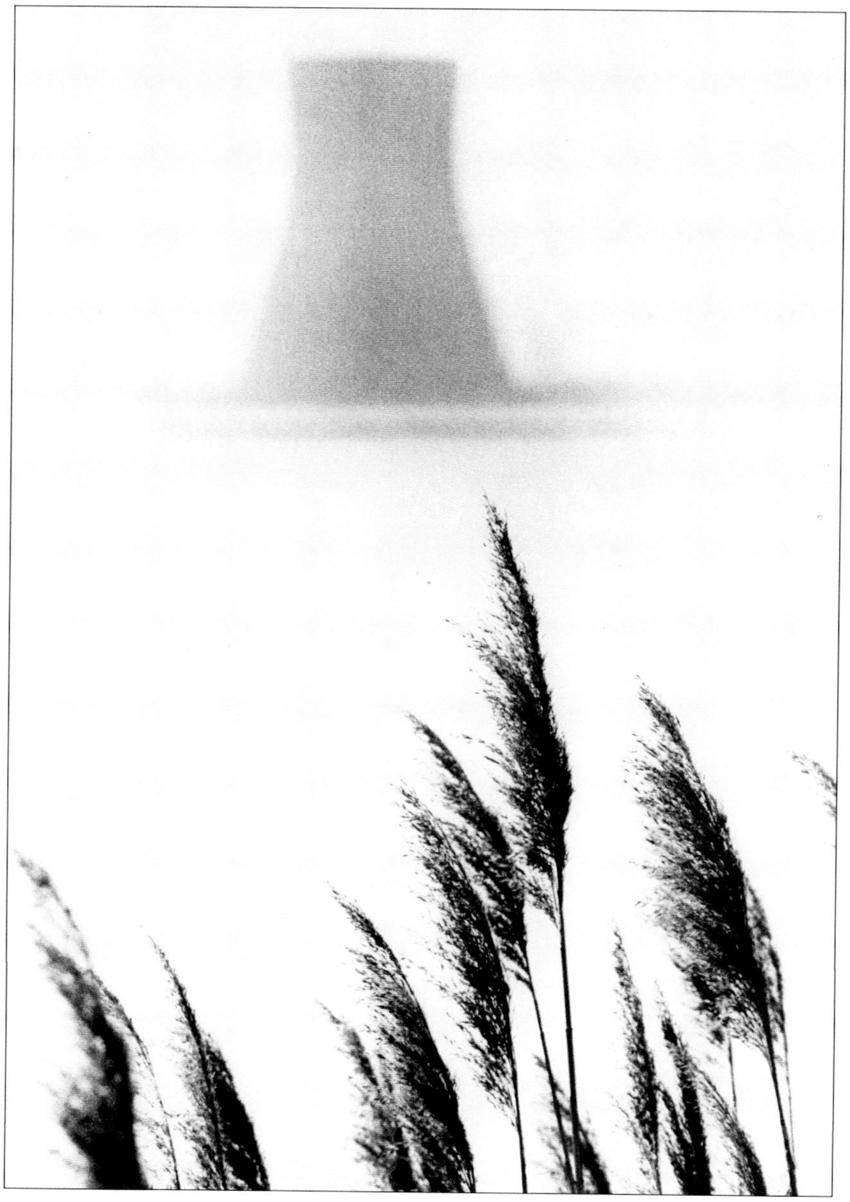

Salem nuclear plant, New Jersey, across the Delaware River from Route 9, 1986

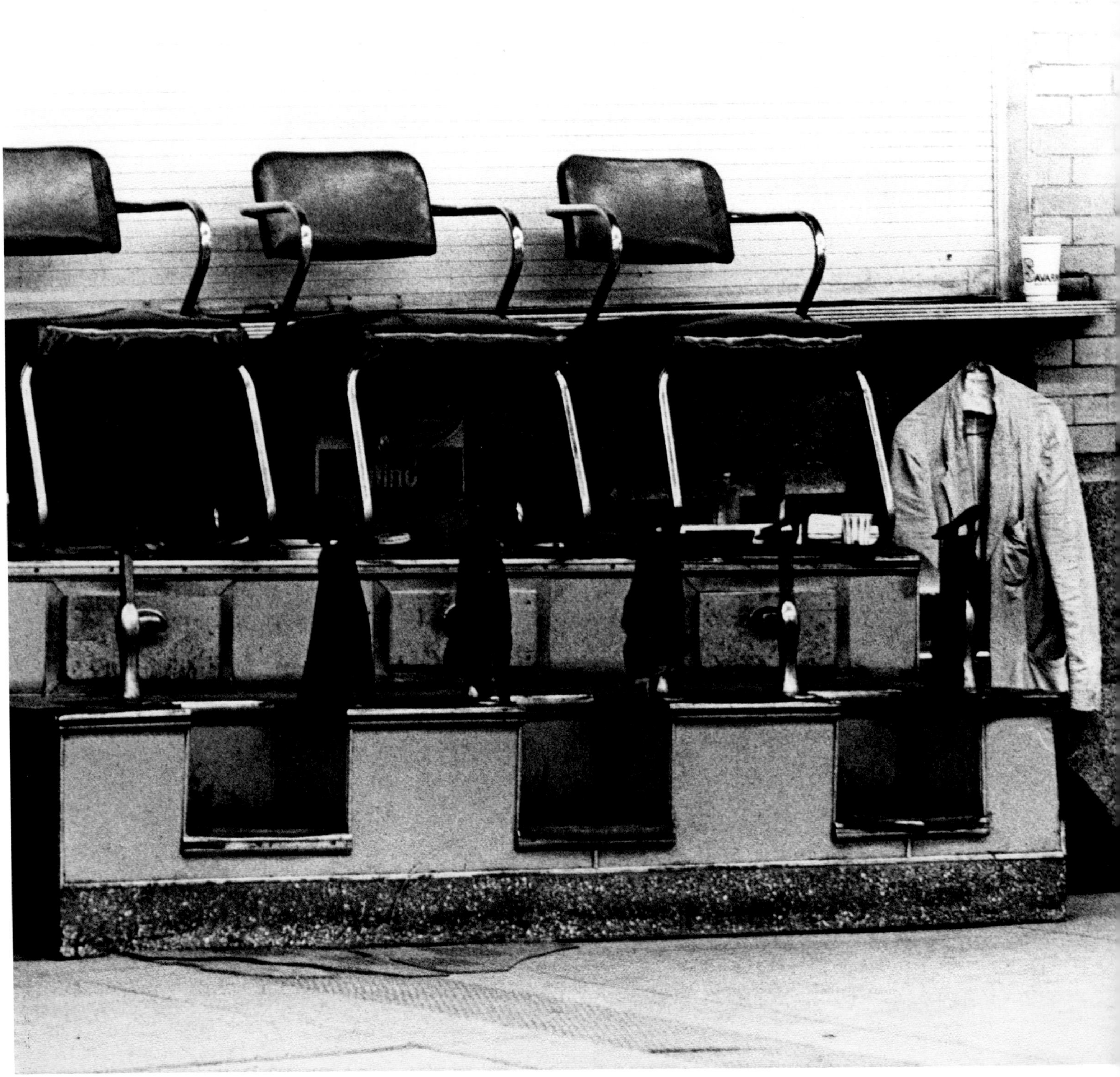

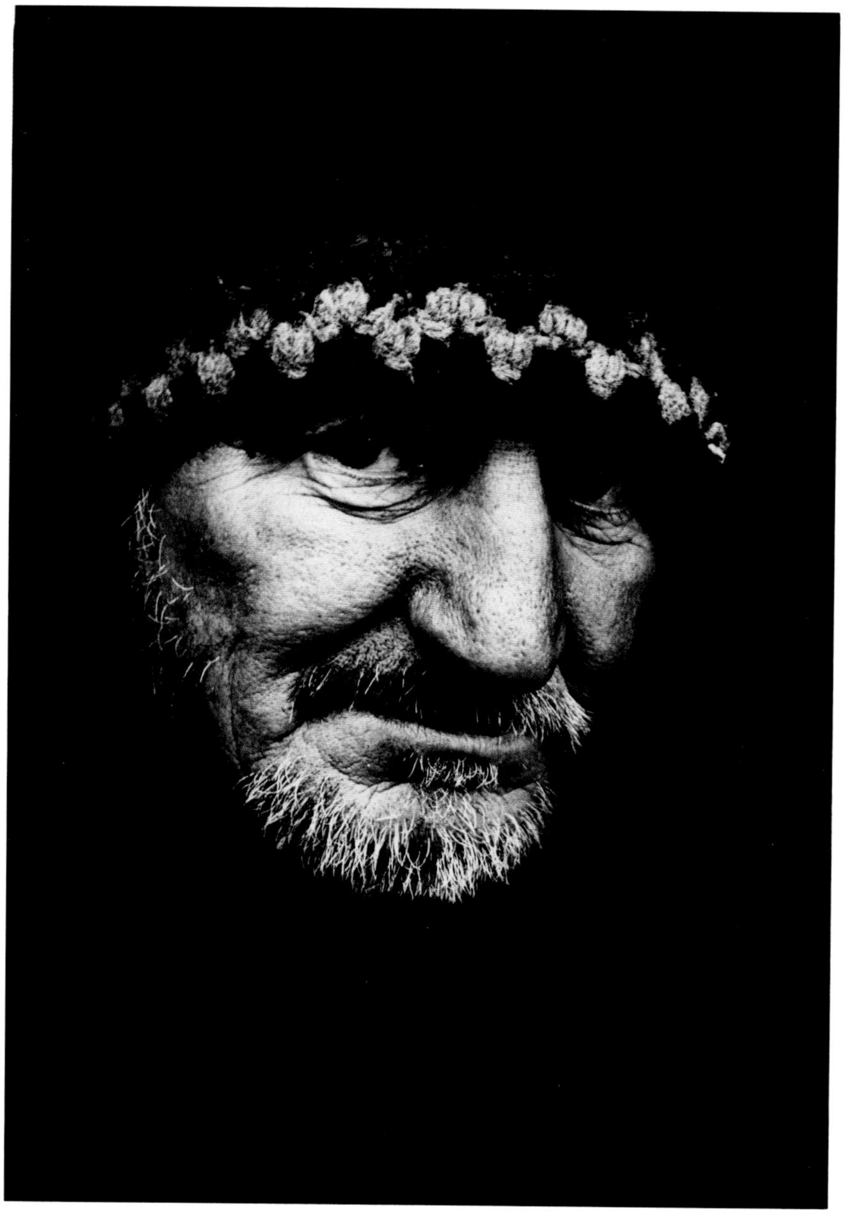

Big nose Sammy, Wilmington, 1973

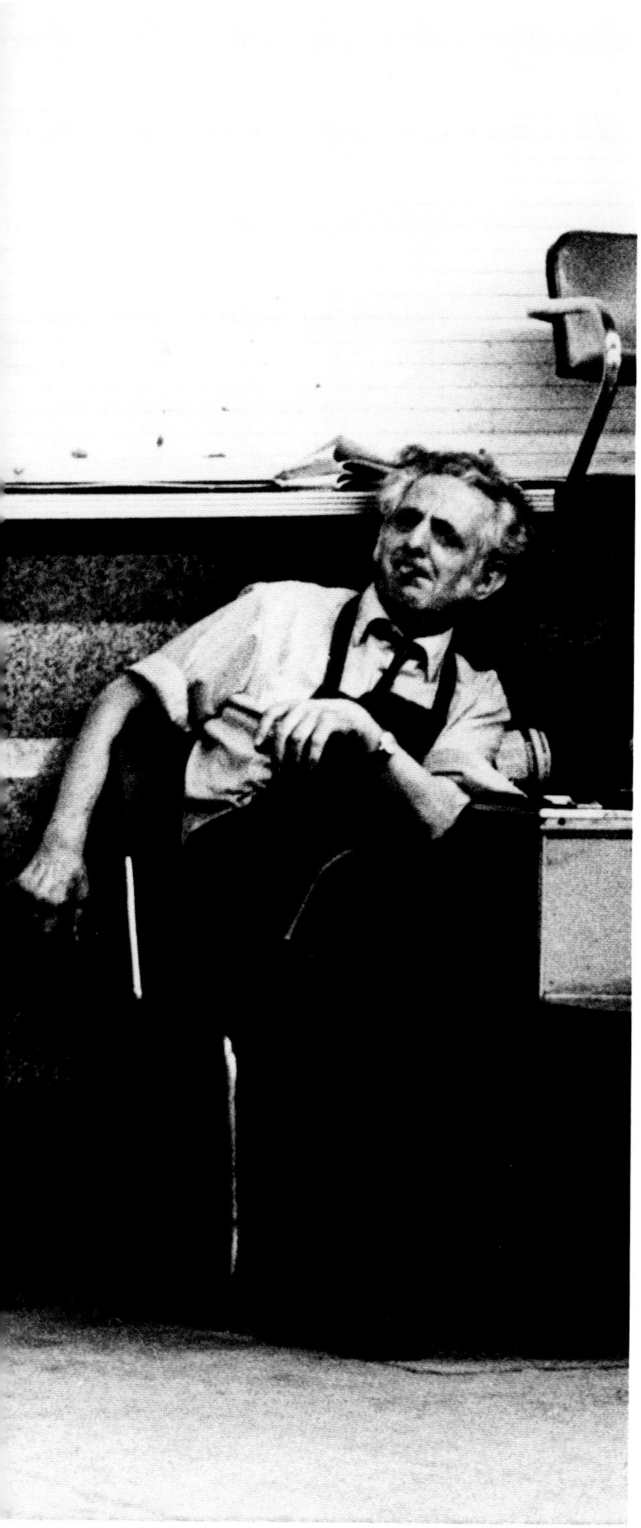

Dominic the shoeshine man, Wilmington Train Station, 1970

Jimmy
Rob
ATHAN
Mike
E-Z
Ric
ADĒ

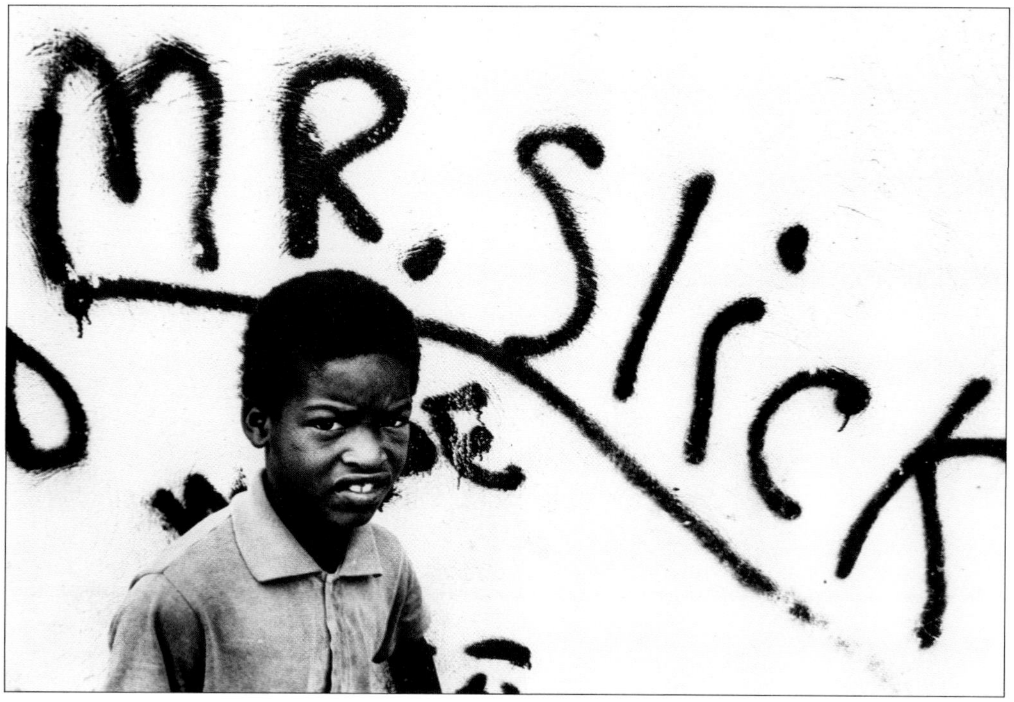

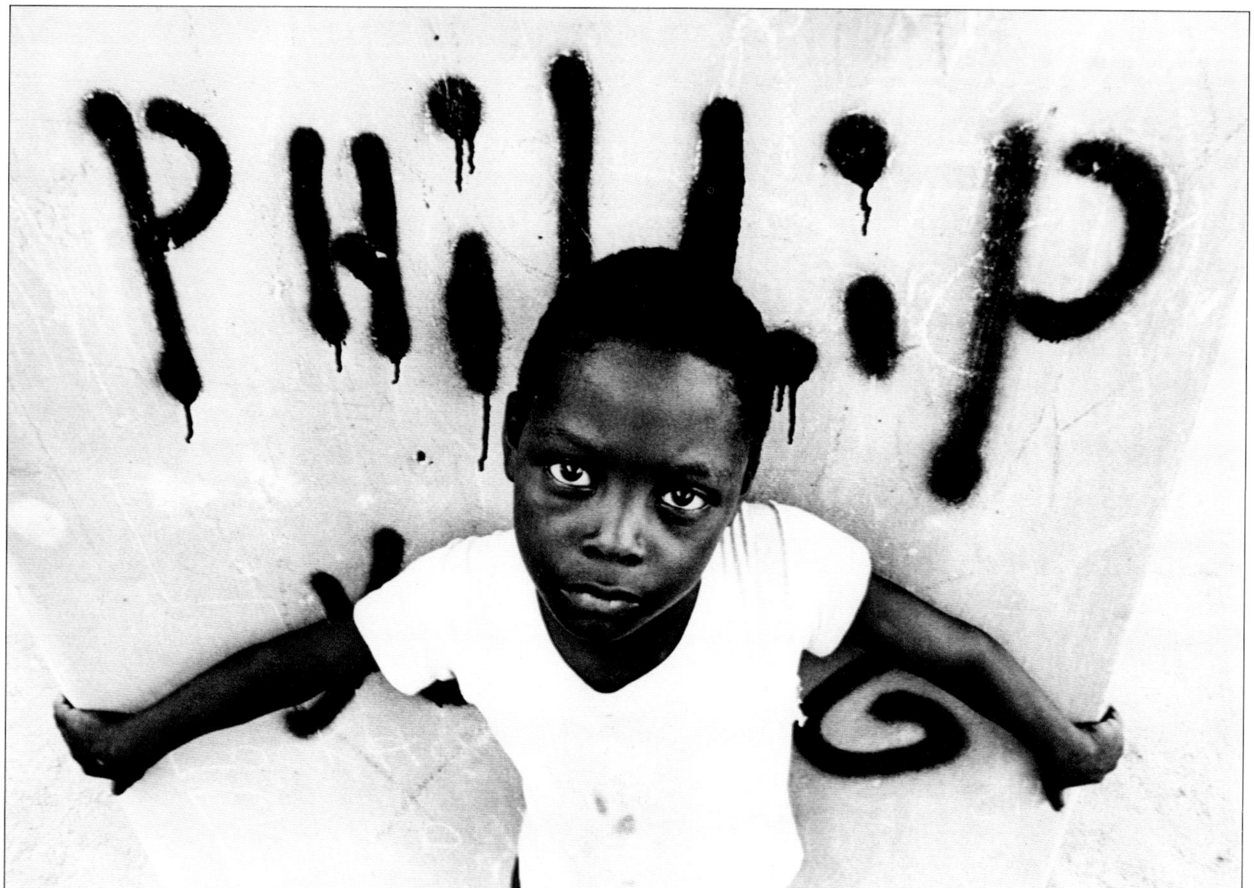

Street graffiti, Wilmington, 1973

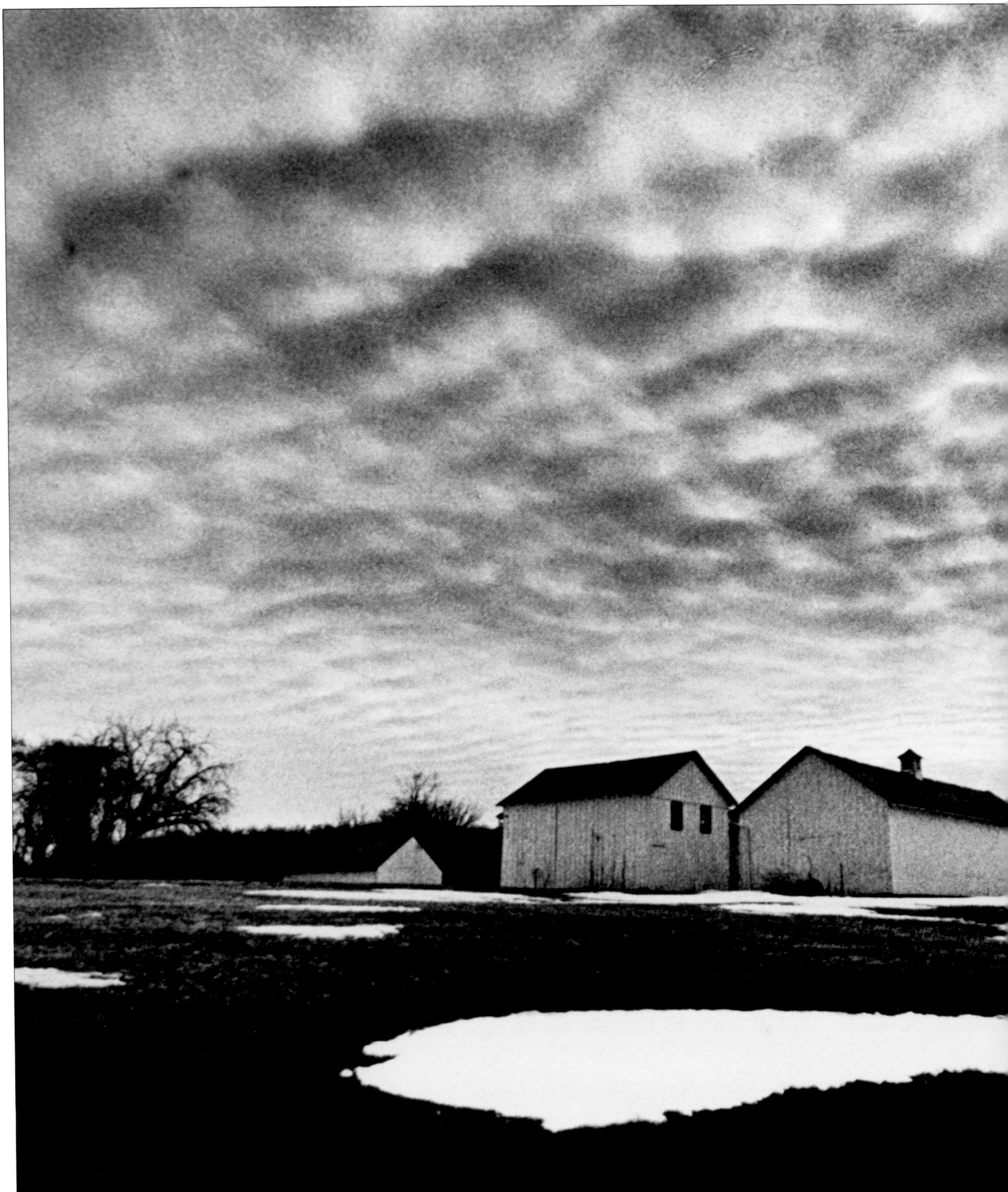

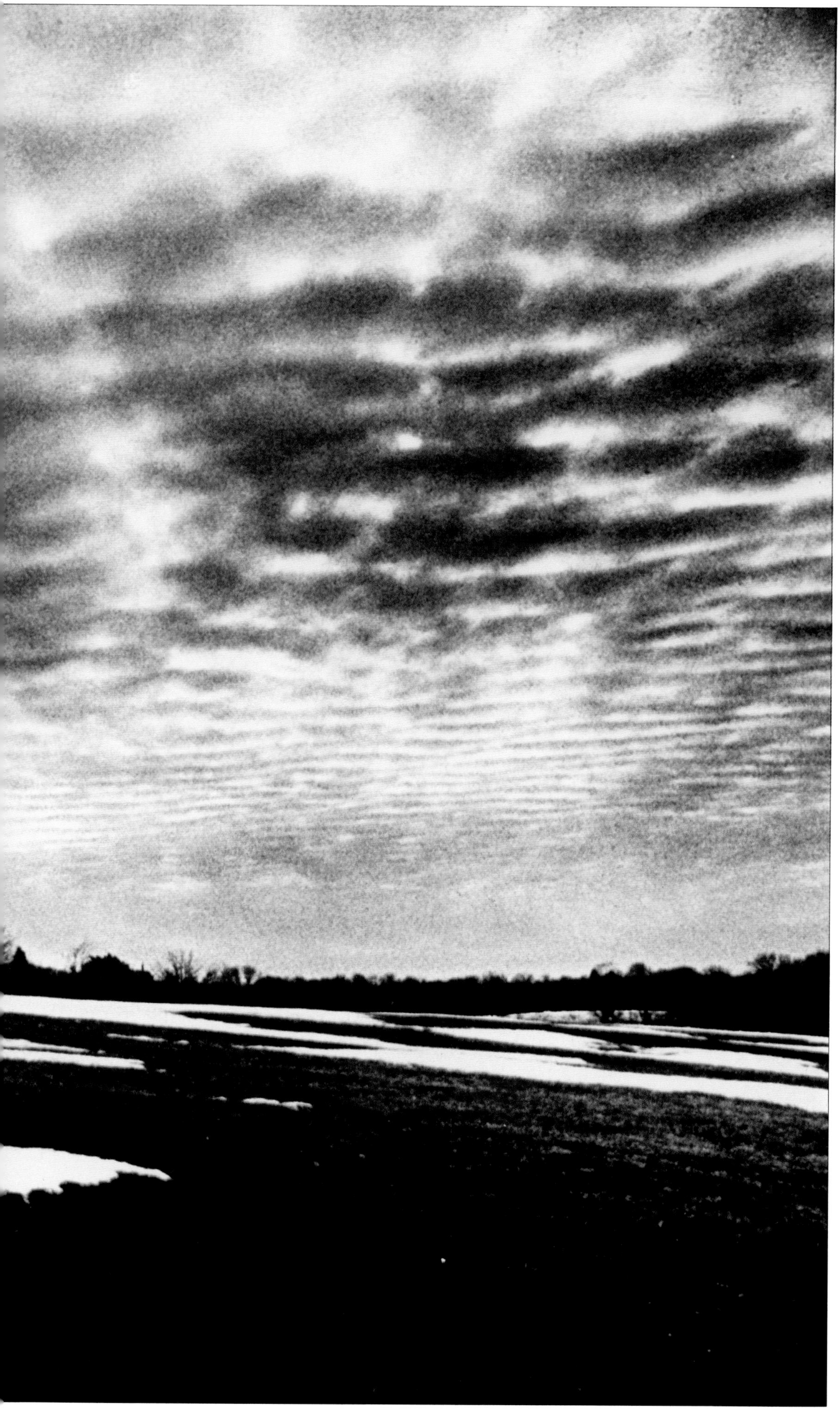

Brandywine Creek State Park, 1987

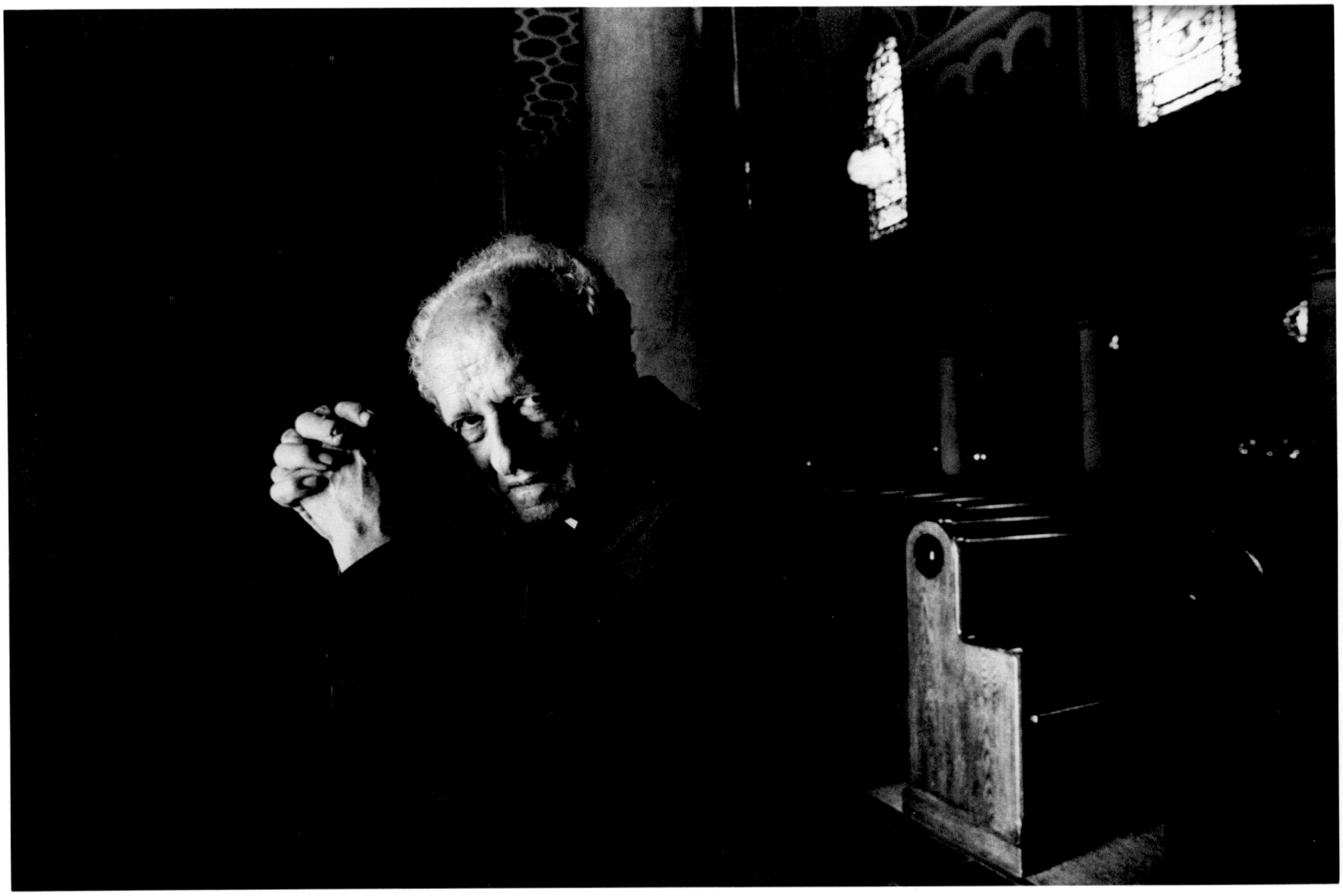

Father Roberto Balducelli, St. Anthony of Padua Church, Wilmington, 1988

Sister Adelaide Nerb, St. Gertrude's Priory,
Ridgely, Maryland, 1988

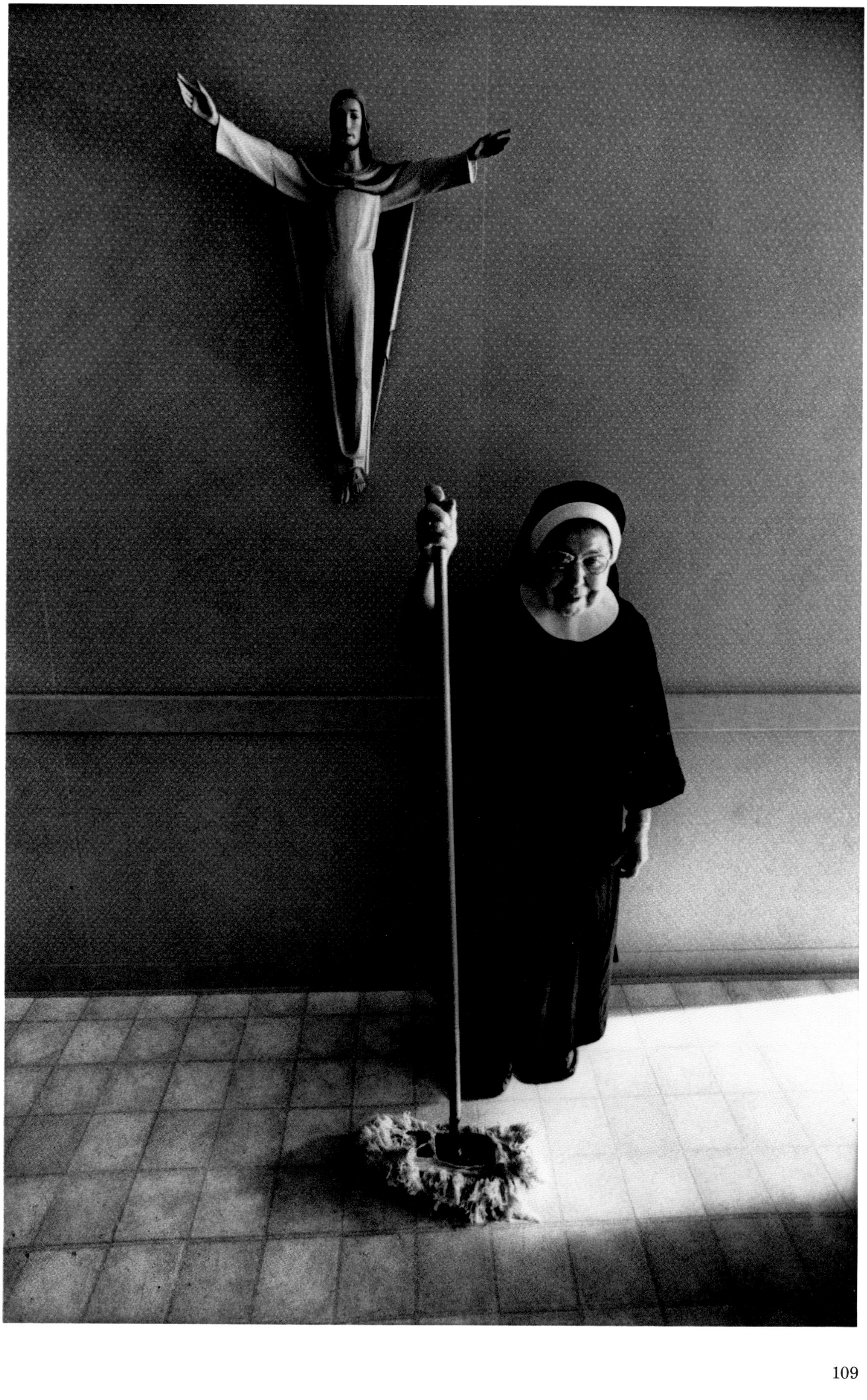

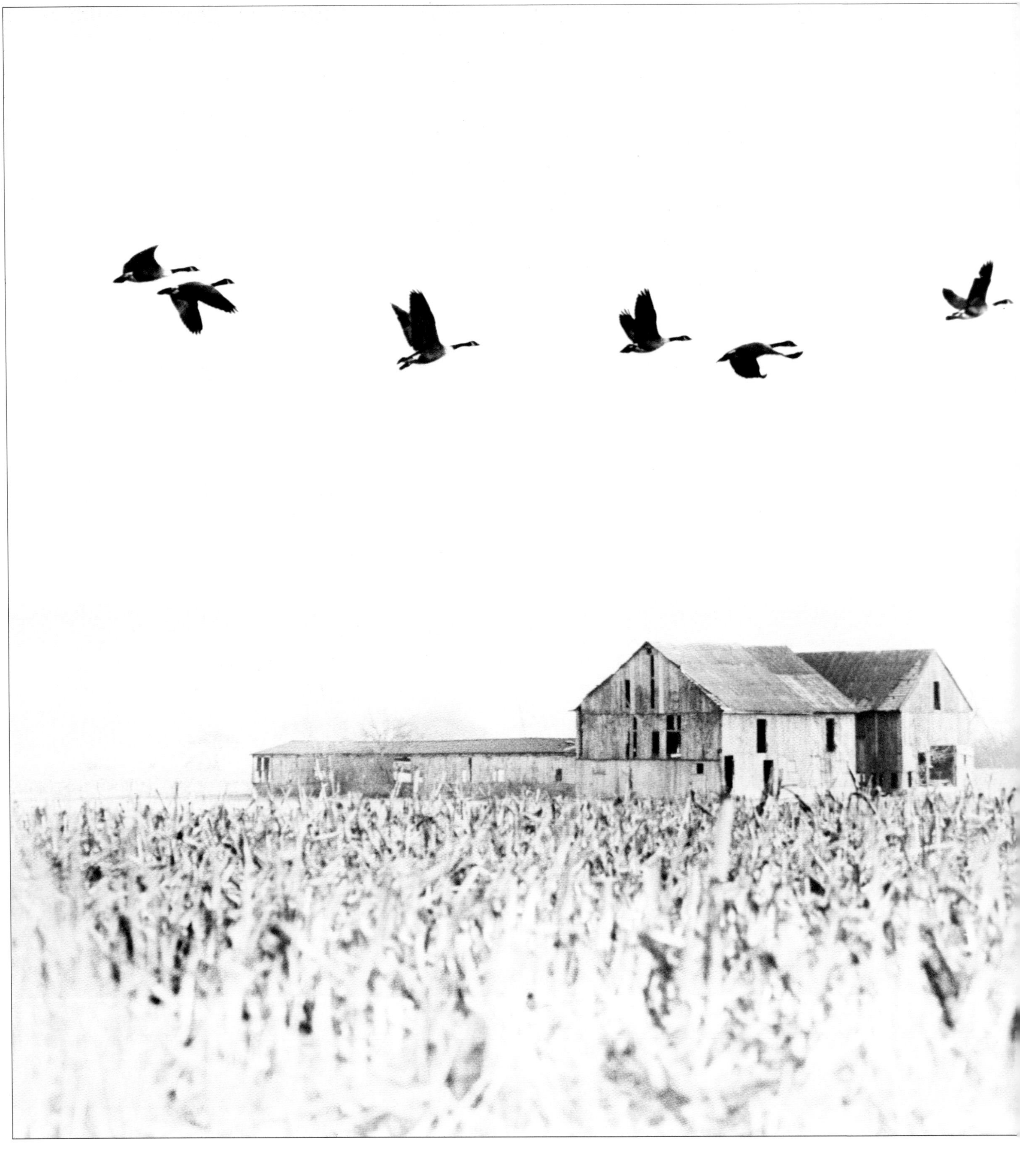

Route 9, Leipsic, 1986

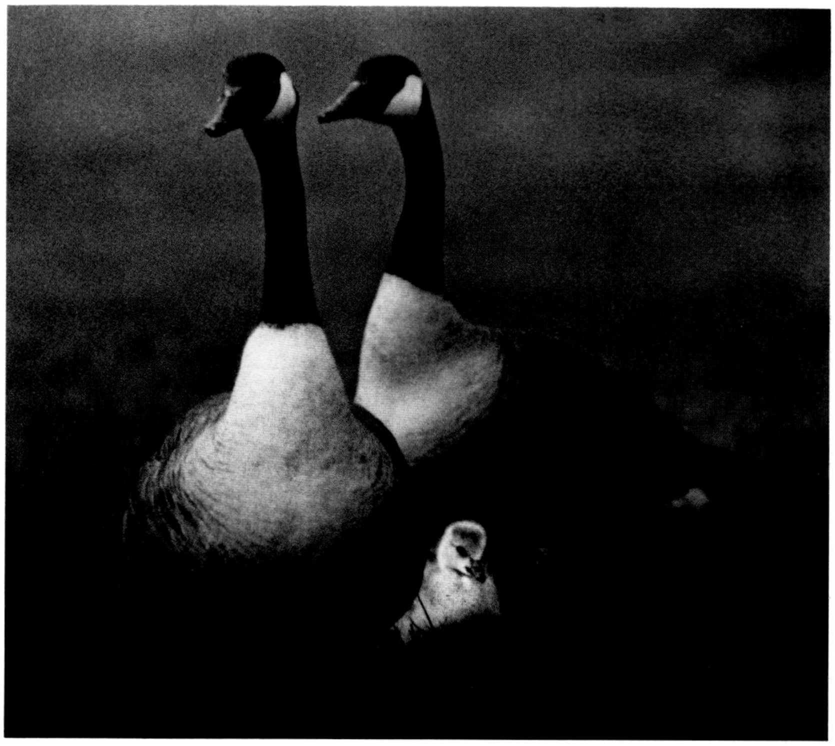

Delcastle Golf Course, 1988

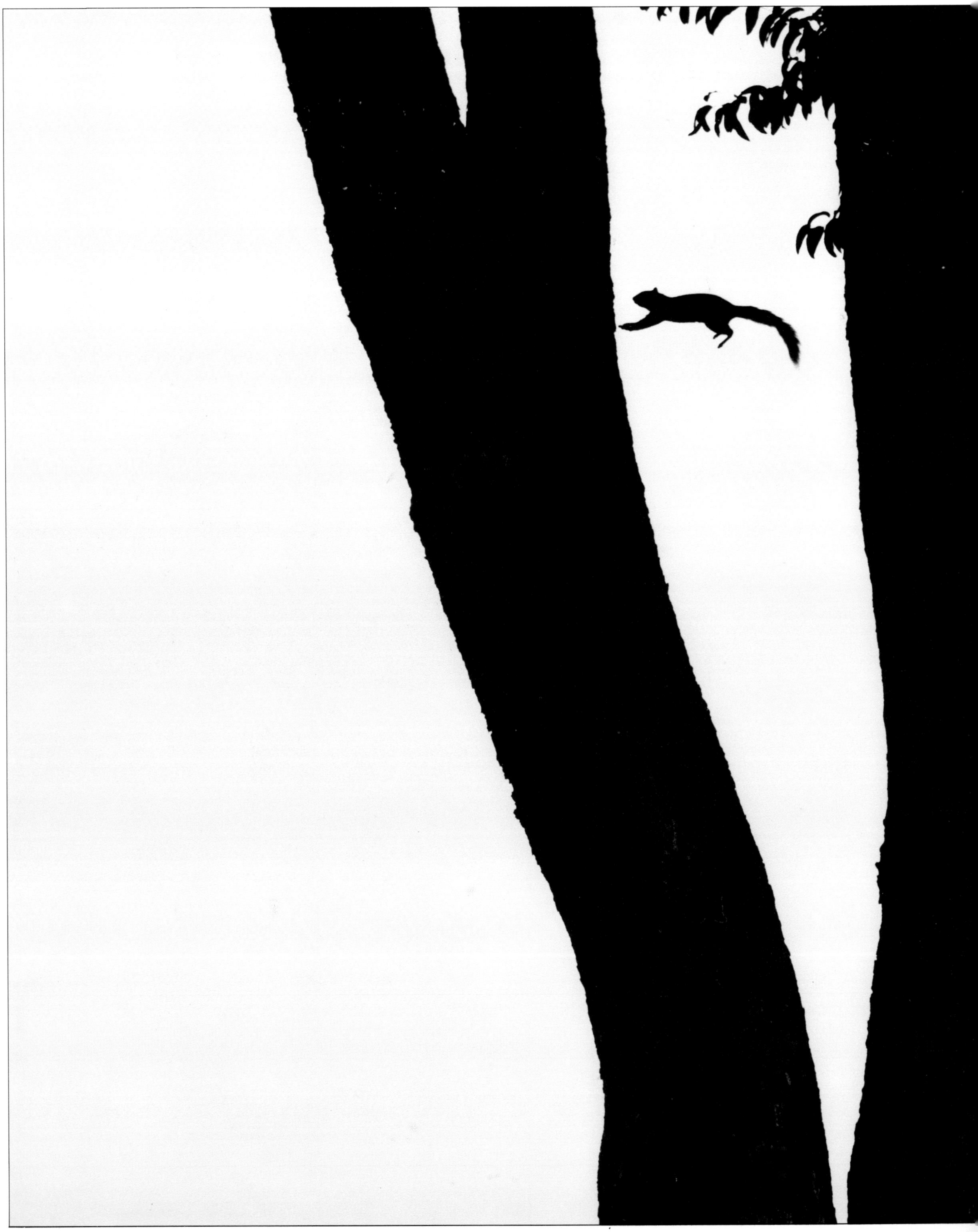

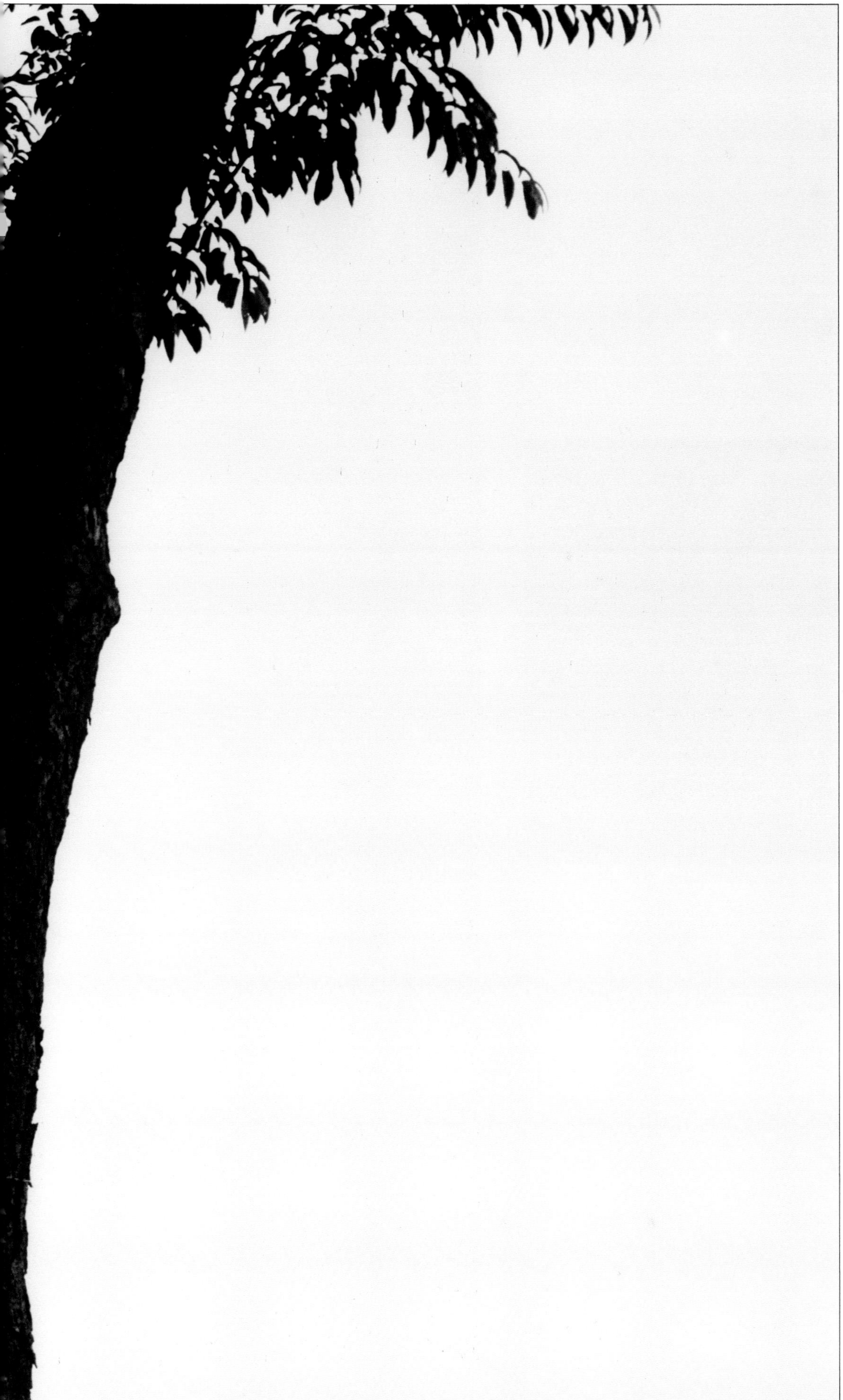

Rockford Park, Wilmington, 1974

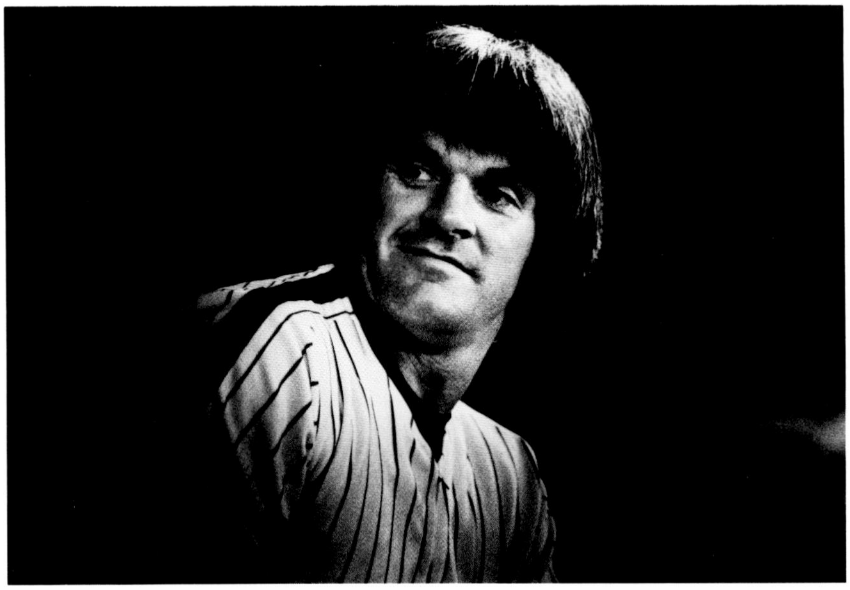

Pete Rose, Veterans Stadium, Philadelphia, 1982

Hank Aaron, Veterans Stadium,
Philadelphia, 1974

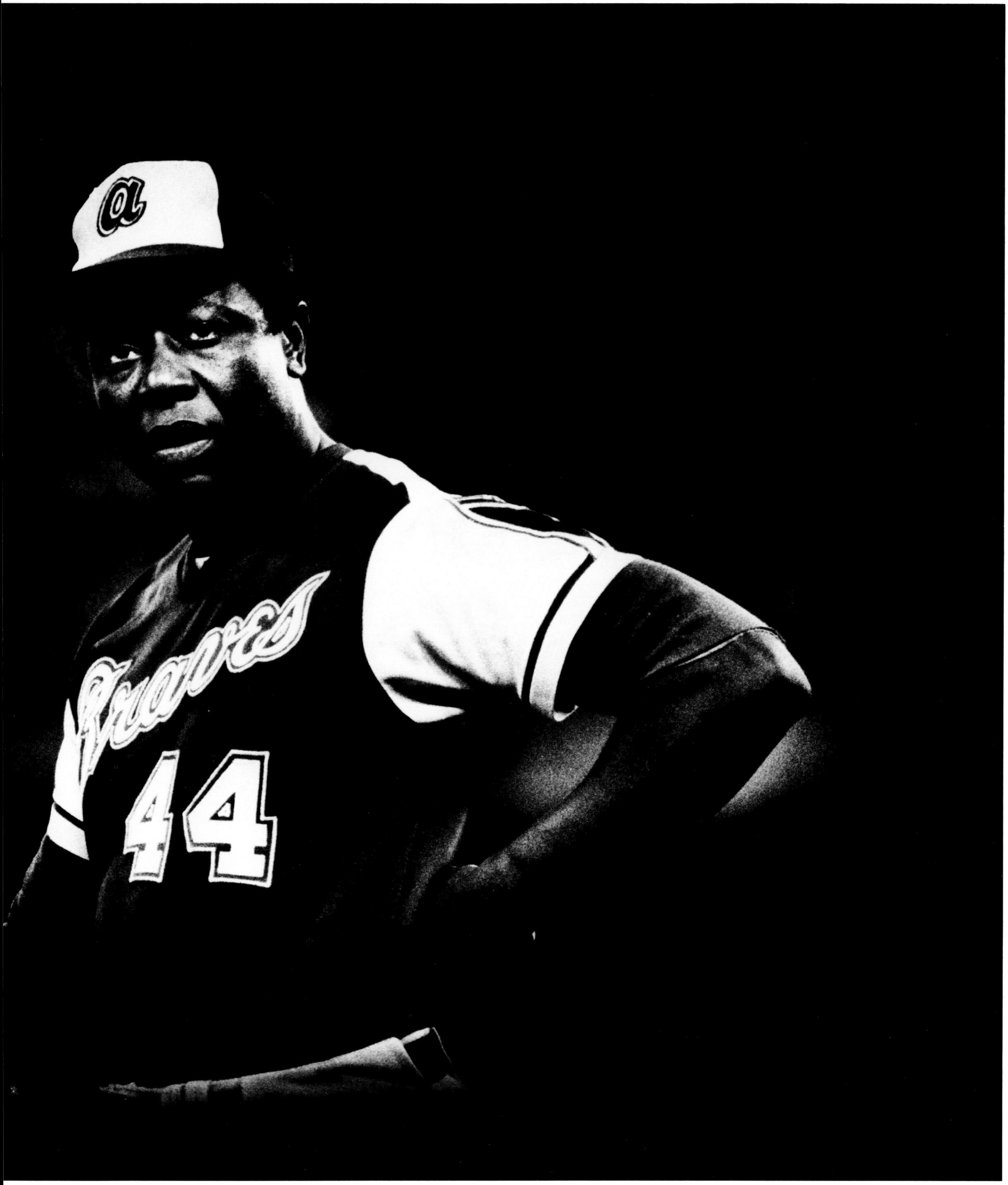
Braves
44

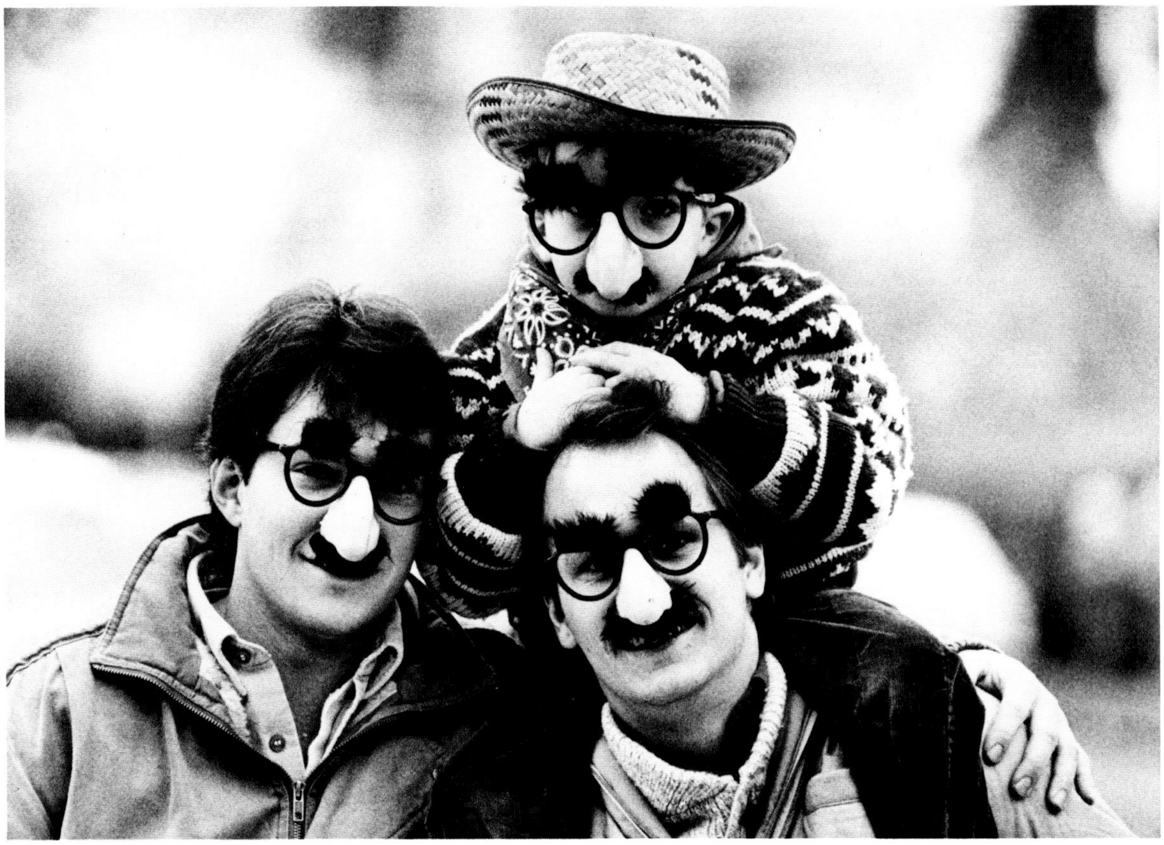

Brian Stanton and Rick Rydzewski – topped by brother Brad, Hummers Parade, Middletown, 1986

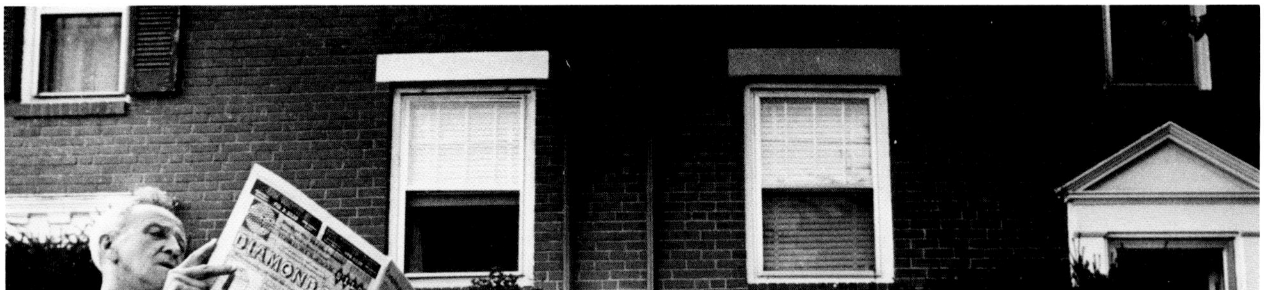

John Payne poolside with neighbor Tammy De Courcelle, Wilmington, 1969

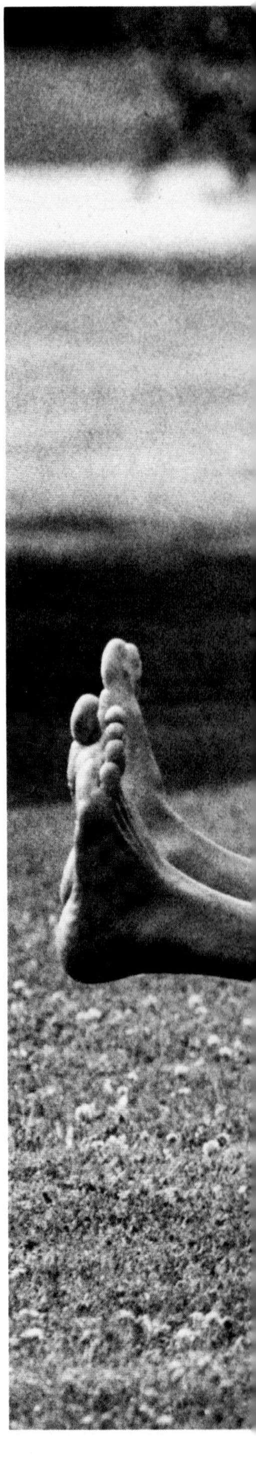

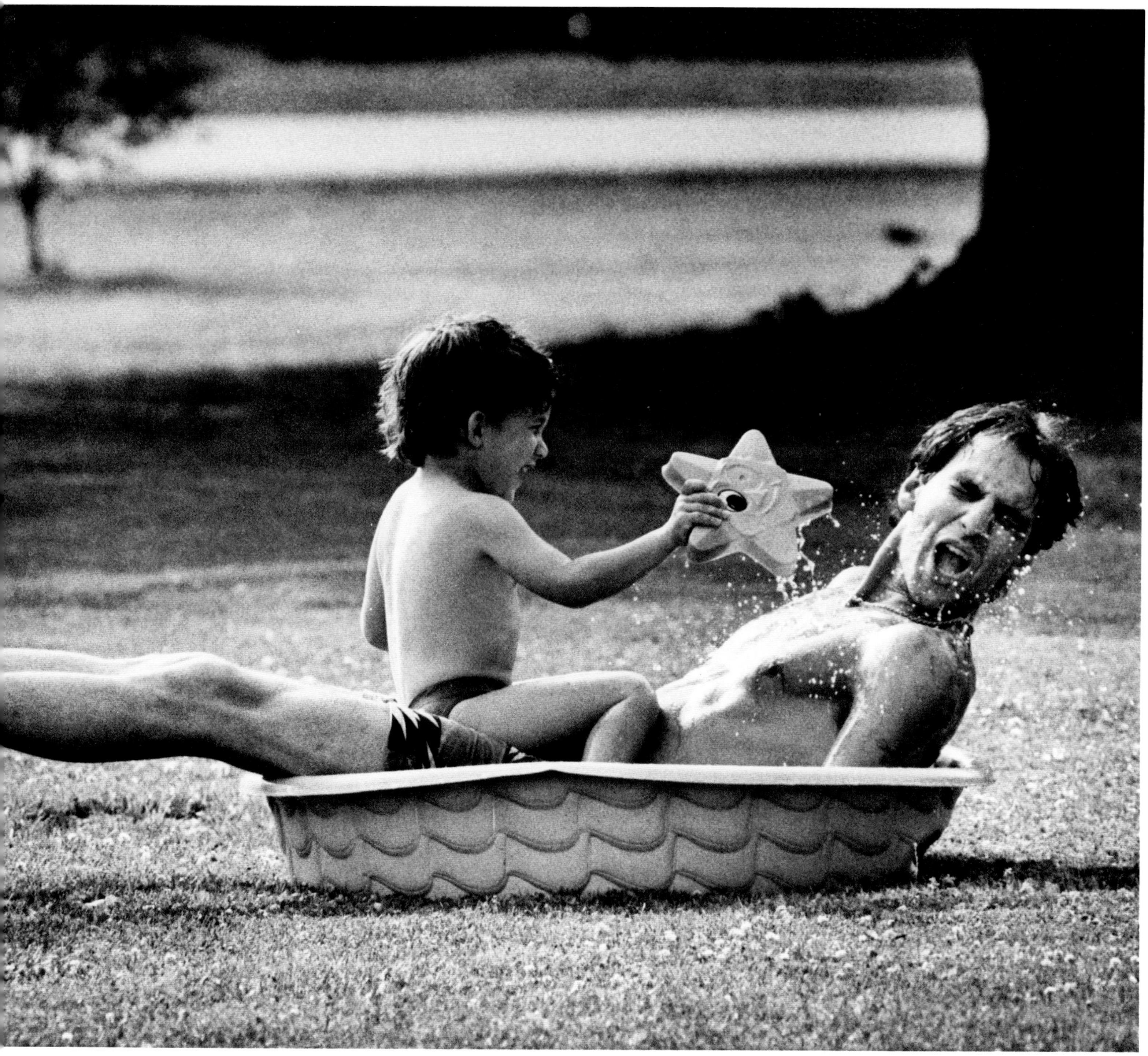

Dino Di Ossi with son D.J., Wilmington, 1986

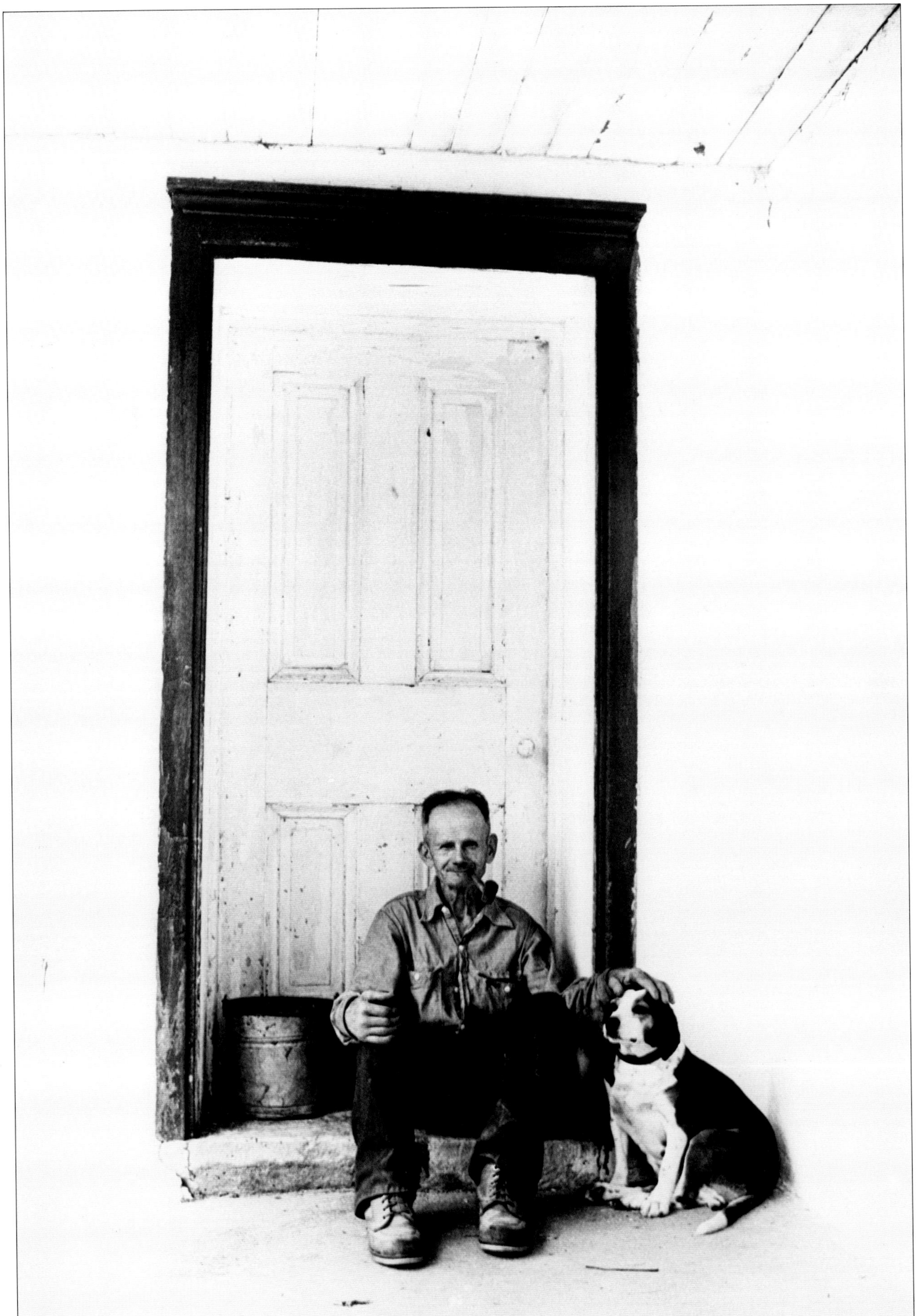

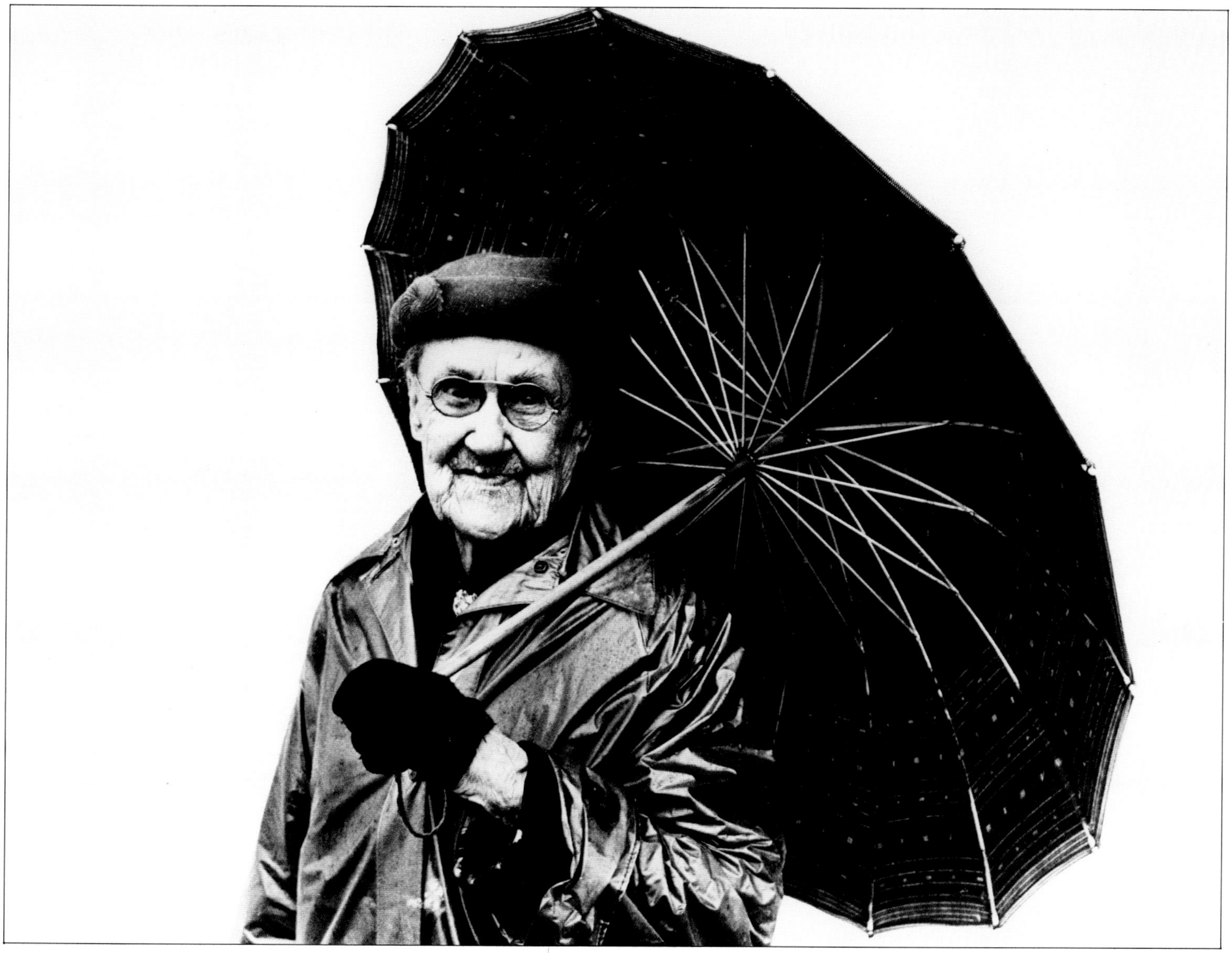

Union Street, Wilmington, 1973

Frank Kelly, North Star, 1973

Chapel of Love 1986

In 1986 I planned to marry my sweetheart, Jane Derby, and went to Elkton, Maryland for our wedding license. At the Cecil County Courthouse I saw two desks, two secretaries, and thousands of wedding documents. The secretaries told me that Maryland law now required a 48-hour waiting period before you could use your license to marry. But once upon a time Elkton had been the "Marriage Capital of the East" – you could breeze into town and marry quick as you pleased. Babe Ruth, Willie Mays, Joan Fontaine, Ethel Merman, David Merrick and Bert Lahr all married in Elkton. So did I.

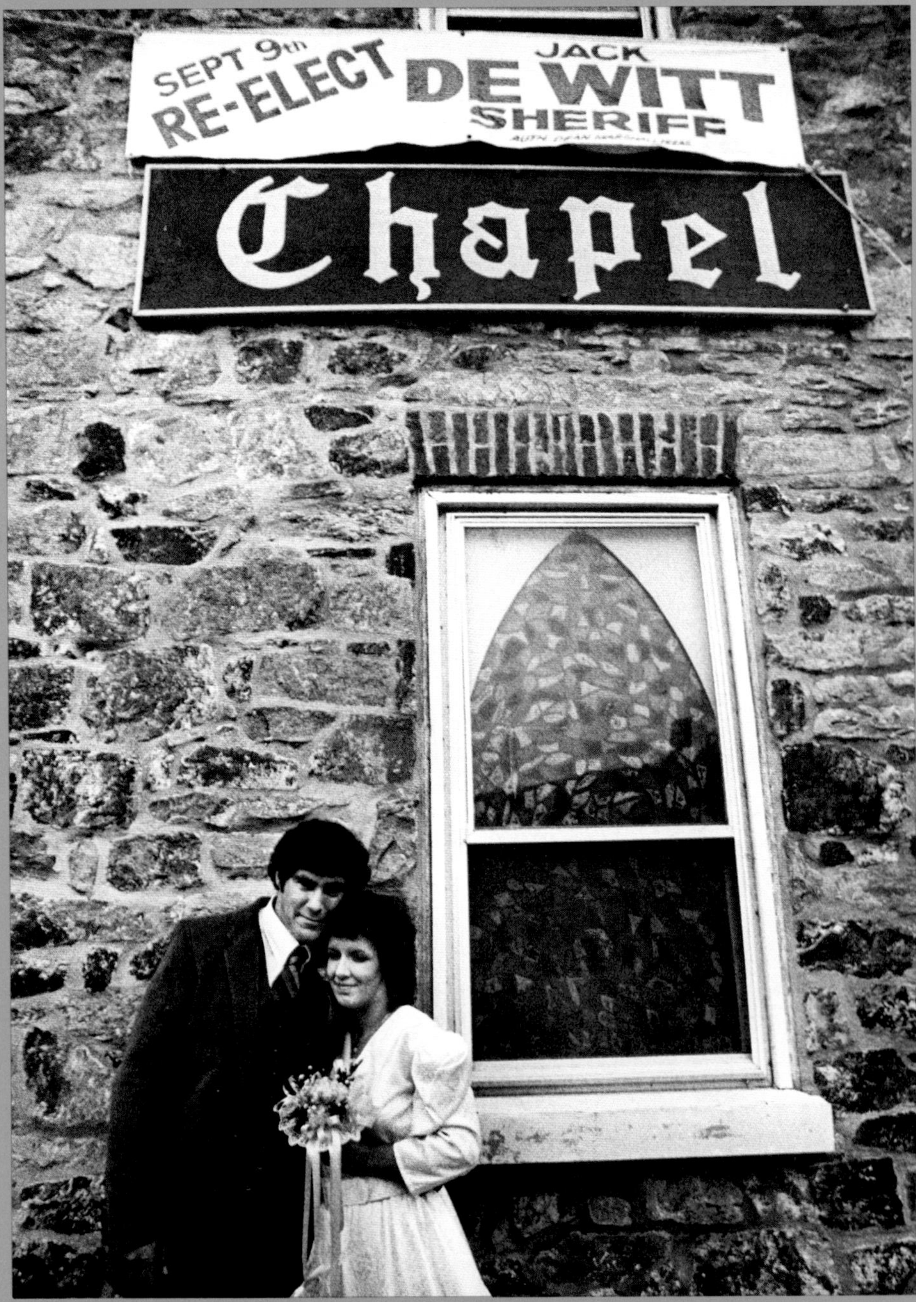

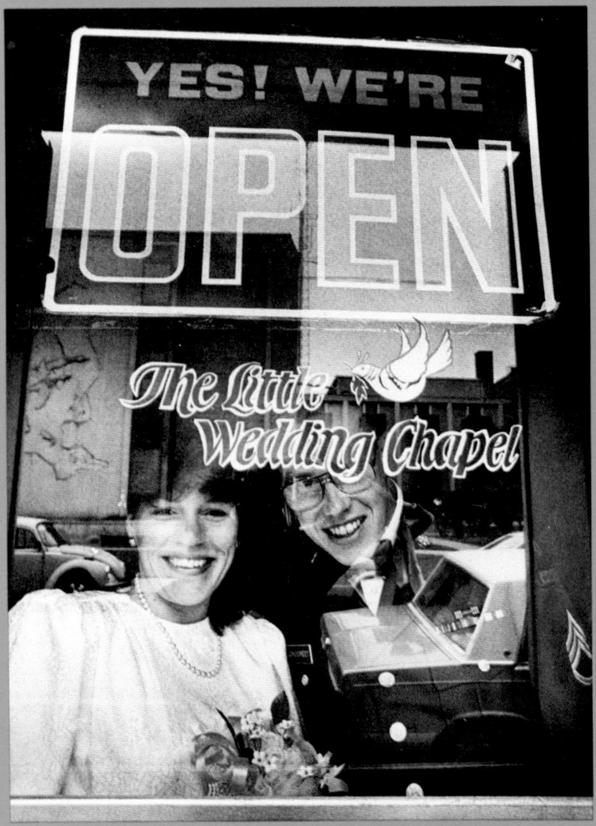

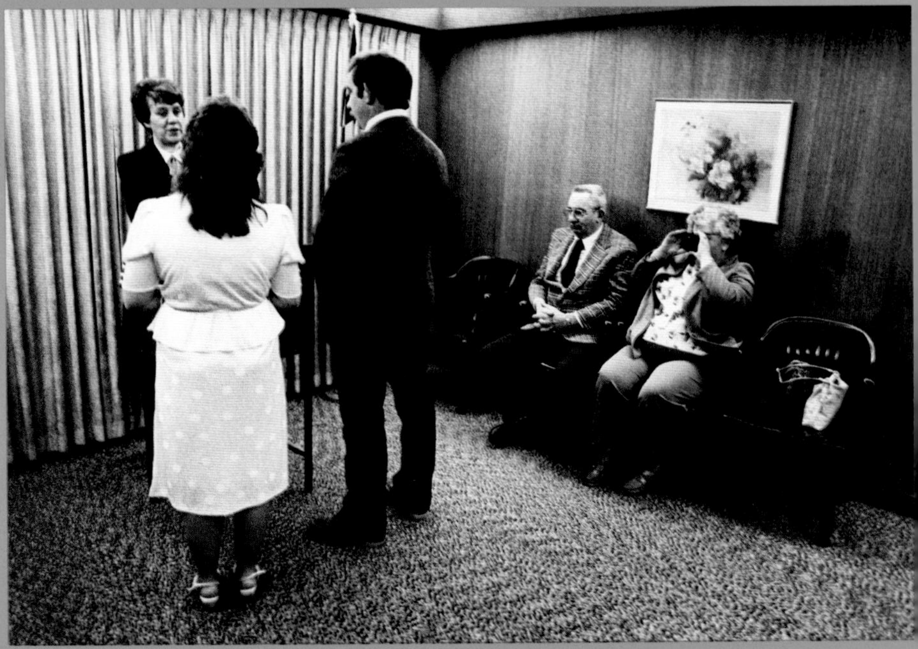

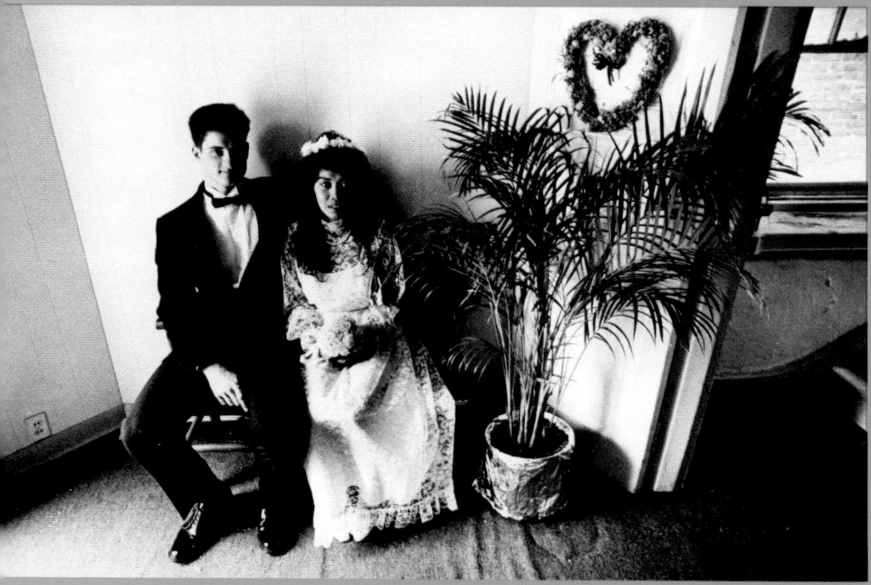

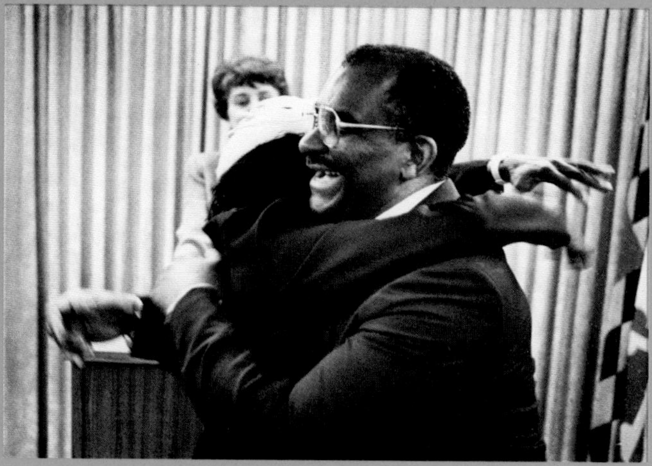

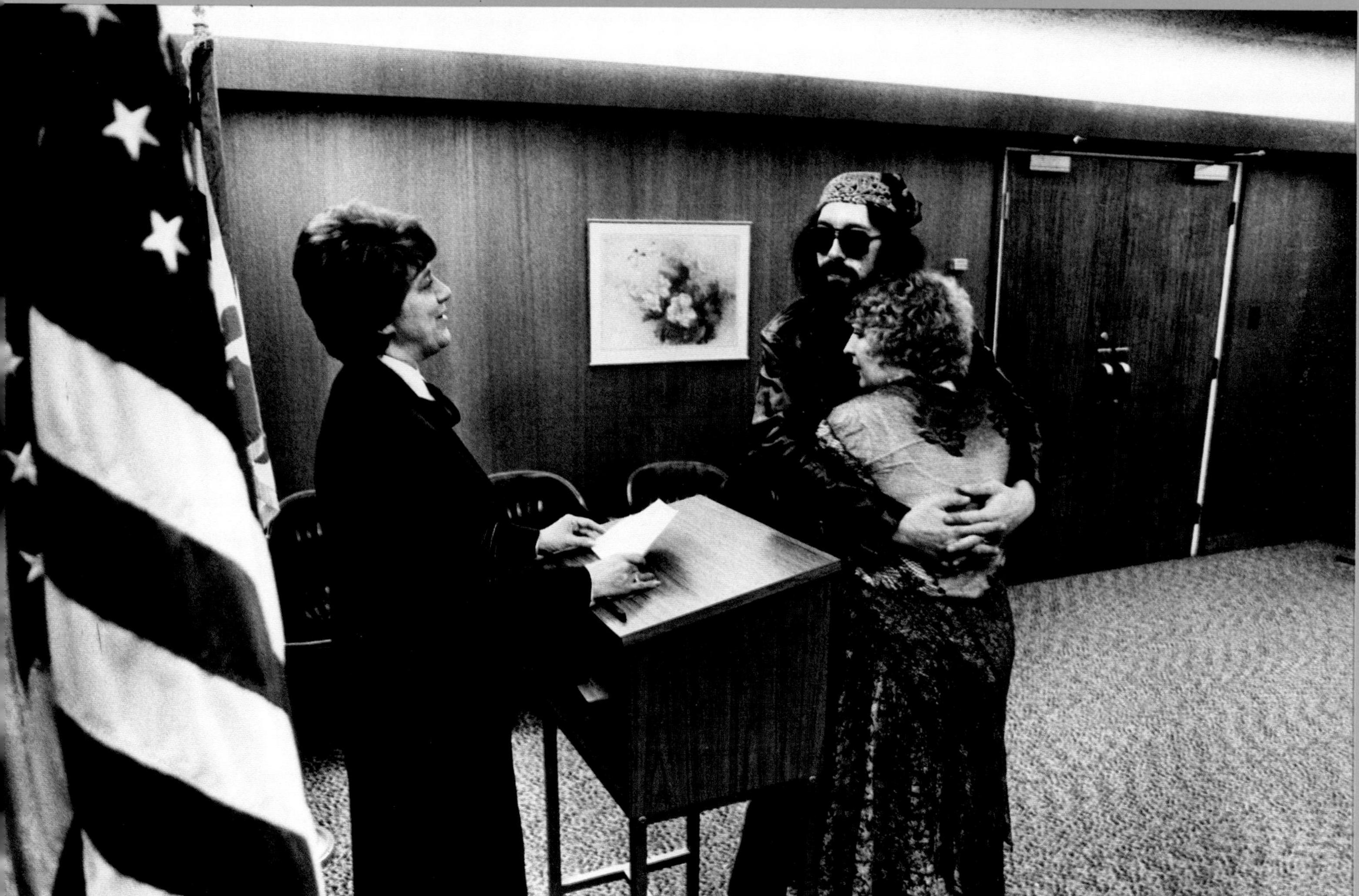

Hoopes Reservoir, 1972

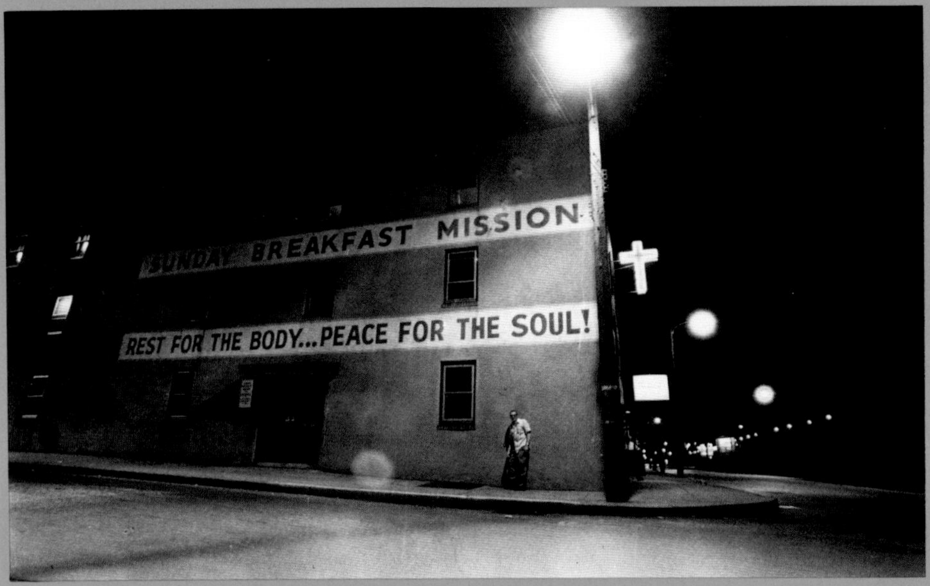

The Mission *1974*

I have been drawn to the homeless and street people since I became a photographer. In 1974 I spent a good bit of time with the men of Wilmington's Sunday Breakfast Mission. Open everyday, despite its name, the mission was at Front and Orange Streets and the Reverend Howard Baxter was in charge. His hopes were written large on the brick facade: "Rest for the body . . . Peace for the soul." What could be more important for us all?

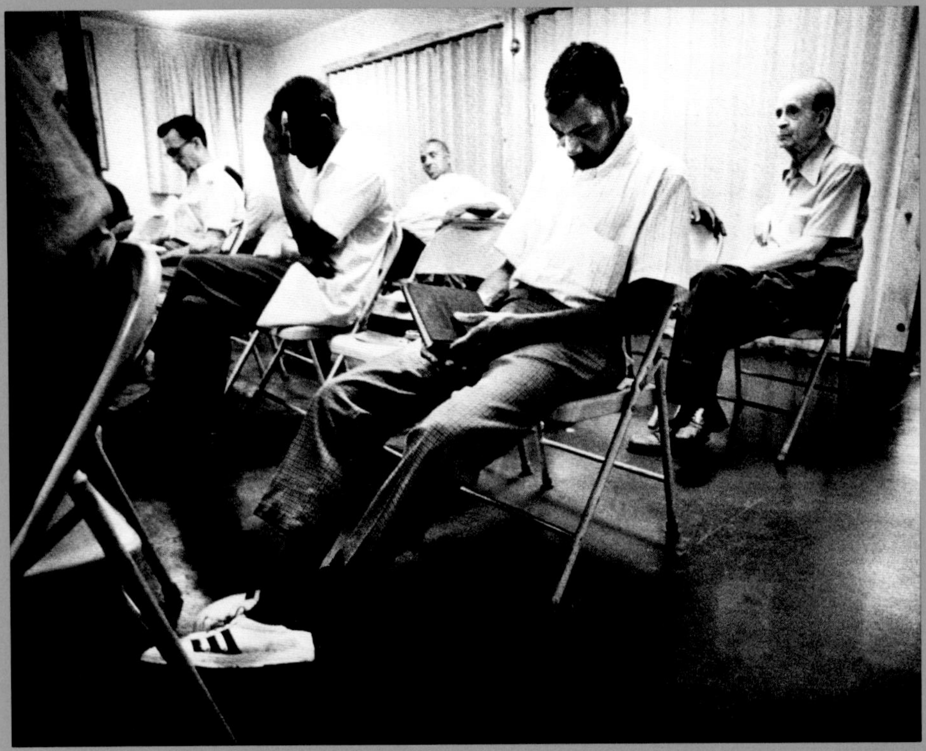

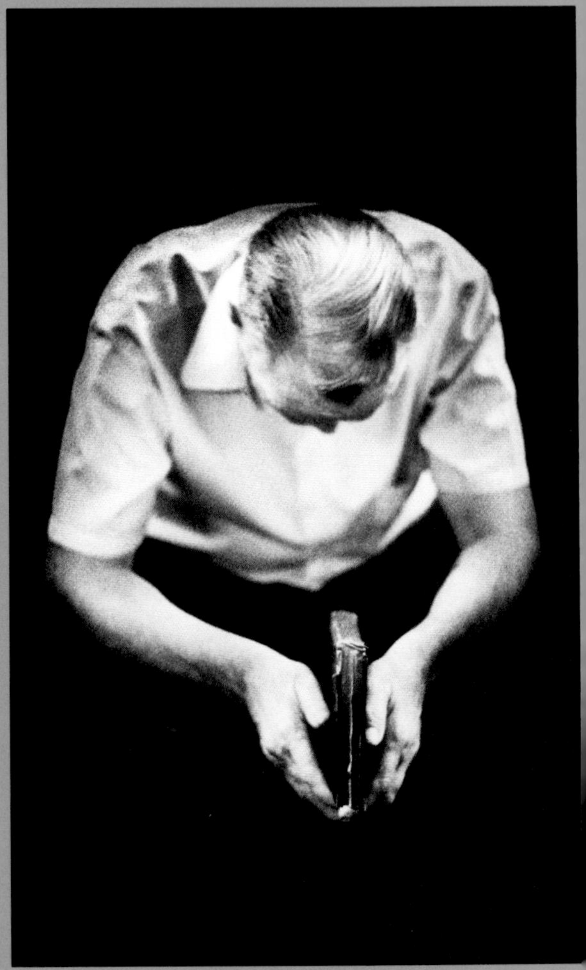

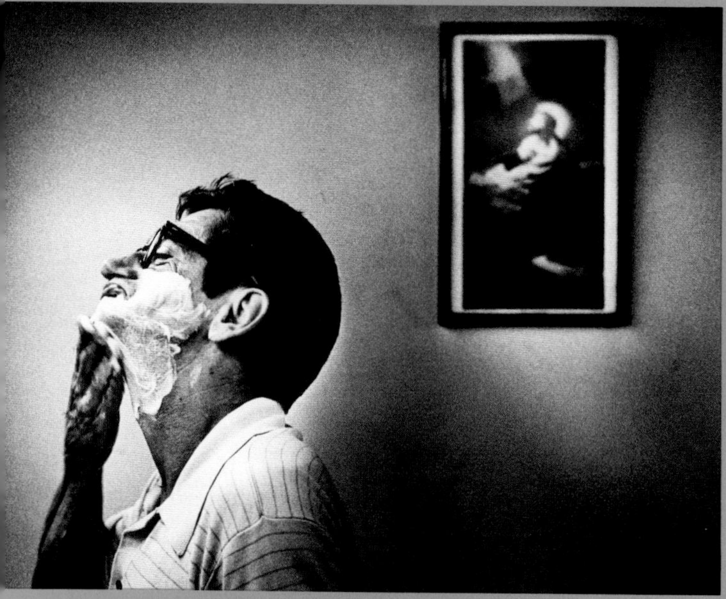

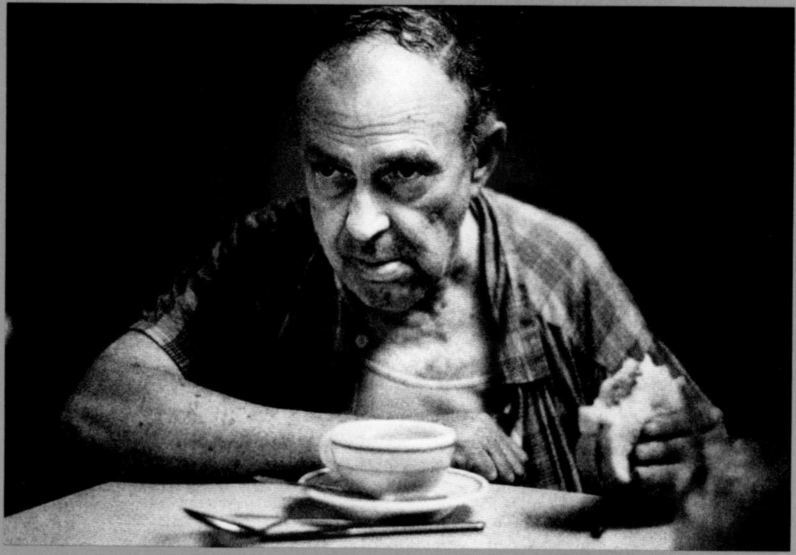

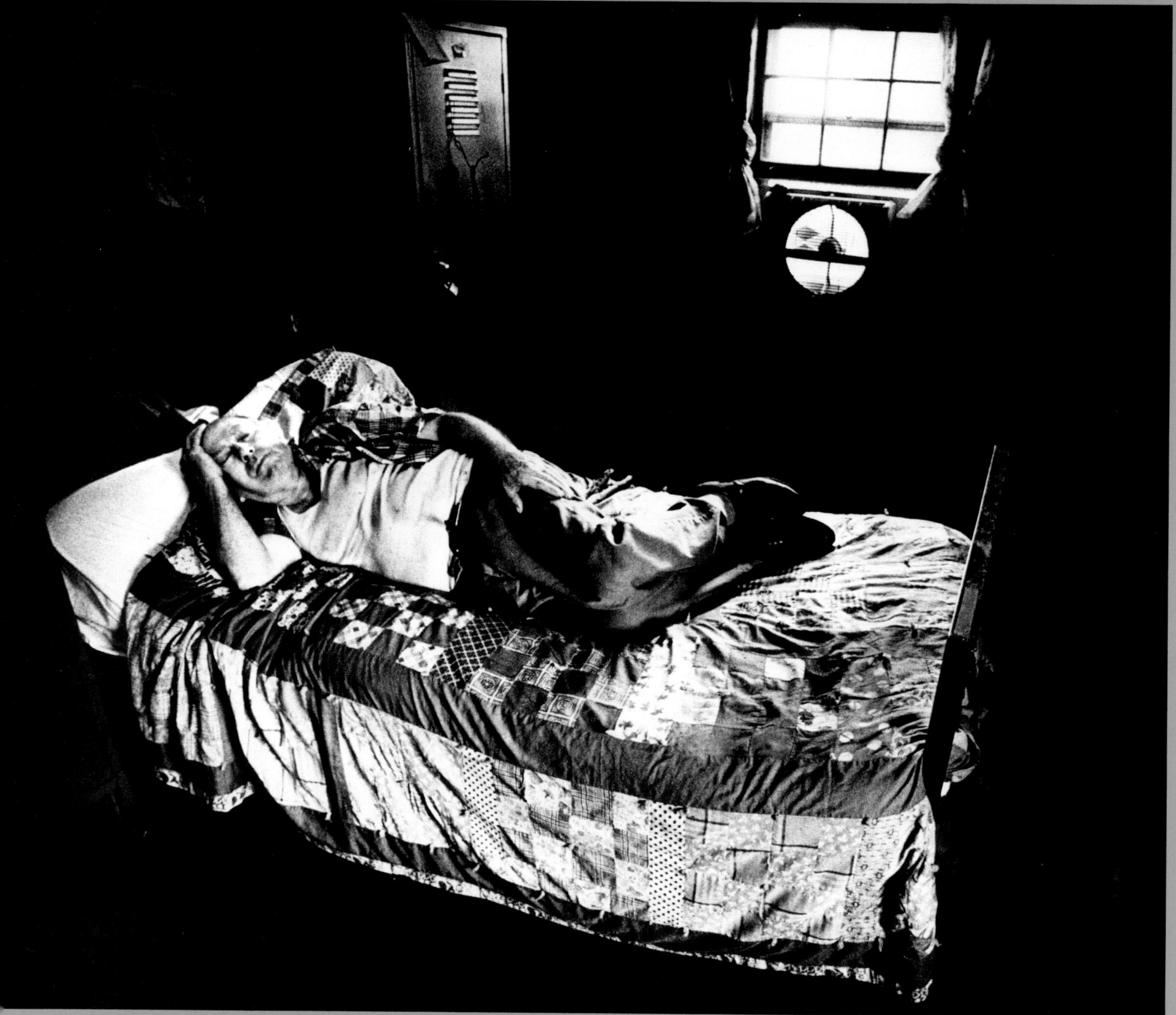

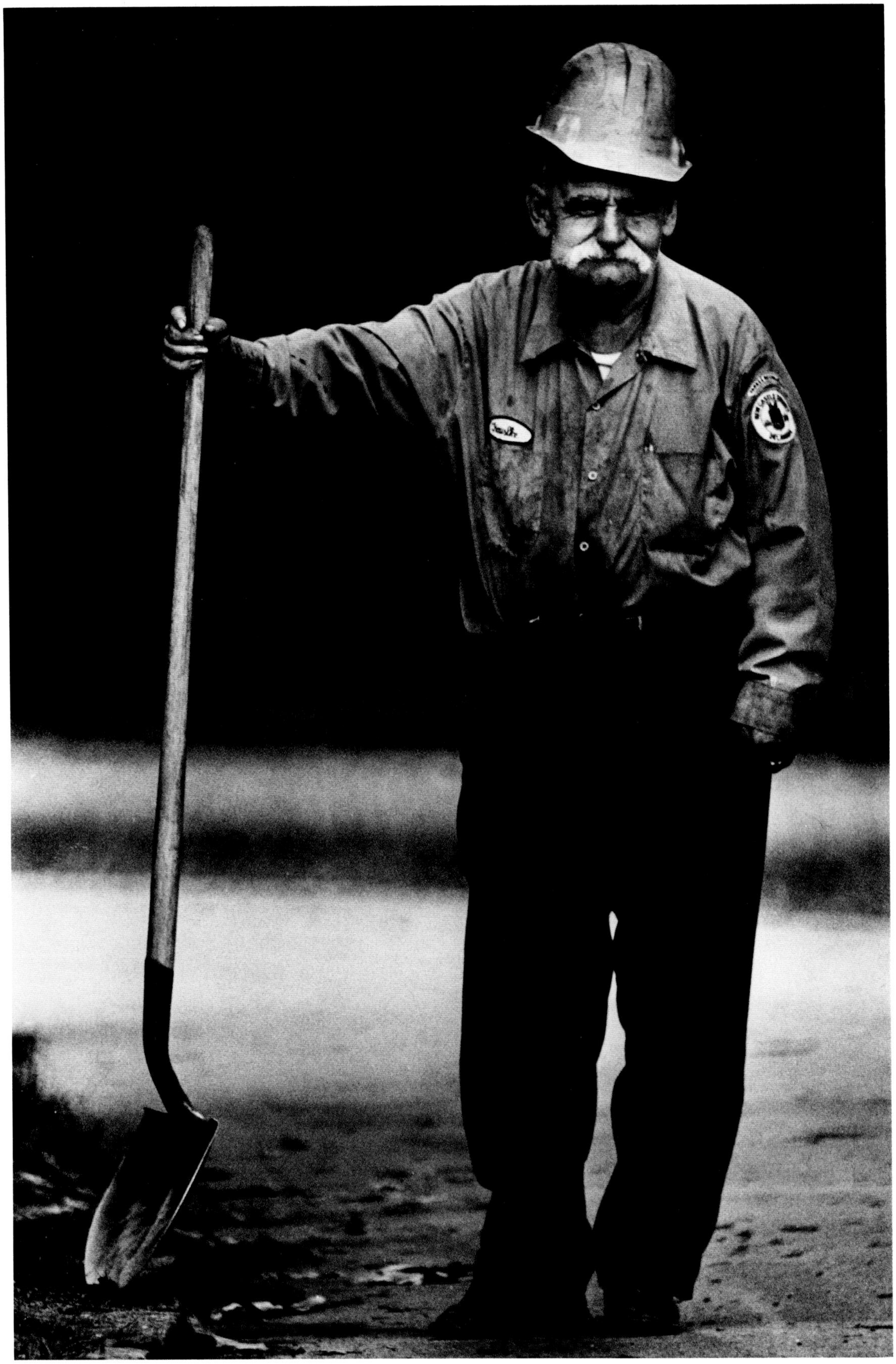

Wilmington city worker, 1974

Greenville gardener, 1987

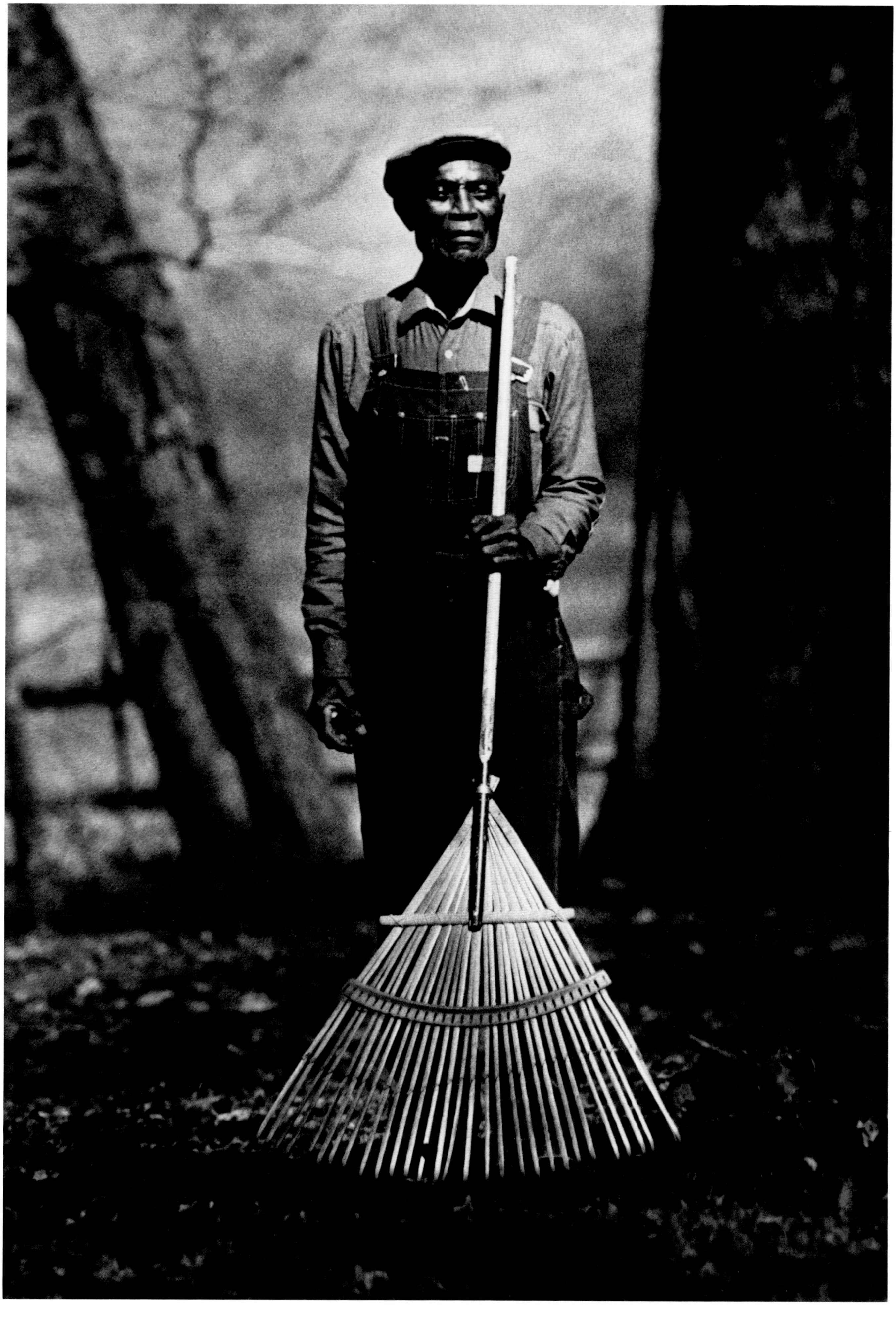

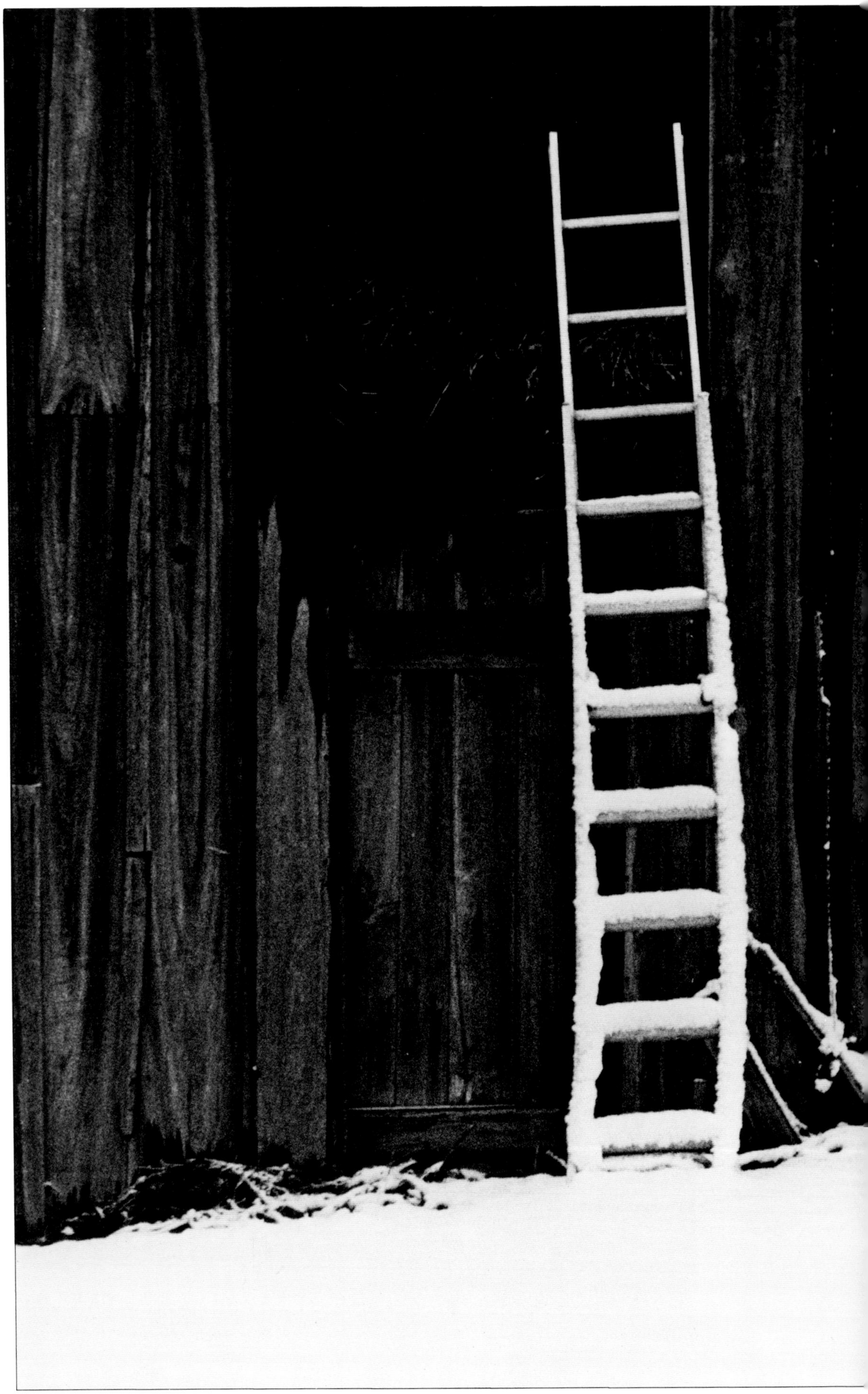

Naamans Road, Wilmington, 1983

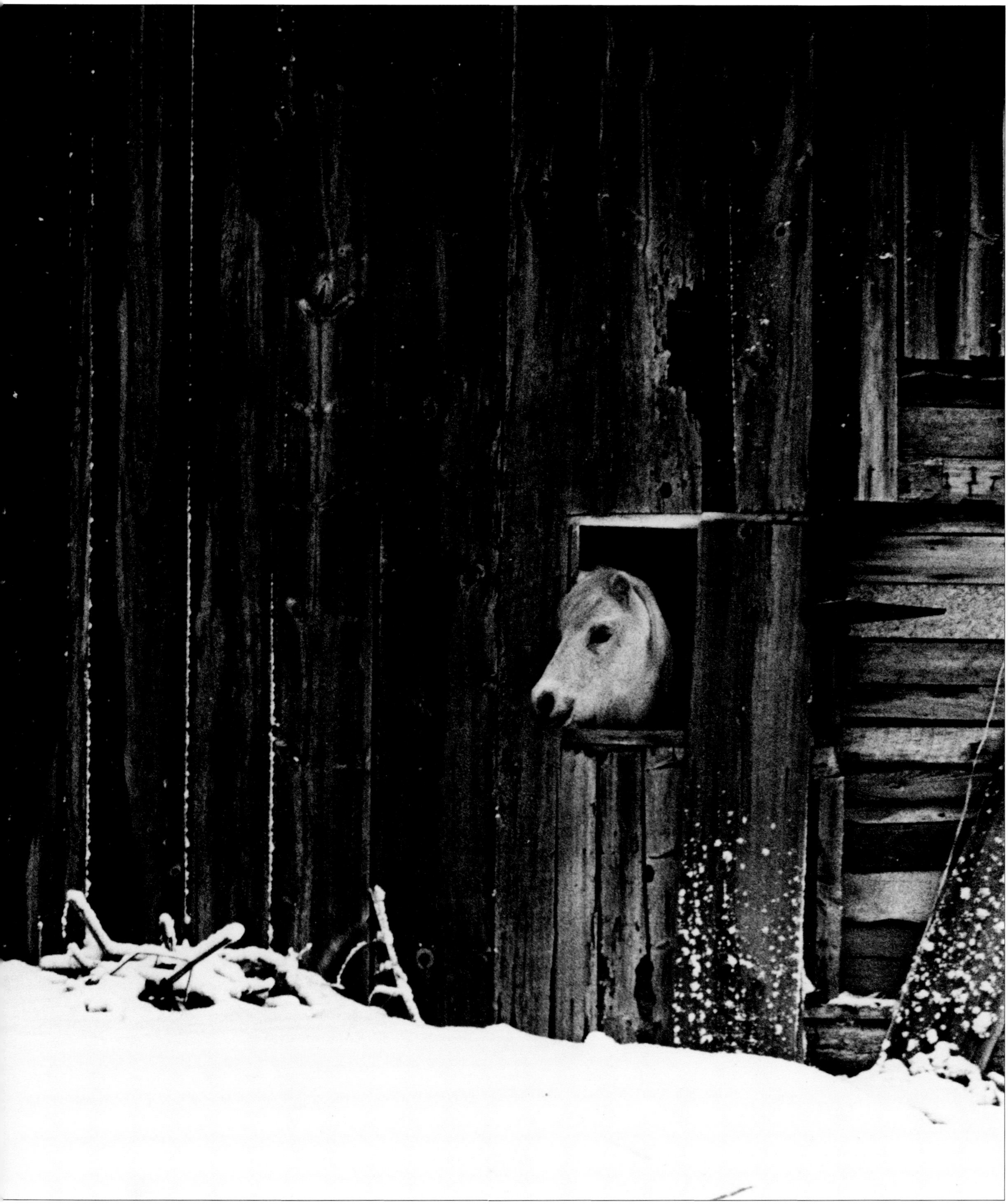

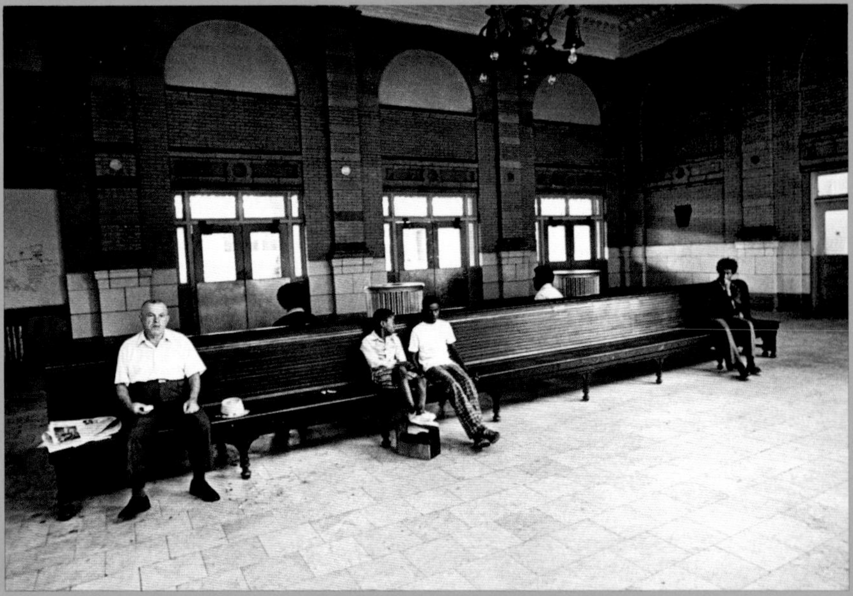

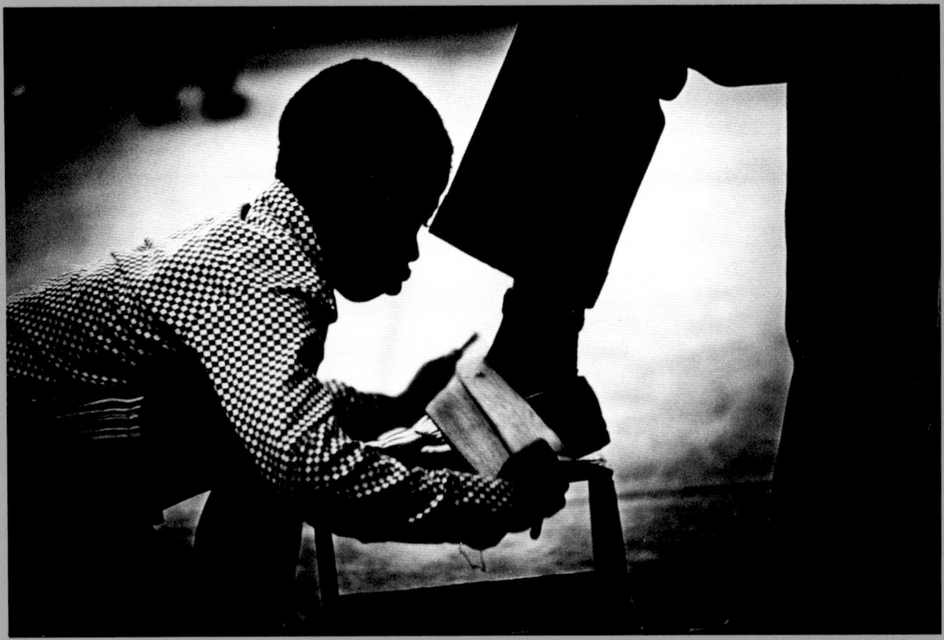

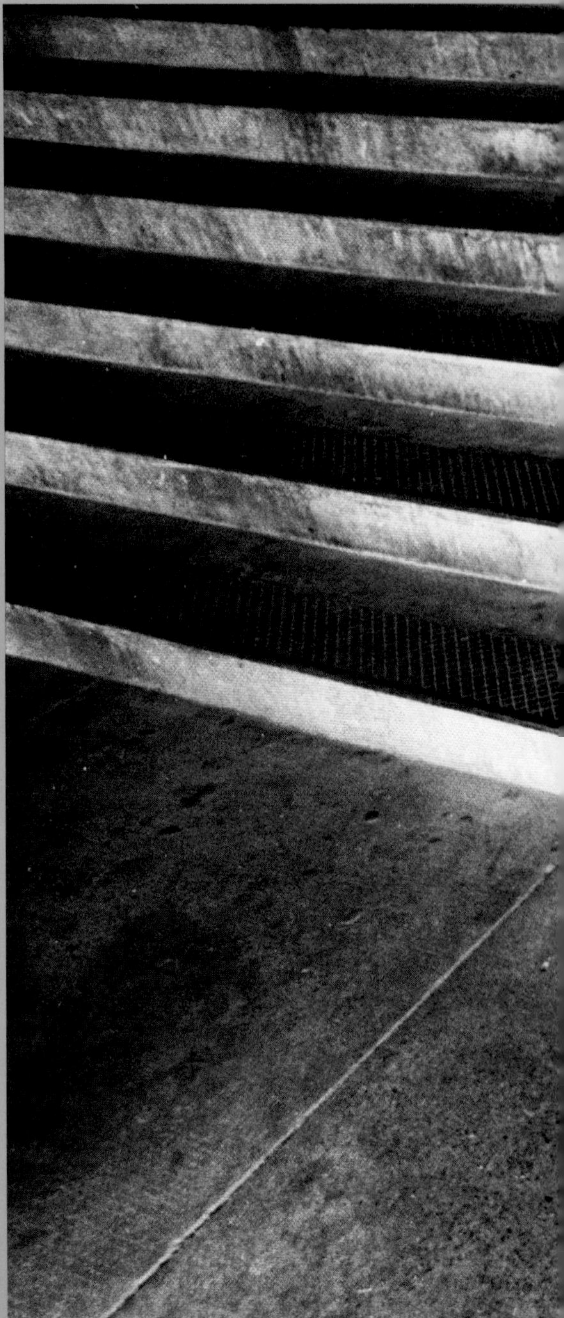

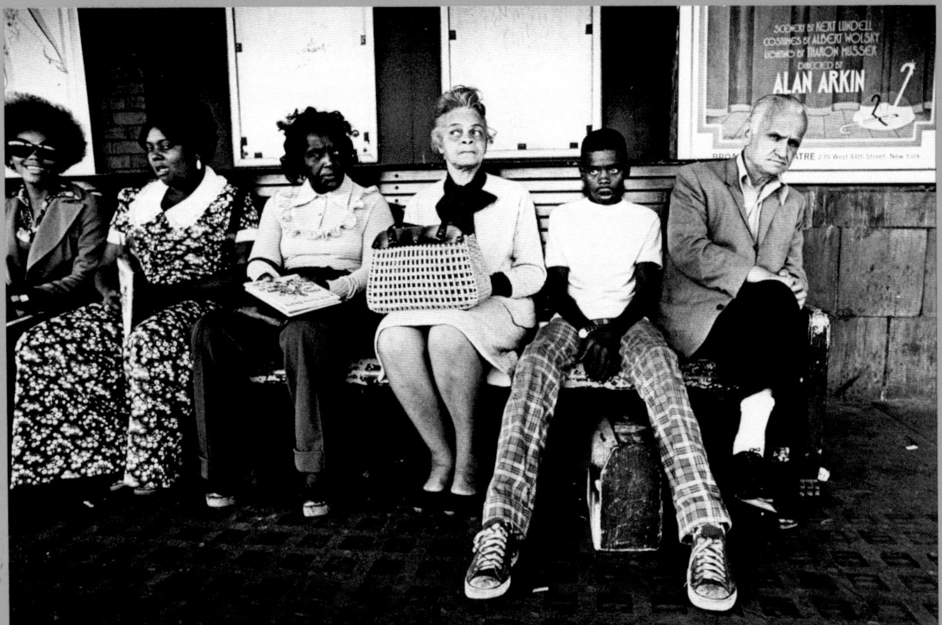
SCENERY BY KERT LUNDELL
COSTUMES BY ALBERT WOLSKY
LIGHTING BY THARON MUSSER
DIRECTED BY
ALAN ARKIN
235 West 44th Street, New York

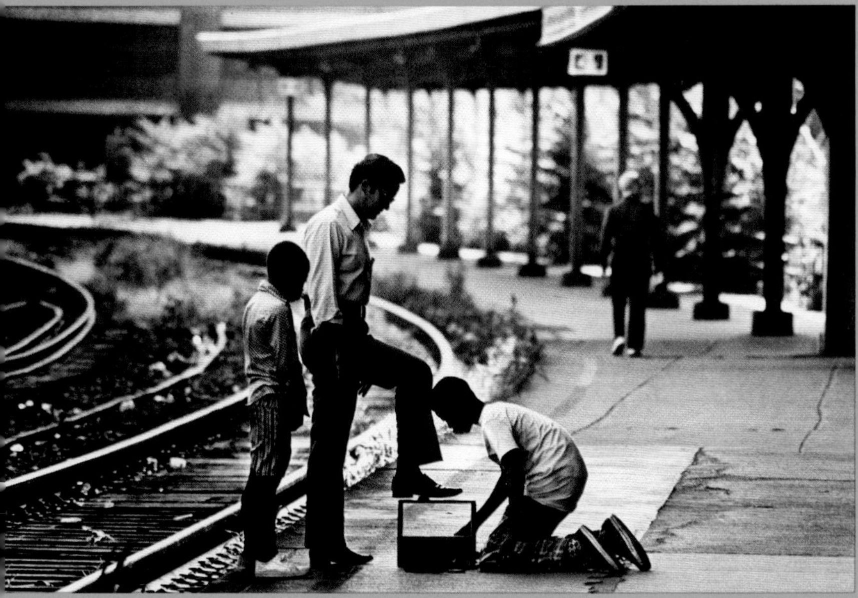

Working the Rails *1973*

I have often visited the Wilmington train station to meet and photograph interesting people. One day I caught sight of Tom Lloyd and his junior business partner, Andre Moody. I learned that theirs was a mobile business. In addition to the train station, they worked the post office and city hall earning $7 a day shining shoes. Pretty good for enterprising school kids.

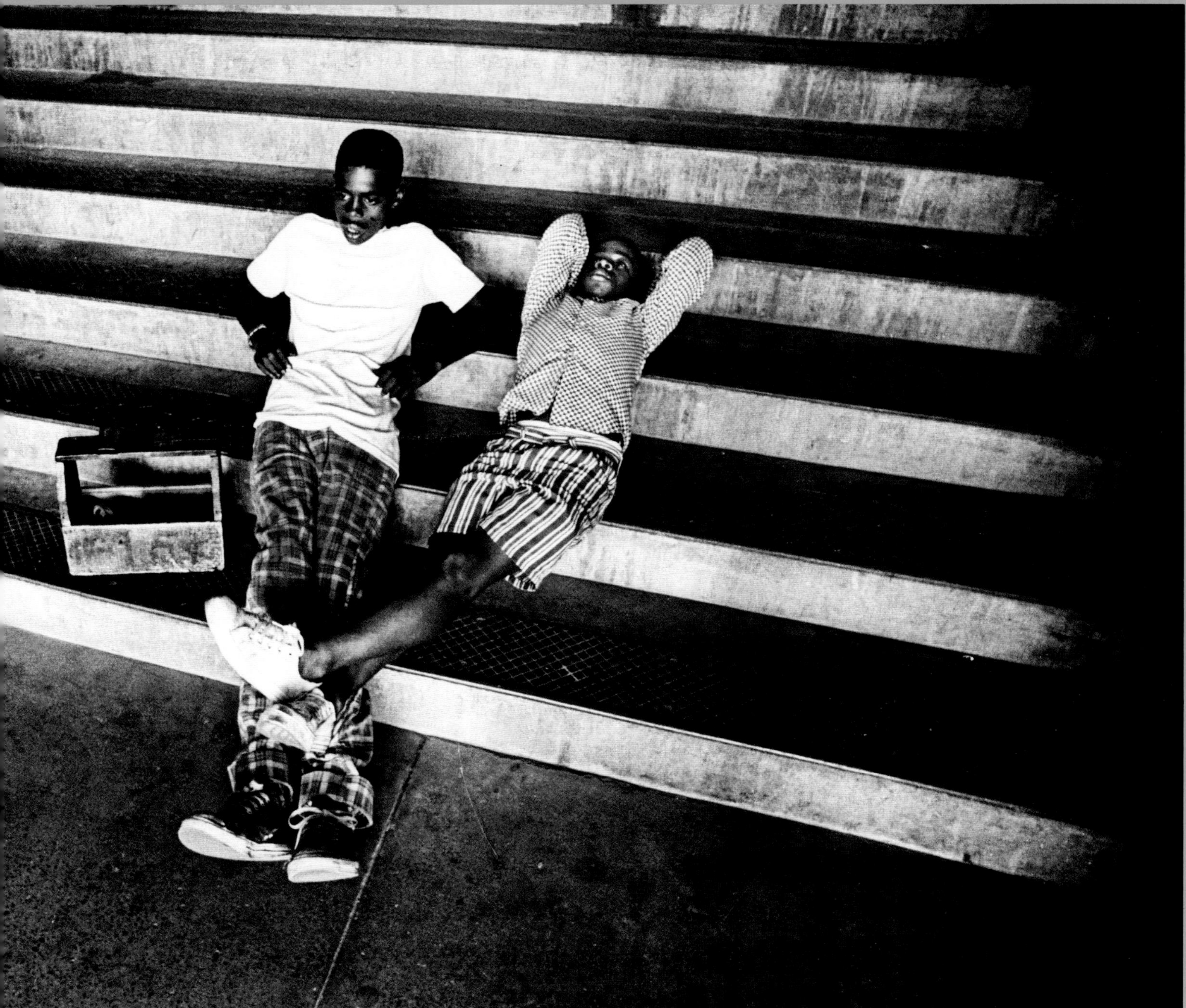

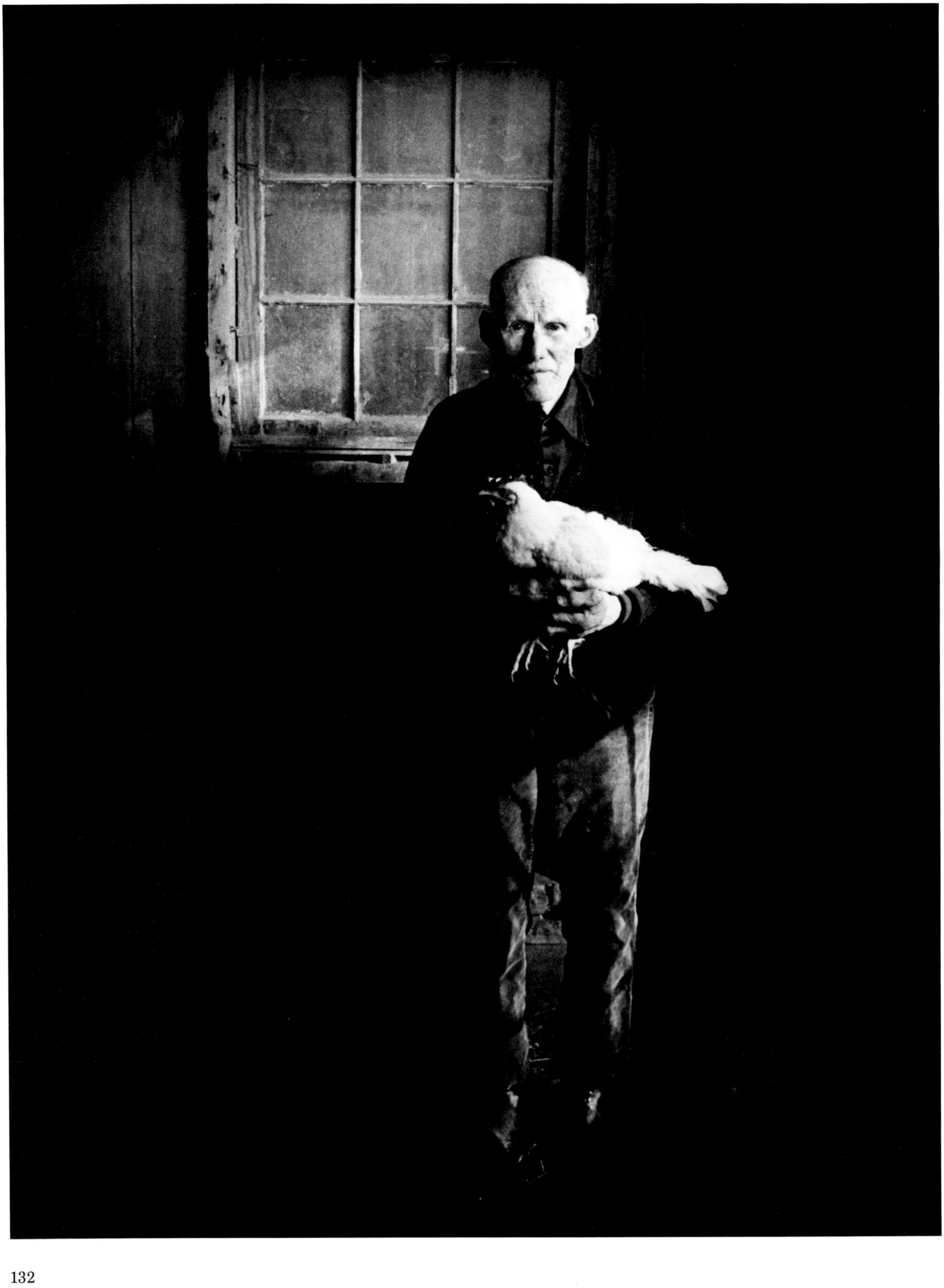

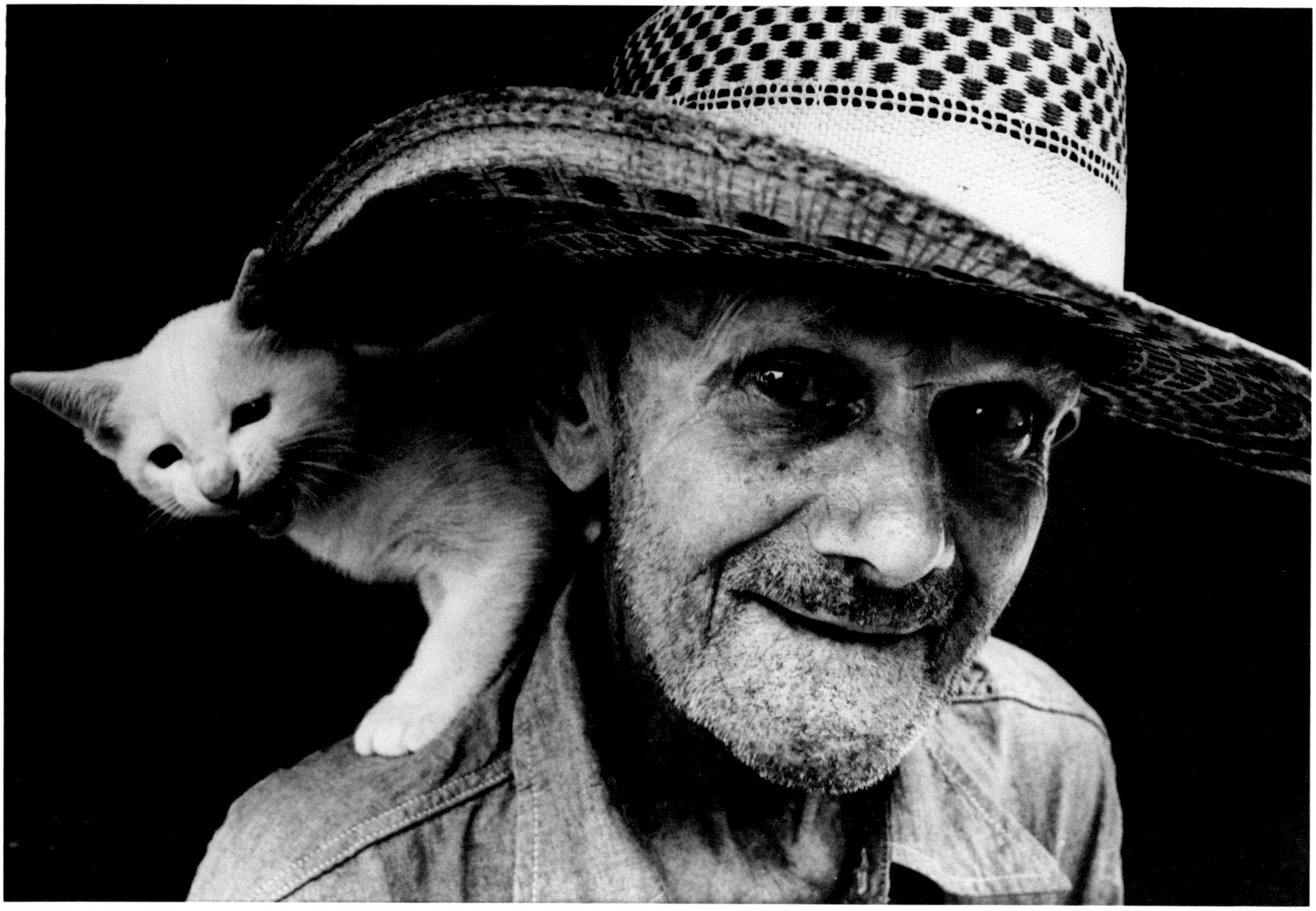

Frank Kelly, North Star, 1973

Wilson Pierson, Hockessin, 1974

Orange Street, Wilmington, 1986

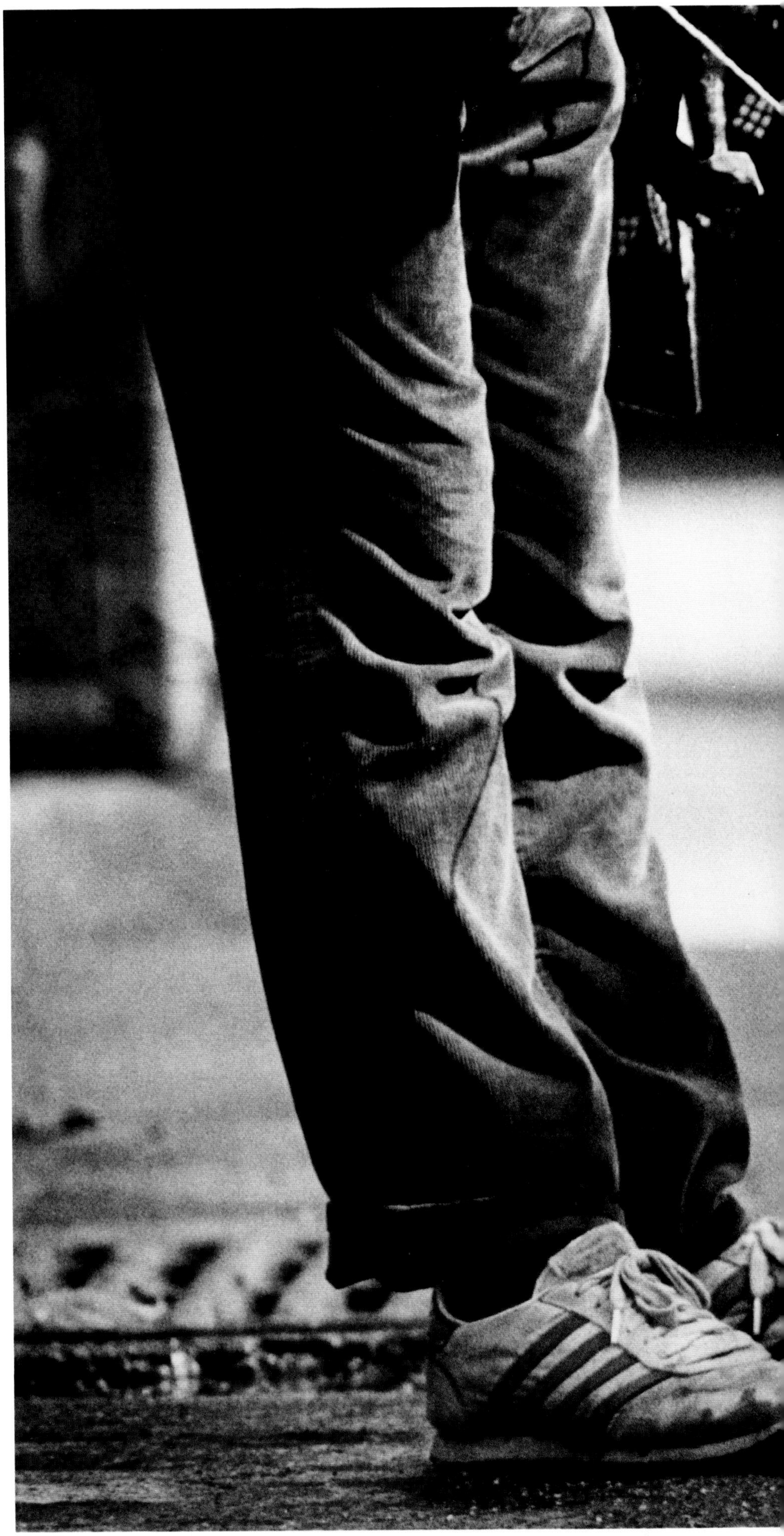

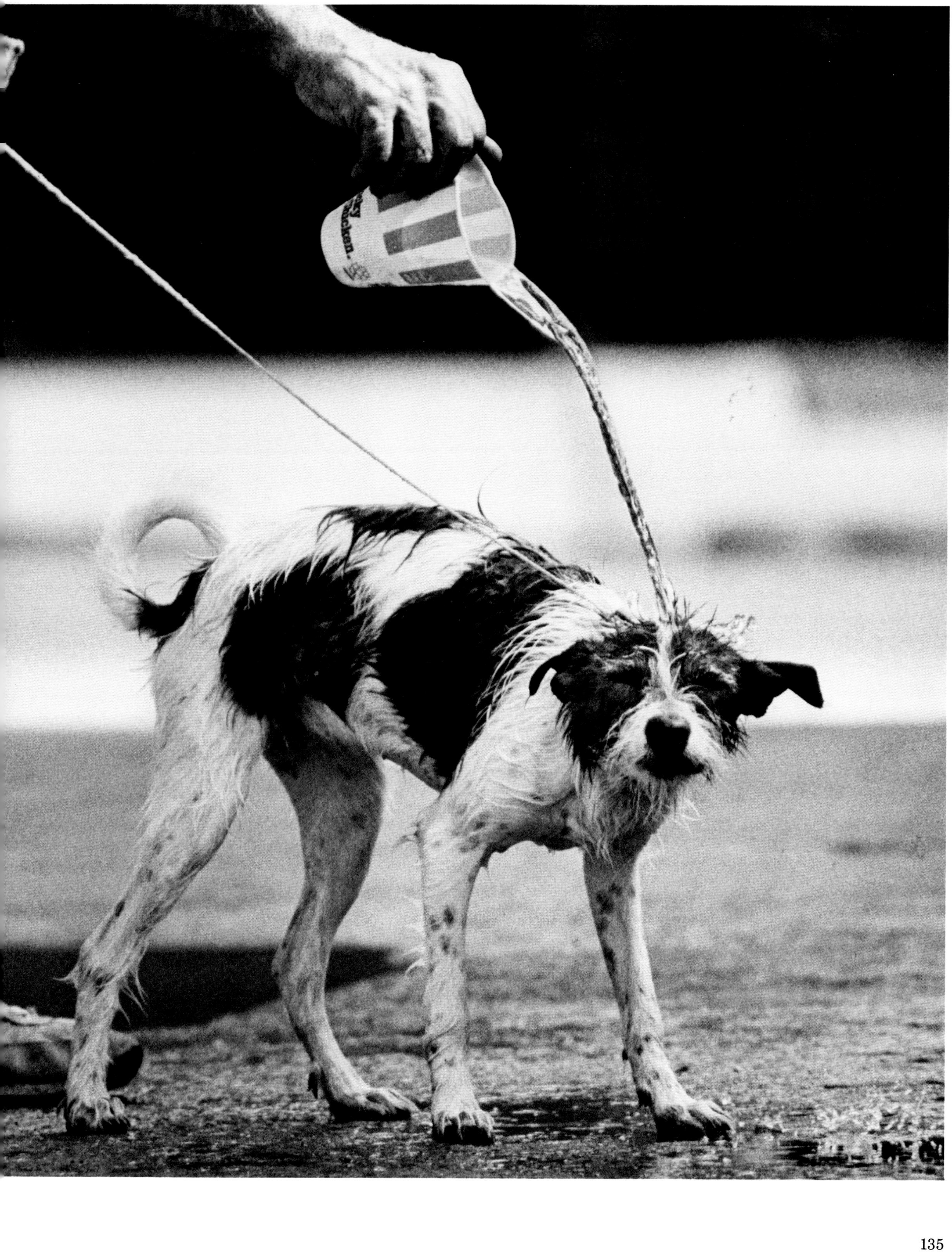

Edited by Jane Vessels

Editorial assistance by Gary Soulsman

Designed by Gerard A. Valerio

Composed in Century Schoolbook and
printed on 100 lb. Lithofect Plus by the
Whitmore Printing Company, Annapolis, Maryland